THE TANAT VALLEY LIGHT RAILWAY

THE TANAT VALLEY LIGHT RAILWAY

PETER JOHNSON

Title page: In the summer of 1954 two Oswestry schoolboys visited the Tanat Valley on their bikes to photograph the railway for modelling purposes. At Blodwel Junction they chanced upon a train being shunted that included wagons loaded with pipes for Liverpool Corporation's pipeline renewal. (John Milner)

Rear of title page: The railway has minimal impact on the landscape throughout its length, especially as it approaches its western terminus, Llangynog. (W. C. Burns/Lloyd, Llanrhaeadr)

Jacket, front: A short passenger train at LLangynog in the 1930s.

Jacket, rear, upper: At Porthywaen, the rails remain in situ on the level crossing of a minor road in 2023.

Jacket, rear, lower: The Tanat valley at Penybontfawr. (W. C. Burns/Lloyd, Llanrhaeadr)

First published in Great Britain in 2024 by
Pen and Sword Transport
An imprint of
Pen & Sword Books Ltd.
Yorkshire - Philadelphia

Copyright © Peter Johnson, 2024

ISBN 978 1 39903 967 3

The right of Peter Johnson to be identified as author of this work has been asserted by him in accordance with the Copyright, Designs and Patents Act 1988.

A CIP catalogue record for this book is available from the British Library.

All rights reserved. No part of this book may be reproduced or transmitted in any form or by any means, electronic or mechanical including photocopying, recording or by any information storage and retrieval system, without permission from the Publisher in writing.

Typeset in Palatino 11/13 by SJmagic DESIGN SERVICES, India.

Printed and bound by Printworks Global Ltd, London/Hong Kong.

Pen & Sword Books Ltd. incorporates the imprints of Pen & Sword Books: After the Battle, Archaeology, Atlas, Aviation, Battleground, Discovery, Family History, History, Maritime, Military, Politics, Select, Transport, True Crime, Fiction, Frontline Books, Leo Cooper, Praetorian Press, Seaforth Publishing, Wharncliffe and White Owl.

For a complete list of Pen & Sword titles please contact

PEN & SWORD BOOKS LIMITED
George House, Beevor Street, Off Pontefract Road, Hoyle Mill, Barnsley, South Yorkshire, England, S71 1HN.
E-mail: enquiries@pen-and-sword.co.uk
Website: www.pen-and-sword.co.uk

or

PEN AND SWORD BOOKS
1950 Lawrence Rd, Havertown, PA 19083, USA
E-mail: uspen-and-sword@casematepublishers.com
Website: www.penandswordbooks.com

CONTENTS

Introduction 6
Welsh place names 8
Acknowledgements and sources 9
Chapter 1   Destination Llangynog 10
Chapter 2   The Light Railway Order 28
Chapter 3   Building the railway 43
Chapter 4   The Tanat Valley Light Railway 68
Chapter 5   Changes of ownership, and closure 95

APPENDICES

Appendix 1   Tanat Valley proposals 118
Appendix 2   Llanfyllin & Llangynog Light Railway – estimate of expenses 1897 119
Appendix 3   Tanat Valley Light Railway – estimate 1897 120
Appendix 4   Tanat Valley Light Railway – local authority advances 121
Appendix 5   Tanat Valley Light Railway – other works 1900 122
Appendix 6   Tanat Valley Light Railway – estimate of expenses 1901 123
Appendix 7   Tanat Valley Light Railway – necessary expenditure 1900 124
Appendix 8   Tanat Valley Light Railway – tenders 1901 125
Appendix 9   Tanat Valley Light Railway – John Strachan's tender 126
Appendix 10   Tanat Valley Light Railway – cost of work done to
               20 November 1902 127
Appendix 11   Tanat Valley Light Railway – details re engineer's commission 128
Appendix 12   Tanat Valley Light Railway – John Strachan's locomotives used
               on contract 129
Appendix 13   Tanat Valley Light Railway – balance sheet, 15 June 1903 130
Appendix 14   Tanat Valley Light Railway – approximate statement of liabilities,
               December 1903 131
Appendix 15   Tanat Valley Light Railway – statement of costs, January 1904 132
Appendix 16   Tanat Valley Light Railway – land purchase costs 133
Appendix 17   Tanat Valley Light Railway – estimated and actual costs 134
Appendix 18   Tanat Valley Light Railway – list of buildings required 135
Appendix 19   Tanat Valley Light Railway – gross traffic receipts to 30 January 1904 136
Appendix 20   Tanat Valley Light Railway – gross traffic receipts from
               6 January 1904 to 30 June 1907 137
Appendix 21   Tanat Valley Light Railway – gross receipts and working
               expenses 1905–1919 138
Appendix 22   Tanat Valley Light Railway – timetables 1913 and 1920 141
Appendix 23   Tanat Valley Light Railway – return to Light Railway
               (Investigation) Committee, loadings 145
Appendix 24   Tanat Valley Light Railway – return to Light Railway (Investigation)
               Committee – mileages 146
Bibliography 147
Index 149

INTRODUCTION

Although the Tanat Valley Light Railway was a product of 1896's Light Railways Act, a government attempt to open up areas considered remote and to improve access to markets, it was not the first attempt to make a railway to Llangynog. Eleven proposals since 1860 had failed for want of financial and/or landowner support. The Act's provisions enabled local authorities to invest in light railways and for the Treasury to make free grants and interest-free loans, and the support of major landowners encouraged Oswestry Town Council to make an application for a Light Railway Order.

Opening in 1904, three years after the Light Railway Order authorising its construction had been made, the timing, coinciding with the post-Boer War depression and high inflation, gave the promoters a rough ride.

Operated by the Cambrian Railways, the railway was not the success they had anticipated and it was in receivership before the first year was out, but was

The target for so many railway schemes, Llangynog is seen here in the early years of the light railway, with a train in the platform, the loco shed, the original water tank and the lead mine spoil heaps dominating the background. (W. C. Burns/Lloyd, Llanrheaedr)

able to carry on with the support of the Cambrian, which took it over in 1921. Under Great Western Railway control from 1922, its passenger service survived the 1930s cull imposed on other railways in the area, lasting until British Railways withdrew it in 1951. The goods service beyond Llanrhaeadr Mochnant was withdrawn in 1952 and beyond Blodwel Junction in 1960; the short section that enabled the Nantmawr quarry to maintain its rail link via Porthywaen remained in use until 1971, and was still in situ at the time of publication.

There was never really the prospect of enough traffic in the valley to justify a railway. If there had been, then raising the capital to build it would have been easy. As it was, any possibility of traffic increasing was soon undermined by the increased availability of motor transport after the First World War. It did play a useful role, however, in the construction and maintenance of Liverpool Corporation's Vyrnwy reservoir pipeline until the 1950s. The Corporation had foreseen the railway's usefulness and had invested in its construction.

The Tanat Valley Light Railway was the triumph of enthusiasm over reason, it had a marginal existence and precarious finances. Although it served the valley for barely fifty years it is remembered fondly by those who knew it.

A contrasting scene in 2023. The lead mine tips can be seen opposite. The caravan park on the left of centre is the site of the light railway terminus, the Llangynog Granite Company's extension ran into the field on the right-hand side of the road.

WELSH PLACE NAMES

Historically, the areas on the Welsh borders west of Shrewsbury and in the Tanat Valley were not inflicted with invasions of English visitors corrupting the spelling of local, Welsh, place names but those who did visit insisted on spelling Blodwel and Llanyblodwel as Blodwell and Llanyblodwell. The correct versions are used here, as are Welsh names of places further away that are occasionally mentioned or quoted, such as Dolgellau or Porthmadog. Llanrhaeadr was spelled Llanrhaiadr in the nineteenth century.

Llanrhaeadr, the terminus since 1951, seen on 12 August 1957, a year before it was closed. The signal posts were installed for the railway's opening. (N. C. Simmons)

ACKNOWLEDGEMENTS AND SOURCES

I first encountered the Tanat valley while en route to a volunteering visit to the Ffestiniog Railway in the 1970s and since then have had the pleasure of driving through it many times.

It was when I was writing my first book on the Shropshire & Montgomeryshire Light Railway (*An Illustrated History of the Shropshire & Montgomeryshire Light Railway*, Oxford Publishing Company, 2008) that I realised how closely linked that railway was to the attempts to build a railway in the Tanat valley, resolving to include 'a chapter' on its railway if the opportunity ever presented to revisit the Shropshire line. The opportunity did present but 'the chapter' turned into five and the story of the Tanat Valley Light Railway became a book on its own.

Researches included the Board of Trade, Ministry of Transport, Treasury, British Railways and Cambrian Railways files at the National Archives, information obtained from digitised newspapers at the British Newspaper Archive (www.britishnewspaperarchive.co.uk), and deposited plans in the Parliamentary Archives.

Biographical information was extracted from www.ancestry.co.uk, the General Register Office's online indices and digitised newspapers. The Bank of England's online Inflation Calculator was used to obtain updates on the value of money.

The railway attracted very little attention by enthusiasts, even when its mixed trains with six-wheeled carriages would have seemed archaic. However, the line's pictorial representation is greatly enhanced by the photographs taken by William Charles Burns, that were published as postcards. Born in Llanrhaeadr in 1886, he probably emigrated to the USA after the 1st World War.

The late Vic Bradley, and John Milner, Joanne Thornton (United Utilities) and Jonathan Williams-Ellis were a great help in providing assistance, support and/or the loan of material or information.

Myself, I have had a fascinating journey trawling through over 150 years of documents and newspapers to uncover the stories of the Tanat Valley Light Railway.

A few of the illustrations are included for their historical interest despite not being technically perfect. It remains for me to say that I accept responsibility for any errors.

Peter Johnson
Leicester
July 2024

CHAPTER 1
DESTINATION LLANGYNOG

The Afon Tanat rises in the foothills of the Berwyns, a range with summits reaching 2,730ft (832m), close to the village of Llangynog, in the old county of Montgomeryshire. Running generally eastwards, it crosses into and out of Denbighshire on either side of Llangedwyn, returning to Montgomeryshire before forming the border with England for a short distance north-west of Llanymynech and joining the Vyrnwy due west of Llanymynech, a distance of about 15 miles. It now lies entirely in the modern county of Powys.

The valley that takes the river's name is quite broad and fertile, its population sparse although there are communities large enough to support schools at Penybontfawr, Llanrhaeadr ym Mochnant and Llangedwyn. In addition to farming there was some mineral extraction at Llangynog. Historically, most of the land was owned by the Williams Wynn family, centred on Llangedwyn, with some at the eastern end owned by the Earls of Bradford and an area around Nantmawr owned by the Earls of Powis. The nearest market was at Llanfyllin, 9 miles and three hours at walking pace from Llangynog, but Oswestry, 17 miles and over five hours, seems to have been preferred.

There were minerals at several locations in the valley, mainly at Llangynog, where a vein of lead containing silver was worked to a depth of 100 yards for over forty years from 1692, until it was flooded, earning a female ancestor of the Powis earldom £20,000 a year. Nearby, slate of durable

A postcard view of Llangynog as it was in the 1920s, with the Rhiwarth slate quarry's lower incline prominent and the wagons visible on the right hinting at the location of the station and yard. (RAP Co. Ltd)

Llangynog, Berwyn Quarries

and marketable quality was quarried from around 1775. The existence of these minerals was as much the motivation for floating the various railway schemes as meeting the needs of the farmers and other residents in the valley.

For tourists there are two long-established attractions in the valley: the waterfall at Llanrhaeadr, and the shrine church in Cwm Pennant. The waterfall, pistill in Welsh, is actually 4 miles from the village from which it takes its name, closer to Llangynog. St Melangell's church, 2 miles south of Llangynog, was established on a Bronze Age site over 1,200 years ago and is Grade I listed; its graveyard is almost circular.

From 1860 there had been several schemes for a railway to Llangynog, from Oswestry, Porthywaen, Llanyblodwel or Llanfyllin (Appendix 1). Some of them went no further than a meeting or two, others deposited Parliamentary Bills that

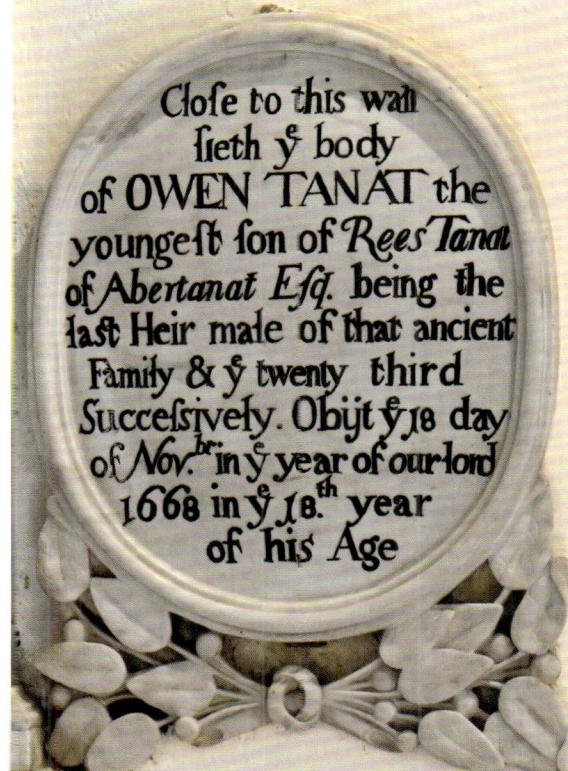

Another 1920s scene at Llangynog, the lead mine tips dominating the hillside. (RAP Co. Ltd)

Memorial to the last of the Tanat family, who died in 1668, in the church of St Michael at Llanyblodwel. There are more recent graves of members of a family named Tanatt in the churchyard and chapel cemetery at Llangynog.

DESTINATION LLANGYNOG • 11

Llanrhaeadr's famous waterfall, only 2½ miles from Llangynog although inaccessible from that place. (William Charles Burns, Llanrhaeadr)

St Melangell's church lies to the south of Llangynog. (William Charles Burns, Llanrhaeadr/ E. C. Burns)

were withdrawn, and others obtained powers. In all cases it was the lack of capital that prevented progress and no work was done on any of them. It was the Light Railways Act of 1896, with its powers for local authorities to promote or finance light railways, that made the Tanat valley's railway possible, and even then, the financial situation was always precarious.

The first proposal for a railway in the Tanat valley, the West Midland, Shrewsbury & Coast of Wales Railway, was intended to be a trunk route for traffic to and from Ireland, the route from a junction with the Shrewsbury & Welshpool Railway being via Ford, Shrawardine, Nesscliffe, Kinnerley, Knockin, Porthywaen, Llanfyllin, Llanrhaeadr, Llangynog, Bala, Dolgellau and Harlech before reaching Porthmadog, where it would connect to a proposed railway to Porthdinlleyn. A tunnel a mile and a half long would have taken the 90-mile route through the Berwyns near Llangynog.

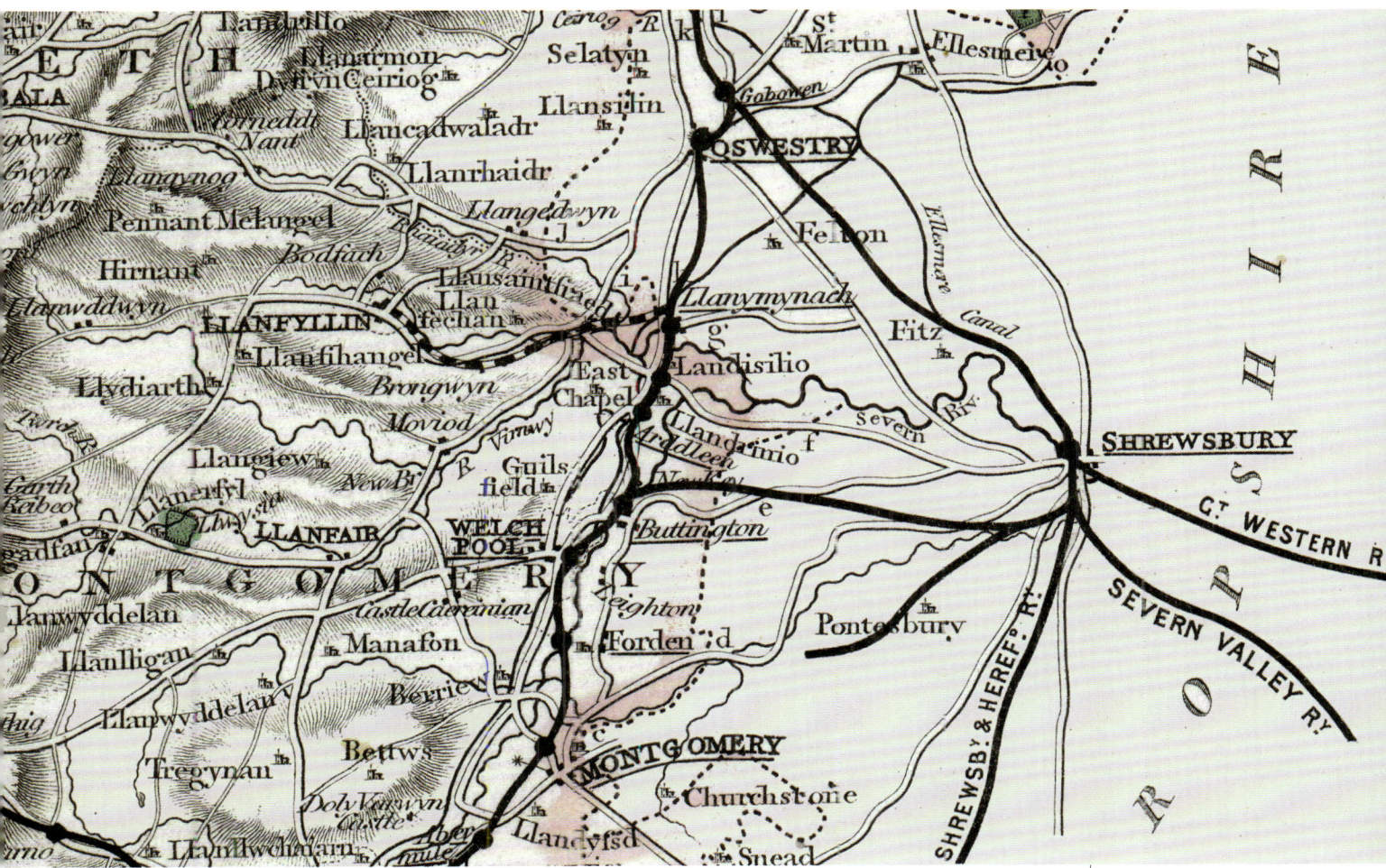

Railways west of Shrewsbury and in Montgomeryshire in the 1860s. (G. F. Cruchley)

One of the West Midland Railway's officials accompanying the survey was Richard Samuel France (1828–83), who became the Potteries Railway's guiding light. The survey opened his eyes, he said later, to the possibilities offered by the Tanat valley. The Bill failed to pass standing orders, however.

The first demand for a railway by the community started in 1862, after the Llanfyllin Railway's promoters, the Oswestry & Newtown Railway, had indicated that they would build 'a tramway' from Llanfyllin to Llangynog. Concerned that this would not meet their needs, on 18 October a group of residents met in Llanrhaeadr and resolved to petition the West Shropshire Mineral Railway, later the Potteries, Shrewsbury & North Wales Railway, for a branch from its intended line at Llanymynech to Llangynog and to send a deputation to France to put their case. By the time the deputation met him in Oswestry on 29 October, it was also armed with 'memorials' from four parishes that would be served by the proposed railway.

France told the deputation that until he had received the request for a meeting the company had had no plans for any extension but that it would be prepared to apply for the necessary powers if there was evidence of support by the principal landowners, which the deputation undertook to obtain (Shrewsbury Chronicle, 24/31 October).

As soon as 13 November the company announced its intention to seek powers for extensions from Llanymynech to Llanyblodwel and from Llanyblodwel to Llangynog and for other purposes (London Gazette, 28 November). The branches

Railway route through the Tanat valley, and branch to Porthywaen, proposed by the West Midland, Shrewsbury & Coast of Wales Railway in 1861. (Parliamentary Archives)

failed to comply with standing order requirements (*Wellington Journal*, 31 January 1863), which might have been a consequence of the haste in which they must have been added to the Bill.

At a meeting held in Llanrhaeadr to support the Bill on 15 February 1864, France described how he had become aware of the valley's possibilities while working on the West Midland, Shrewsbury & Coast of Wales Railway proposal in 1860, resolving to build a direct route to Wales by instalments after the Coast of Wales Bill had failed. Most of the meeting's speeches having been made in Welsh, France's joke that while his education had not considered it essential to teach him the language, the railway company was doing what it could to teach English to the Welsh was met with cries of 'Oh, oh' (*Eddowes's Journal*, 24 February). The *Shrewsbury Chronicle* (19 February) acknowledged the assistance of two bi-lingual audience members, enabling it to report on the meeting.

In the following session, the West Shropshire Mineral Railway (New Lines) Act, enacted on 30 June 1864, authorised branches to Llanyblodwel, Llangynog and Nantmawr, the last two springing out of the first.

Following the Mineral Railway's reinvention as the Potteries, Shewsbury & North Wales Railway in 1866, financial difficulties ensured that the Llangynog extension would not be built, although the Llanyblodwel and Nantmawr branches were. The Oswestry & Newtown Railway did not proceed with its proposal for a line from Llanfyllin.

Below: Llanrhaeadr, the largest village in the Tanat valley, pushed for a railway but when it arrived a combination of geography and economics meant that it was a mile away. (Lloyd, Llanrheaedr)

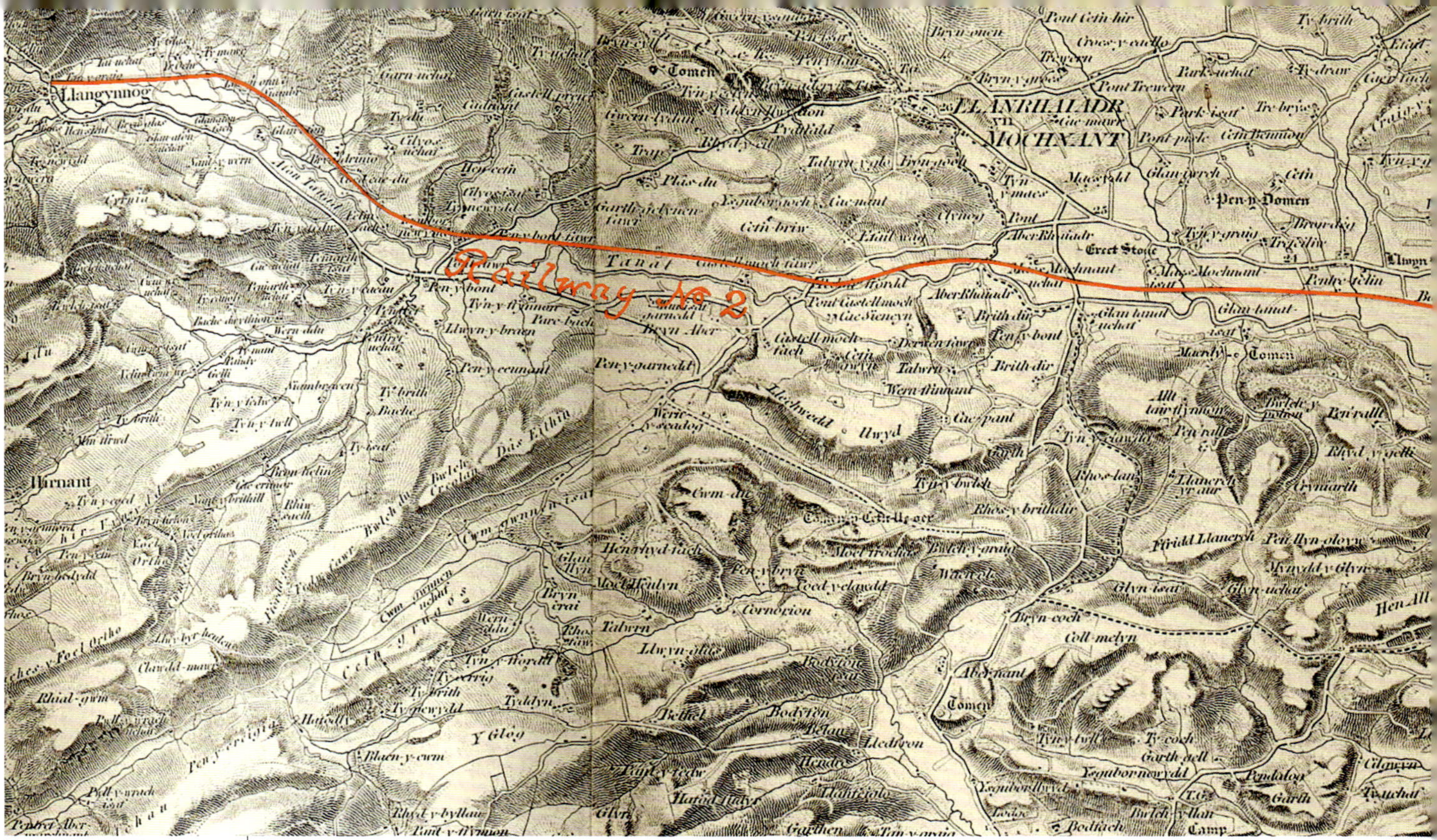

The West Shropshire Mineral Railway's 1863 proposal for a railway to Llangynog, complete with a tramway to Nantmawr. (Parliamentary Archives)

Sir Watkin Williams Wynn, the 6th Baronet, owned the land around Llangedwyn. (*Vanity Fair*)

The next scheme for a railway to Llangynog was launched on 18 October 1869, when meetings were held in Llanrhaeadr and Llansilin to discuss a proposal for the Oswestry & Llangynog Railway, a 2ft-gauge railway routed via Llansilin (*Wrexham & Denbighshire Advertiser*, 23 October).

Its engineer was Thomas Edward Minshall (1837–1907), a member of a long-established Oswestry family. He had been Benjamin Piercy's resident engineer on the Llanidloes & Newtown, the Oswestry & Newtown, and the Wrexham, Mold & Connah's Quay railways. Since 1867 he had been working for himself, chiefly occupied on Parliamentary work.

The scheme was rather unusual, in that it was hardly mentioned in the local press and its promoters were not named. A Bill was deposited but determined opposition from one of the landowners, Sir Watkin Williams Wynn (1820–85, 6th Baronet), despite a petition signed by four hundred residents, caused it to be withdrawn (*Wrexham Advertiser*, 19 February 1870). He had argued that if the Bill was delayed by another year the money market would be easier and 'important alterations' could be made (*Llangollen Advertiser*, 25 February). It was not revived, of course, which was probably what Sir Watkin wanted. John Thomas, then mayor of Oswestry, said in 1878 that all the landowners had objected (*Cambrian News*, 29 November).

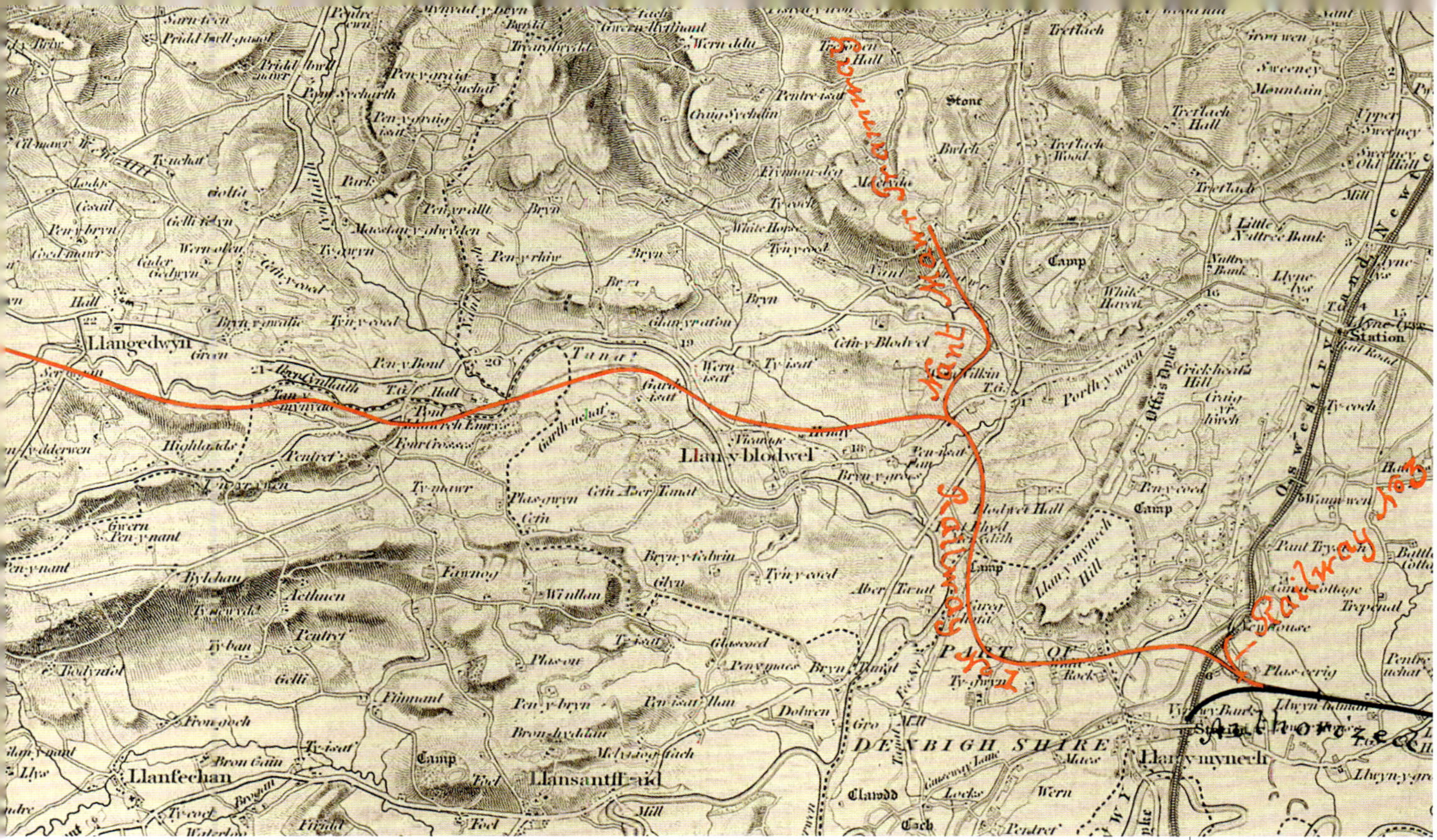

Schemes from both Llanfyllin and Oswestry were proposed in 1872. The first, which would also have been narrow gauge, was the subject of a meeting

The station and yard at Llanfyllin.

DESTINATION LLANGYNOG • 17

The Oswestry & Llangynog Railway's 1873 route. (Parliamentary Archives)

held in Llanfyllin on 27 August, those attending including George Hammond Whalley (1813–78), who had driven the construction of the Cambrian Railways' constituents, George Owen (1835–1917), the Cambrian's engineer, and Thomas Savin (1826–89), the contractor. The landowners were said to be in favour and the clerk did not anticipate any objections. Savin pointed out that as the Llangynog slate and lead mines were being developed, the question was not whether a railway should be made but whether it should run to Llanyfyllin.

Whalley said that the choice of narrow gauge was supported by the success of the Festiniog Railway, which itself had been validated by the recent visit of the Russian delegation representing the Czar (*Cambrian News*, 30 August).

Very much a Cambrian-supported initiative, its supporters claimed that it could be built for £2,000 a mile and would be much cheaper than a longer line to Oswestry. At another meeting, at Llangynog on 6 September, that had to compete with the attractions of the Llangedwyn flower show for an audience, the cost of a competing line, standard gauge, was put at £8,000 a mile (*Cambrian News*, 13 September). This scheme was obviously intended to keep Llangynog within the Cambrian sphere of influence. While it would have been very good for Llangynog residents who actually wanted to go to Llanfyllin, for those who wanted to go to Oswestry it would have been a 'round the houses' route.

Oswestry's mayor put the case for an Oswestry–Llansilin–Llangynog railway at the Town Council's meeting on 7 October, saying that while the Llanfyllin proposal was better than nothing, it ran the risk of diverting Llangynog traffic from Oswestry to Shrewsbury and the council should therefore push for a route that protected its interests. The council resolved to send a deputation to see Sir Watkin's solicitors to ascertain his views on the matter (*Shrewsbury Chronicle*, 11 October 1872).

A deputation from Llansilin met the mayor on 21 October, when he said that whether the railway was built or not was simply a question of money and it would be necessary for the deputation to go out and canvas support, to find out how many shares the public would be willing to subscribe. As a narrow-gauge line, the railway would cost £50,000, while

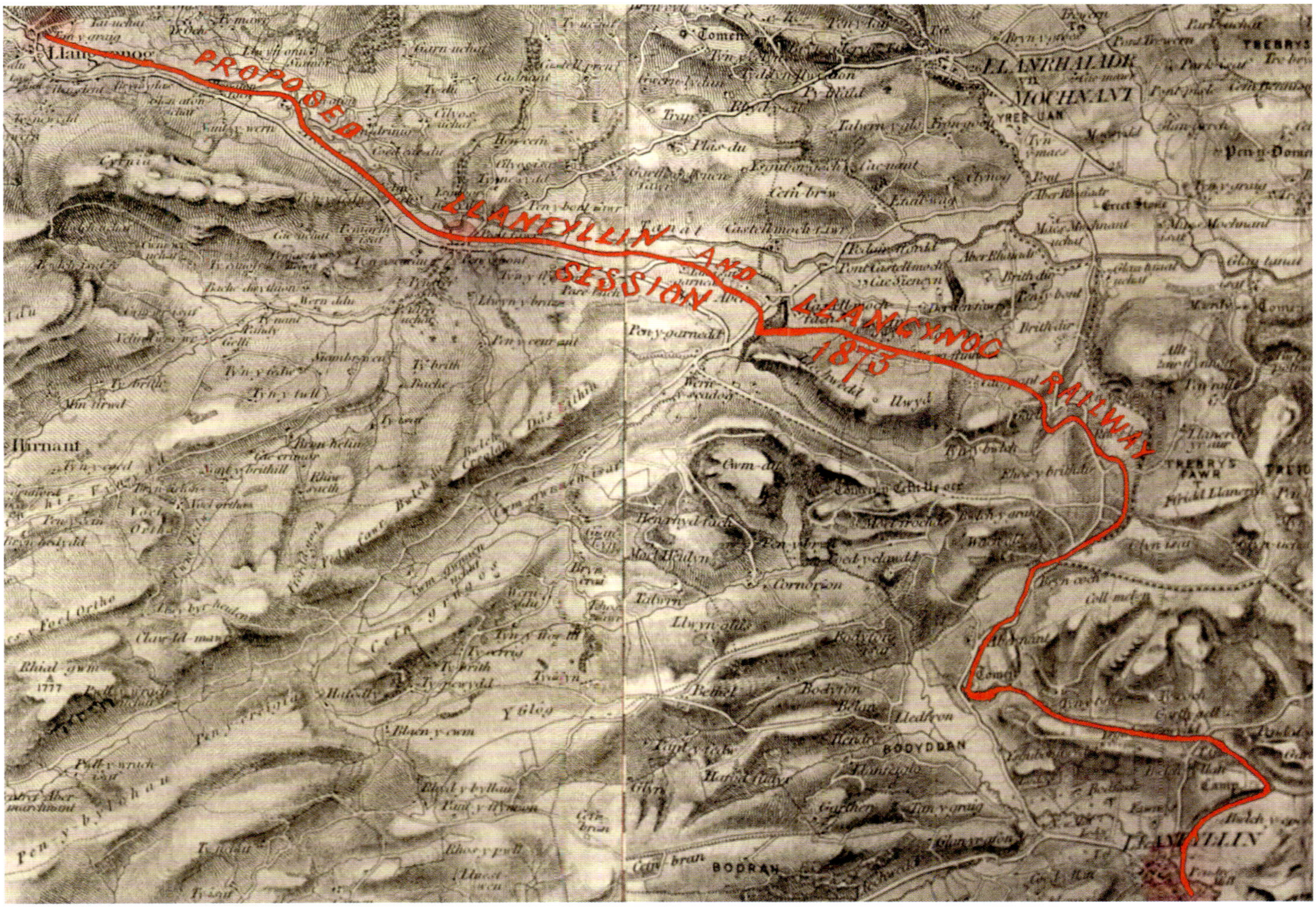

The Oswestry & Llangynog Railway was in competition with the narrow-gauge Llanfyllin & Llangynog Railway. (Parliamentary Archives)

DESTINATION LLANGYNOG • 19

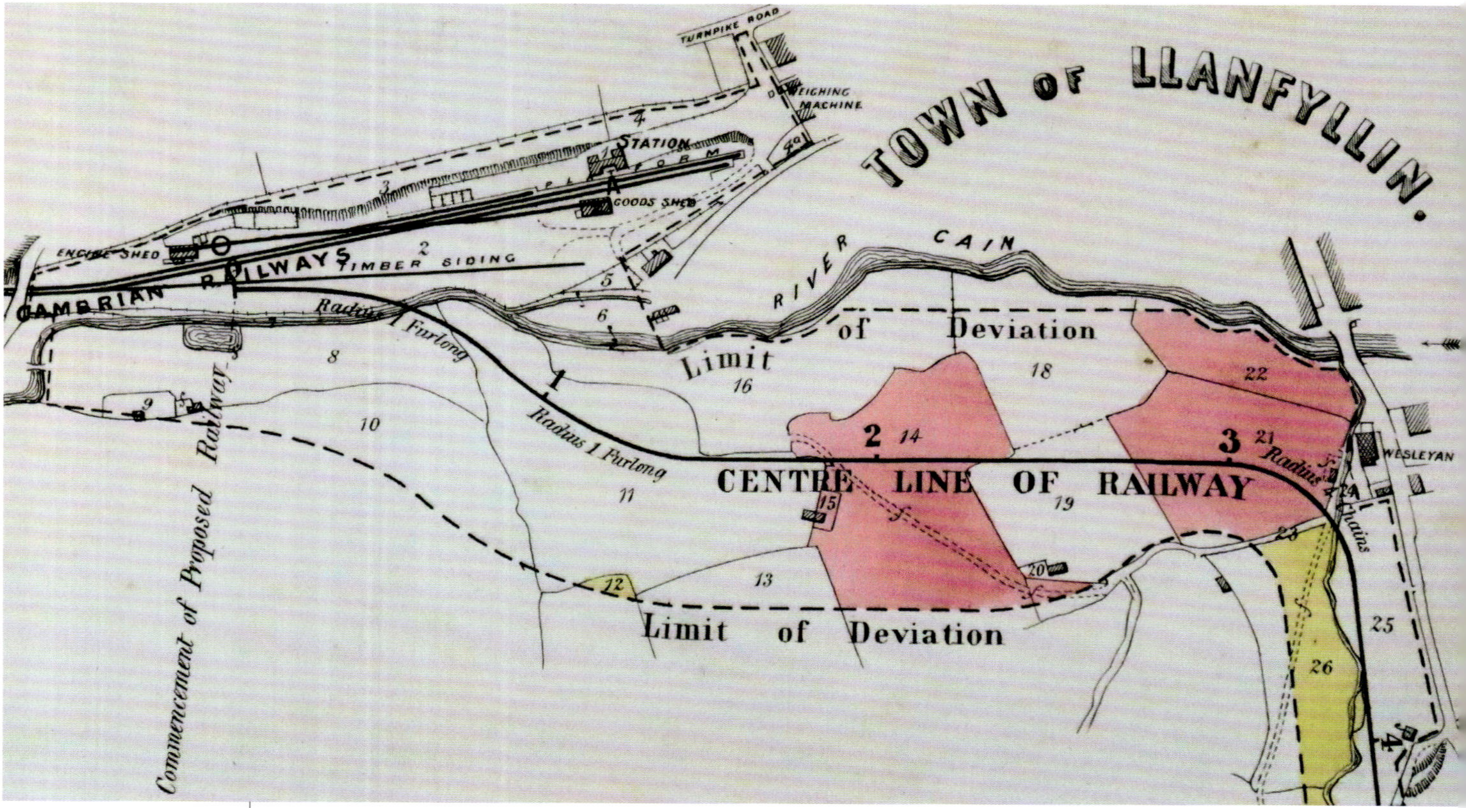

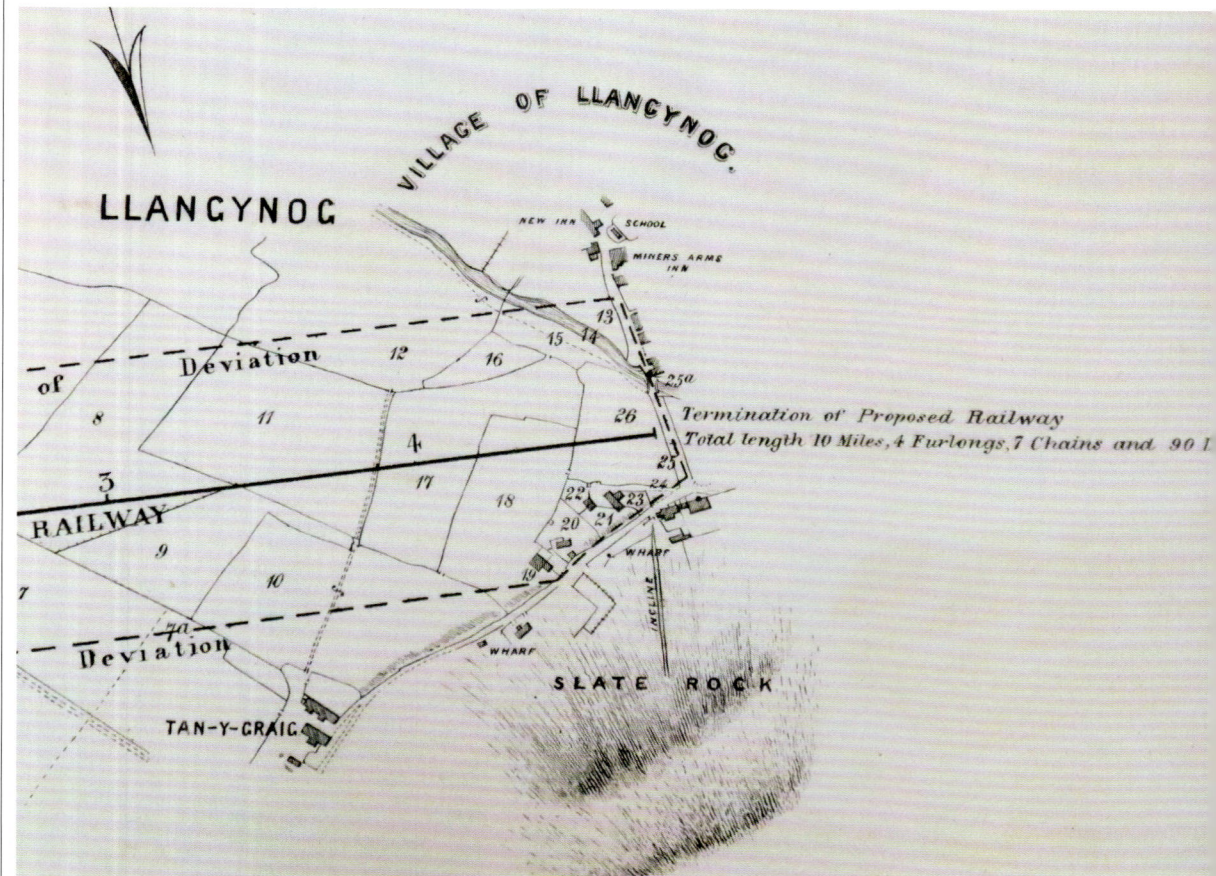

Detail from the Llanfyllin & Llangynog Railway's deposited plans showing the proposed arrangements at Llanfyllin. (National Archives)

The Llanfyllin & Llangynog Railway's proposed Llangynog terminus. (National Archives)

20 • THE TANAT VALLEY LIGHT RAILWAY

another £30,000 would be required to make it standard gauge. Some deputation members expressed a preference for standard gauge, claiming that cattle and timber could not be carried by narrow gauge (*Cambrian News*, 25 October). By 8 November (*Cambrian News*) £6,000 had been promised in shares and £400 towards the preliminary expenses.

Owen, who had attended the 7 October meeting, presented his plans for the Llanfyllin route in Oswestry on 5 November, when it was resolved to submit a Bill to Parliament and to issue the appropriate notices (*Cambrian News*, 8 November).

Notices about the intention to deposit Bills for both railways were advertised in November 1872 (*London Gazette*, 22/26 November). The Oswestry scheme also included a branch to Llanymynech and shorter lines to connect with the Potteries Railway's Nantmawr tramway and the Shropshire Union Canal but for an as yet unknown reason its Bill was withdrawn in January 1873 (*London Evening Standard*, 30 January). The Llanfyllin Bill was processed without difficulty, despite containing a clause to permit the use of a non-standard gauge, and received royal assent on 16 June.

The Act named the promoters as Thomas Openshaw Lomax (1837–82), Edward Evans, John Jones and Cadwalader Richard Jones (1829–1902) and the first directors as the first two of them plus one other. Article 34 specified the gauge as 2ft, except that it could be altered to any gauge up to standard with the Board of Trade's approval. The first meeting of shareholders was held on 12 December and adjourned (*Cambrian News*, 19 December 1873).

The next recorded activity of the company came on 23 November 1875, when it published a notice of intention to deposit a Bill seeking powers to abandon its undertaking (*London Gazette*). The Bill's preamble stated that no capital had been raised and no powers had been exercised. Assent was given to the Act on 27 June. No explanation was offered for the failure to raise capital and exercise the powers, and no published comment on the failure to continue with the railway or its abandonment has been found.

In 1878 the Oswestry Highway Board prosecuted Thomas Savin, the former contractor, for committing nuisances and 'destroying roads' with his traction engines between Porthywaen and Llangynog, a protracted case heard in several courts. The decision eventually went against him at the Court of Appeal in 1880 and he had to pay £500 damages (*Eddowes's Journal*, 22 December).

Before the case was concluded Oswestry architect and surveyor William Henry Spaull (1840–1915) decided that another attempt to promote a railway between Oswestry and Llangynog, via Llansilin, was justified, calling a meeting held in Llangedwyn on 7 November 1878 (*Cambrian News*, 15 November).

Previously attendant at meetings held in support of the 1872 schemes, Spaull was married to one of the daughters of Charles Mickleburgh, the Montgomery land agent and surveyor who had trained the engineers Benjamin Piercy and George Owen, who had also married his daughters.

Opening the 1878 meeting, Sir Watkin Williams Wynn said that while traction engine users should contribute towards the cost of road maintenance, no powers had been given to the Local Government Board. Those who would most benefit by the railway, he said, Llangynog residents, should demonstrate their support for it but there were none of them present. He concluded that he would make any of his land required available at agricultural rates providing his offer was taken up within three years.

Spaull said that while a railway would reduce the cost of highway maintenance, a standard-gauge railway would not pay for itself for a long time, so he was proposing a narrow-gauge line, citing the Festiniog and Talyllyn railways. He thought the cost of transhipment would be reduced if it used the same gauge as that used in the quarries.

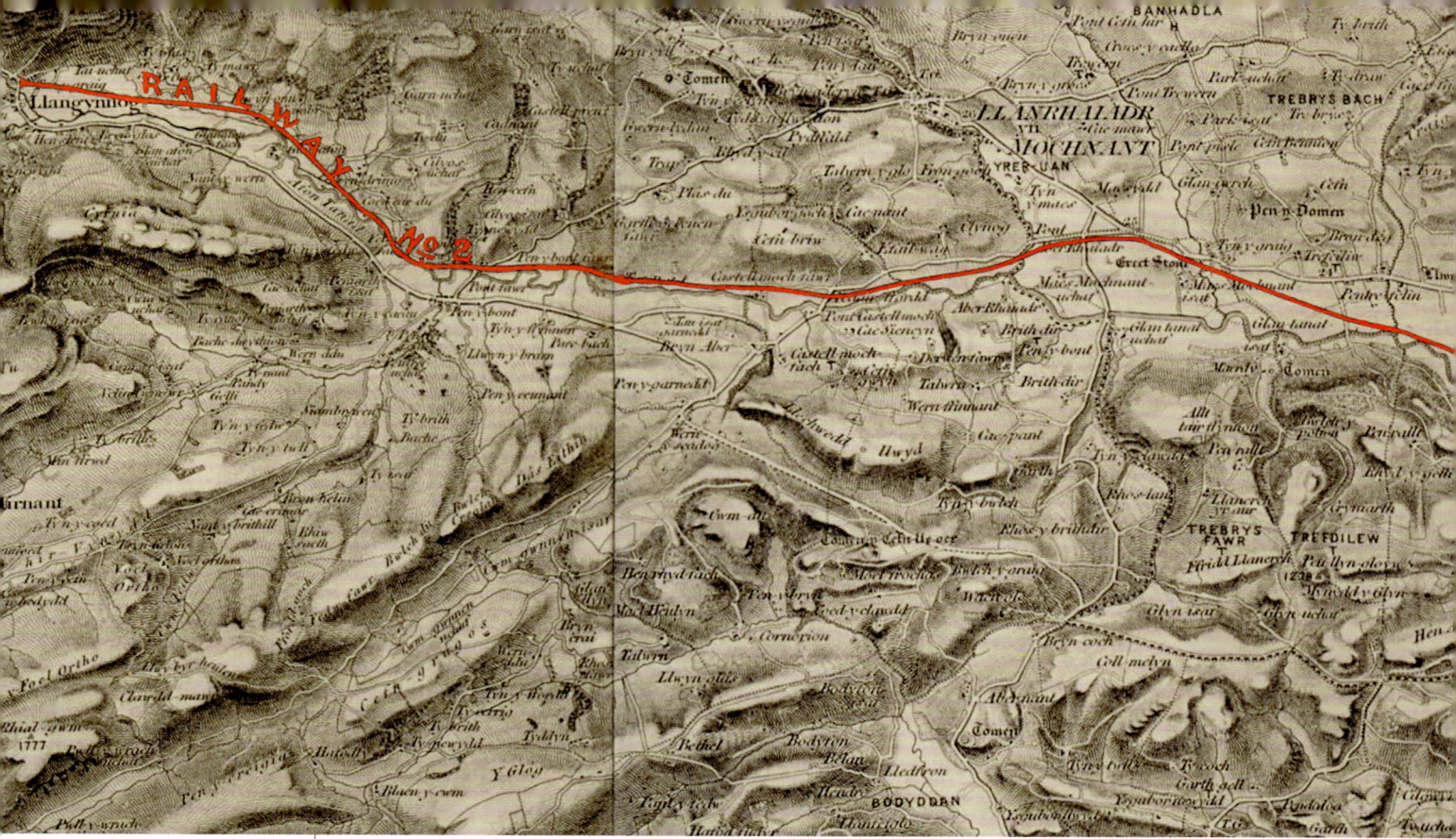

The 1882 version of the Oswestry & Llangynog Railway had many of the features adopted by the light railway. (Parliamentary Archives)

He also thought that it would be useless spending much money on promotion and obtaining powers until they had evidence that the capital could be raised. (*Cambrian News*, 15 November).

A committee was formed, and meetings held in Llanrhaeadr and Oswestry, the latter being more comprehensively reported. Spaull explained that of the proposed £50,000 capital, £20,000 would be allocated to landowners for their land, leaving the remainder to be raised in cash. One of the speakers supported Spaull's approach, effectively to raise the capital and let the promotional budget take care of itself. He added that this was a once in a lifetime opportunity to build a railway, for not only were the landowners united in support, but iron and labour were cheap, and everyone must support it by subscribing for shares, not leaving it for others, which was as true of previous proposals and of future ones as it was of the present one.

John Thomas (1834–1910), the mayor, said that he had spent time and money in supporting earlier schemes. In 1872, for example, £1,000 had been raised in Oswestry, but not £10 in Llangynog. Although an Oswestry committee was appointed to solicit share subscriptions in the town, no further reports relating to this scheme have been found and it faded out of existence. (*Wrexham Guardian,* 23 November / *Cambrian News*, 29 November).

Notwithstanding its dire financial straits and being subject to its 1881 Winding-up Act, later in the year the Potteries, Shrewsbury & North Wales Railway deposited a Bill for an Oswestry & Llangynog Railway, which intended to make use of running powers over the Cambrian Railways between Oswestry and Porthywaen. Similar to the later light railway, a new railway connected the Porthywaen branch with the Potteries Railway to the east of Llanyblodwel and then the 'main line' struck off for Llangynog to the west of Llanyblodwel, the new company having been given the right to make the connecting section of the Potteries Railway fit for public traffic.

Transferred to the unopposed list after Sir Watkin had withdrawn what he said was a formal objection to ensure the inclusion of clauses for his benefit (*Wrexham Advertiser*, 25 March 1882), the Bill received royal assent on 10 August. With the company to be named the Oswestry & Llangynog Railway, Thomas Dyne Steel (1823–98), John Deveraux Pugh

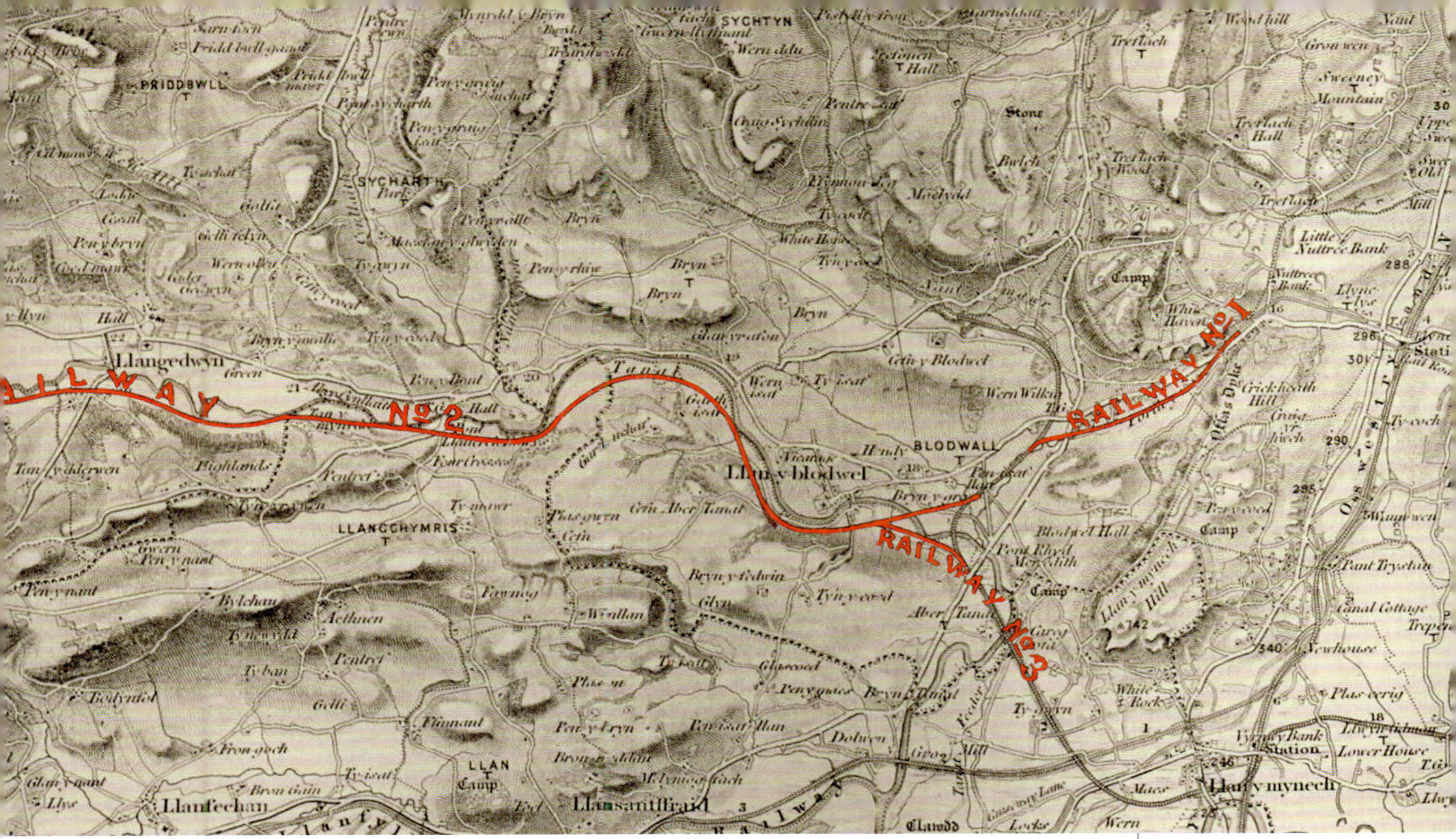

(1822–91) and John Beattie were named as the promoters and first directors.

Steel was a civil engineer based in Newport, Monmouthshire, who built a number of bridges. Pugh was a solicitor in Wrexham who in 1886 was made bankrupt (*Cheshire Observer*, 19 June) and in 1887 was struck off for misappropriating trust funds (*Carlisle Journal*, 25 March). Beattie has not been positively identified but a man with that name was the chairman of the North Staffordshire Tramways Company and a director of the Southwark & Deptford Tramways Company (*Daily Telegraph & Courier*, 12 January 1882).

Sir Watkin's clauses enabled him to appoint a director, required the company to build 'a passenger station of an ornamental character' in Llangedwyn and permitted no part of the railway to be opened until it was connected to the Porthywaen branch unless he had given his approval in writing.

The company made no obvious effort to raise capital, start work or promote itself. There was virtually no comment about it in the local press, the *Wrexham Advertiser*'s erroneous report (28 October 1882) that forecast the start of work in April 1883 being one of the few items about it. On 14 August 1884 the Cambrian's solicitor reported that he had been served with a notice to treat for land required for the intended junction, but no sale was made.

The Oswestry and Llangynog Railway (Extension of Time) Act was enacted on 25 June 1886 and on 9 July 1896 the

[45 & 46 VICT.] *Oswestry and Llangynog Railway Act*, 1882. [Ch. cxcviii.]

CHAPTER cxcviii.

An Act for making railways in the counties of Salop Denbigh and Montgomery to be called the Oswestry and Llangynog Railway and for other purposes. [10th August 1882.]

A.D. 1882.

WHEREAS the construction of the railways herein-after described would be of public and local advantage:

And whereas the persons herein-after named with others are willing to carry the undertaking into execution and it is expedient that they be incorporated into a Company and that the requisite powers be conferred upon them:

And whereas it is expedient that the Company so to be incorporated (in this Act called "the Company") and the Cambrian Railways Company be authorised to run over work and use the railway and portion of railway herein-after in that behalf mentioned:

And whereas it is expedient that the Company and the other Companies in that behalf in this Act mentioned be empowered to enter into and carry into effect traffic and other agreements as herein-after provided:

And whereas plans and sections showing the lines and levels of the railways authorised by this Act and also books of reference containing the names of the owners and lessees or reputed owners and lessees and of the occupiers of the lands required or which may be taken for the purposes or under the powers of this Act were duly deposited with the clerks of the peace for the counties of Salop Denbigh and Montgomery and are herein-after respectively referred to as the deposited plans sections and books of reference:

And whereas the purposes of this Act cannot be effected without the authority of Parliament:

May it therefore please Your Majesty, that it may be enacted and be it enacted by the Queen's most Excellent Majesty by and with the advice and consent of the Lords Spiritual and Temporal and

[*Local.–198.*] A 1

The Oswestry & Llangynog Railway Act, 1882.

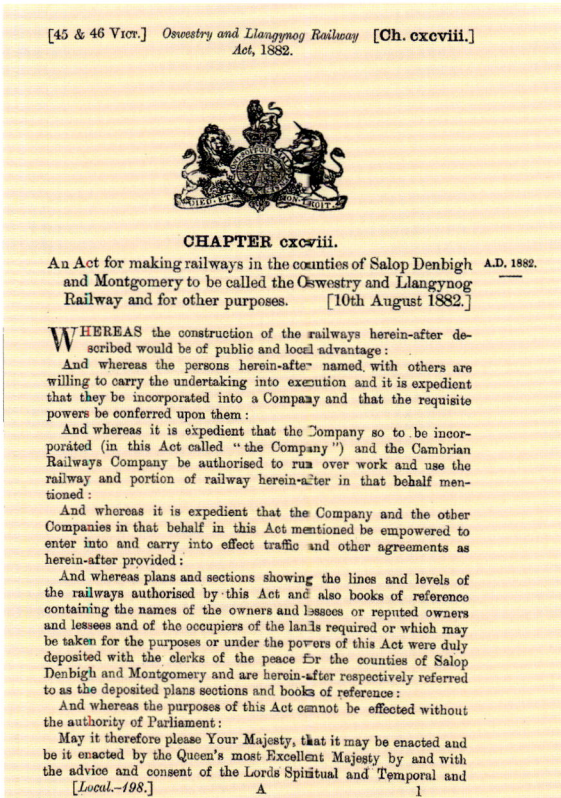

Right: The Oswestry & Llangynog Railway Act, 1886.

Far right: The Oswestry & Llangynog Railway (Abandonment) Act, 1889.

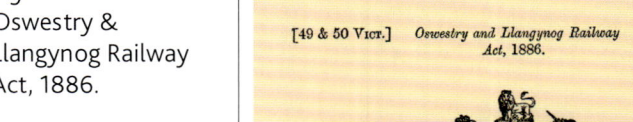

Cambrian was asked if it would assist in carrying out the Act's objectives, either with cash, a guarantee of interest on preferred stocks or by making a working agreement for a 'moderate' percentage of traffic receipts. Cambrian manager John Conacher took the request seriously and recommended it to his directors, although he noted that with £200,000 capital the proposed line would require traffic of £1,045 per mile per year to be capable of paying 4% interest or dividend after deducting 45% for working expenses, when in 1880 the nearby Llanfyllin branch serving similar country had earned only £400 per mile, increased to £500 a year after the Vyrnwy reservoir construction had started in 1881. The scheme came to an end with the Oswestry and Llangynog Railway (Abandonment) Act obtained in 1889.

A scheme that would have brought rails into the valley, if not to Llangynog, was an initiative of Liverpool Corporation, which in 1881 was planning for the construction of its Vyrnwy reservoir and associated works. The Corporation wanted to install a temporary roadside tramway between the Shropshire Railways' Llanyblodwel station and Penybontfawr, 10 miles, to carry equipment and materials. The Llanfyllin, Llangollen and Oswestry Highway Boards said that it would have to be 3ft 6in gauge, laid on the left-hand side of the road, presumably when heading westwards, and worked by horses. The surface between the rails would need to be made good for normal traffic, sold to them at valuation when no longer needed or removed and the road reinstated as the Boards determined, for a charge of £15 per mile per annum (*Eddowes's Shrewsbury Journal*, 23 February 1881). Nothing more was said about the scheme so presumably the Corporation found the terms too onerous and not worth the effort of trying to change. It did use tramways in connection with its works

Vyrnwy Embankment.

Burns, Photo.

The Vyrnwy dam. Its construction had been managed by W. H. Bickerton, the engineer who had worked for R.S. France on the Potteries Railway in the 1860s; after the dam had been completed he had also been in charge of laying part of the first pipeline (*Shrewsbury Chronicle*, 13 September 1907). (William Charles Burns/Burns & Son, Llanrheaedr)

in the Oswestry area (*Oswestry Advertiser*, 20 March 1889).

The next attempt to promote a railway to Llangynog was initiated when Owen Roberts (1836–1902), manager of the Rhiwarth slate quarry, started a letter writing campaign in June 1890. It made sufficient momentum that a public meeting held in Oswestry on 26 August voted to form a committee to take the preliminary steps towards the formation of a company and to report on its preferred route. Unlike the previous attempt, where the landowners had objected, now they were all in favour, the meeting was told. Roberts played very little part in the meeting, which had been called by the mayor in response to requests by 'notable persons' in the town (*Oswestry Advertiser*, 25 June/27 August).

On 27 August the *Oswestry Advertiser* also reported that the newly established

> **BOROUGH OF OSWESTRY.**
>
> **LLANGYNOG RAILWAY.**
>
> A MEETING of all Persons interested in the promotion of Railway Communication between Oswestry and Llangynog will be held in the Guildhall, Oswestry, on Tuesday, the 30th December, 1890, at Five p.m., at which the Plans of the Promoters will be explained by Sir Richard Green-Price, Bart., and others.
>
> The Chair will be taken by A. Wynne Corrie, Esquire, Mayor.

Advertisement for a meeting regarding the Shropshire Railways' proposed route, *Oswestry Advertiser*, 10 December 1890.

DESTINATION LLANGYNOG • 25

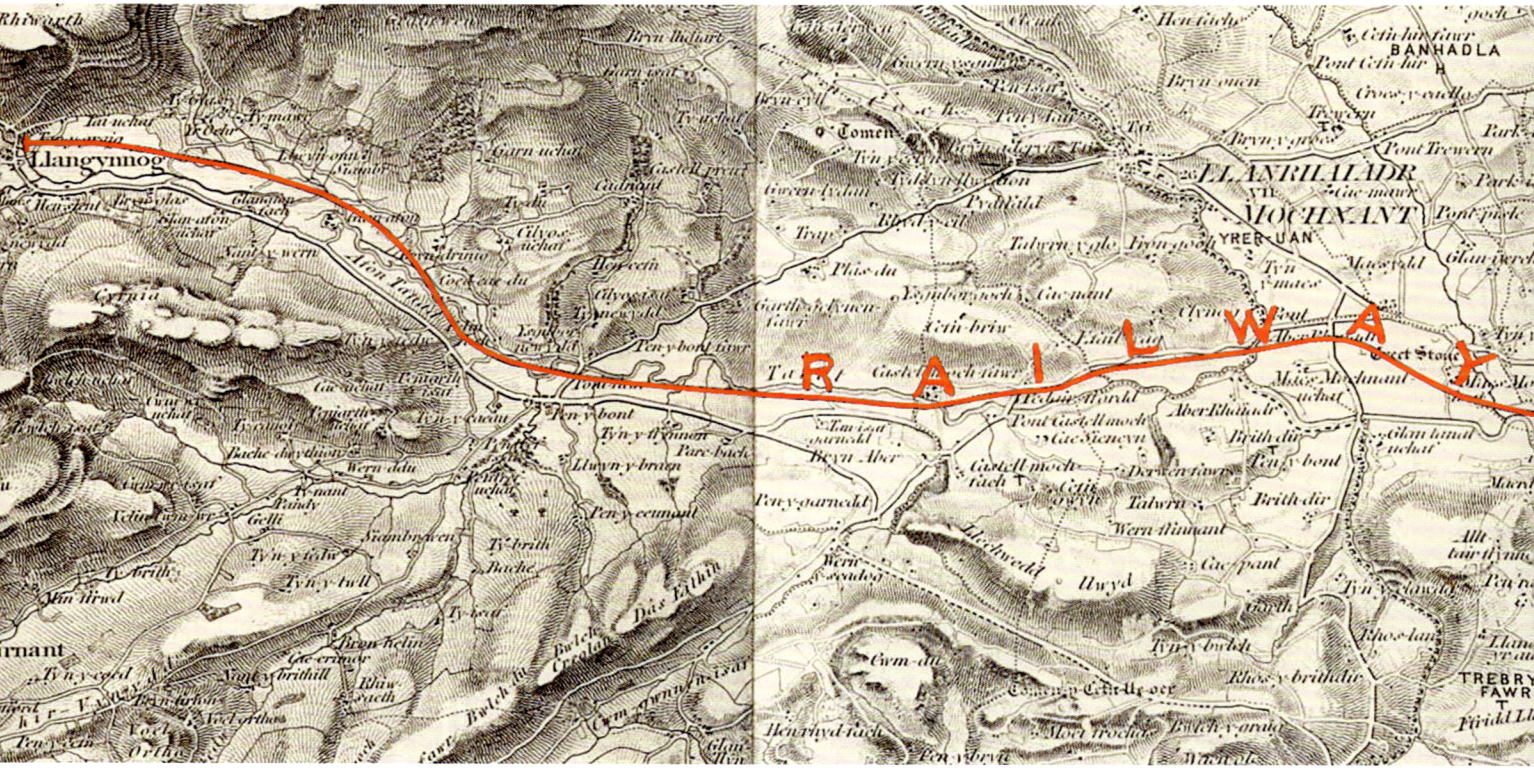

The Shropshire Railways' 1891 route to Llangynog.

Shropshire Railways was contemplating extending its line to Llangynog. With regards to this, Sir Richard Green-Price, the company's chairman, attended a meeting in Llangynog on 18 October, saying that he also had the landowners' support and that he did not anticipate any opposition in Parliament, unless it came from Oswestry. He made a great play of having liquidated the Potteries Railway's £1,390,000 debt with a sum of £350,000 without admitting that the latter sum was not represented by cash but by share and debenture certificates. The Shropshire Railways would, he said, raise the capital for the railway's construction but looked to the residents to defray the promotional expenses, which he expected to be less than £1,000. The meeting voted to support the scheme. (*Oswestry Advertiser*, 22 October).

Powers for a Llangynog extension were sought in the Shropshire Railways' notice of intention to deposit a General Powers Bill published on 10 November (*London Gazette*, 21 November 1890) and by the time Sir Richard attended a meeting in Oswestry on 30 December, which also voted to support the extension, £700 had been raised, £500 from landowners and directors (*Oswestry Advertiser*, 31 December 1890). However, the Bill was withdrawn when the company had failed to raise sufficient for the deposit (*Wellington Journal*, 8 August 1891). The active promotion of the Shropshire Railways' scheme seems to have brought an end to the scheme supported in Oswestry on 26 August 1890.

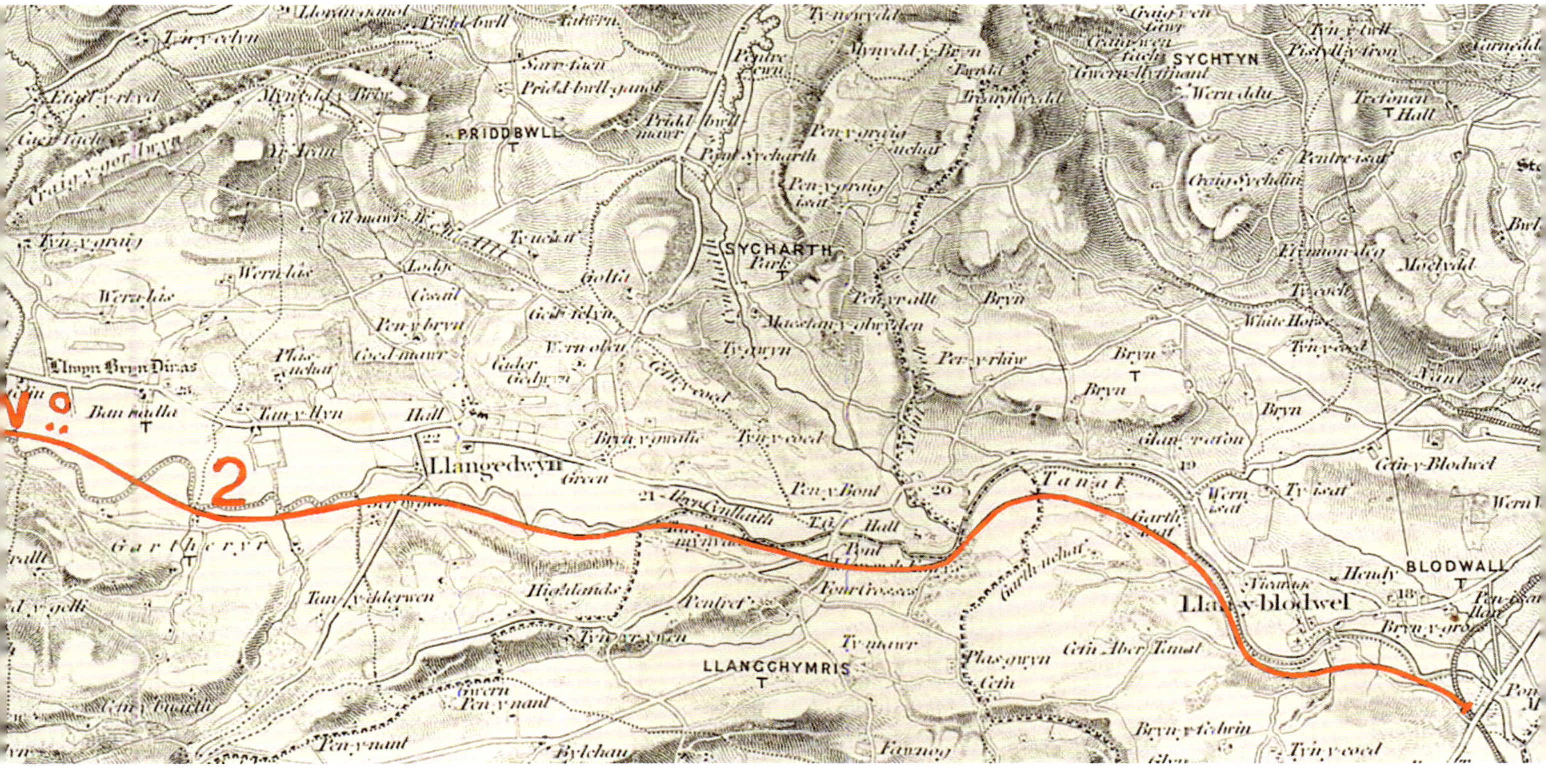

Llansilin Road station at Penybont Llanerch Emrys, truly a wayside station. The road behind the fence on the left was built by the railway to divert an existing road and avoid having two level crossings in close proximity

CHAPTER 2
THE LIGHT RAILWAY ORDER

Strange as it might seem, but the eventual construction of a railway in the Tanat valley had its origins in the Irish potato harvest failure and consequent famine of the 1880s. In its aftermath the Light Railways (Ireland) Act, 1889, was enacted, enabling light railways to be approved by the Lord Lieutenant by means of an Order in Council, for the Treasury to make grants or loans from funds provided for the purpose and for local authorities to guarantee dividend payments.

Agriculture in England and Scotland being also in depression, county councils campaigned for powers to promote light railways with a view to develop 'remote areas' and improve conditions for agriculture. A resolution on the subject was circulated between councils (*Oswestry Advertiser*, 12 February) but it was a while before the government acted.

One of the deterrents to the use of railways to aid the development of rural areas with sparse populations was that the Board of Trade imposed the same standards on country branch lines as it did on busy main lines. Another was the cost of obtaining powers. Legislation to address these issues had been attempted twice before. 1864's Railways Construction Facilities Act provided that where no compulsory purchase powers were required, the Board of Trade could issue a draft certificate for approval by Parliament. However, its requirement to have the consent of all landowners and other affected parties and no opposition from any railway or canal company meant that no use was made of it, and its 1870 amendment giving objectors the right to address Parliament merely increased its cost to applicants. The Regulation of Railways Act, 1868, contained powers for light railways, including restricting axle weights to 8 tons and speeds to 25mph, but little use was made of them.

There were many letters to newspapers deprecating the red tape and expense imposed on 'ordinary' railways by the Board of Trade, some contrasting the UK with the Continent, where there were, it was said, light railways in abundance. Among the letters, a writer to *The Times* (7 November 1894) said that his friend had been killed because he had tried to board a moving train, not by the height of the platform [imposed by the Board of Trade], adding that 'until we are allowed low-priced works, cheap fencing, abolition of unnecessary staff, and some respite from the circumlocution department, we shall never get light railways in England'.

The Times took the credit for setting the ball rolling, with a series of articles published in March 1894. Later in the year a 'voluntary committee' was established in the House of Commons and in November a light railways conference was appointed under the auspices of the Board of Trade, meeting for the first time on 6 December. It obtained the views of county councils as to whether there should be light railways under an improved system of procedure and regulations, the desirability of state and local aid to private enterprise and 'the mode of construction of light railways, as to gauge, etc.' and made recommendations to the government.

Concurrently, the royal commission on agriculture took evidence on the subject in July 1894 and in February 1895. On the latter occasion the newly elected MP for Montgomeryshire, Arthur Charles Humphreys-Owen (1836–1905), said that powers should be given to county councils to promote light railways, as already existed for borough councils in respects of tramways. He also said that in Montgomeryshire there were two valleys eminently suitable for being worked by cheap railways. One ran from Welshpool to Llanfair, and the other from a point on the Cambrian Railways to Llangynog (*Liverpool Mercury*, 8 February). Humphreys-Owen was also a director of the Cambrian Railways and had inherited the Glansevern estate, near Welshpool, where his aunt had played a part, not always constructively, in the development of the Newtown & Llanidloes Railway.

A Bill was introduced in the House of Commons in April 1895, but its progress was ended by a general election on 12 August. The conference was resumed on 28 November, where there were some who held that the state should not be involved, and one county had responded that whatever was done 'they must not obstruct for hunting' but the meeting resolved to urge the government to introduce legislation authorising light railways with an improved system of procedure and regulations, and adding state and local aid to private enterprise.

A second Bill was introduced in February 1896. Speaking in its support, the president of the Board of Trade, Charles Thompson Ritchie (1838-1906), said that the proposal was not a panacea for agricultural depression but by reducing costs and bringing consumers and producers closer together it would do something to mitigate the issue. The government, he said, accepted that light railways would not be made without some aid, both from the localities and the state; the absence of financial support had been a criticism of the 1895 Bill.

He had been to France and Belgium to see how things were done there. In France, so-called light railways, he thought, were really secondary railways, built to complete major trunk routes, whereas in Belgium light railways were steam tramways, mainly based on the use of public roads with occasional use of cross-country routes. There were few signals, hardly any stations and simple branches served particular farms and industries. A thousand miles had been built over ten years. Funded by the state, provinces, communes and outside subscribers, the returns had been satisfactory.

He favoured the Belgian system, questioning how it could be applied to Britain. Hitherto, the main difficulties had been the reluctance of Parliament to devolve the power to authorise compulsory purchase and the expense of meeting the Board of Trade's requirements for public safety. He hoped that Parliament would release its grip on the approvals process and that landowners would be content with a 'simply organised enquiry' without insisting on appeals to the legislature. Regarding safety, the public must decide, if it wanted light railways, to exercise a certain amount of caution and not insist on the elaborate precautions necessary on trunk lines.

During the Bill's committee stage in June a member complaining about the lack of a definition of the term 'light railway' was told that as localities varied widely, attempting a definition 'would greatly embarrass the working of the Bill'. Those who called for all railways to be 4ft 8½in gauge appear to have been ignored and royal assent was given on 14 August 1896. The Locomotives on Highways Act was enacted at the same time, exempting 'light (road) locomotives' from certain provisions while imposing restrictions regarding weight, traction and other matters. Two very different Acts with very different purposes, but one would have a great influence on the outcome of the other.

The Light Railways Act comprised twenty-nine clauses and three schedules. Briefly, it established the Light Railway Commission and charged it with facilitating the construction and working of light railways. Applications for orders could be made by any council through which the proposed railway was to pass, by any individual, corporation or company, independently or jointly.

Councils could contribute to a railway's capital either by loan or by shares, in which case the Treasury could lend an amount not exceeding a quarter of the total amount required or the amount being advanced by the council, providing that at least half of the amount required was share capital and at least half of that had been subscribed and paid up by persons other than local authorities. If the Board of Agriculture or the Board of Trade certified that a light railway would benefit agriculture or the development or maintenance of a specified industry, the Treasury could also make a special advance not exceeding half of the amount required, either by a free grant or a loan or a combination of both, provided that the land required had been provided without charge. The Treasury was allocated £1 million to disburse, of which not more than a quarter could be by free grants. Local authorities could fund their contributions by borrowing.

Any order made by the commissioners had to be submitted to the Board of Trade for confirmation and once confirmed would have effect as if enacted by Parliament and was to be treated as evidence that the requirements of the Act had been complied with. The Board of Trade decided that the cost of making an application should be £50, an amount that remained unchanged until the legislation was replaced in 1992. Orders could include powers to take land compulsorily without recourse to Parliament.

To qualify for a Treasury grant a railway would have to be built and operated by an existing company. The former was something of a charade, for the client company would raise capital and issue tenders for the parent company to approve; when work started the parent's engineer would certify the work for payment to his employers, who would pass the money on to the contractor. As regards the operation, this was expected to reduce costs, as the client company did not normally have to purchase its own rolling stock, as it would be supplied from the parent's existing pool, and thus reduce the amount of capital required. The downside was that there was no single individual responsible for the light railway's traffic, with an interest in expanding it or finding new sources.

Reporting of the Bill's progress had attracted much interest in areas that thought they might benefit from the legislation and Montgomeryshire became a hotbed of agitation for the promotion of light railways. Not surprisingly, with regards to the Tanat valley, the mayor of Oswestry, Charles Edmondson Williams (1861–1935), was the first off the line, responding to requests from residents of Llanrhaeadr, Penybontfawr, Llangynog and Llansilin as well as his own town for a meeting on the subject. This was held on 18 May, a few weeks before the legislation came into effect. Without specifying which route it should take, the meeting passed a motion in support of a light railway between Oswestry and Llangynog (*Wrexham Advertiser*, 23 May).

At another meeting, held in Oswestry on 21 July, a route via Llansilin was favoured and George Owen showed how a standard-gauge line could be achieved but the vicar of Llanrhaeadr's suggestion that the meeting should be adjourned to a future date at Llanrhaeadr to give the rural community a chance to contribute was accepted.

At Llanrhaeadr on 18 August, therefore, the resumed meeting was joined by a party of nine from Oswestry and with some of it conducted in Welsh, a motion in support of the Llansilin route was passed (*Montgomery County Times*, 25 July, 1/22 August).

In Llanfyllin, meanwhile, news that Oswestry residents were pushing for a light railway to Llangynog was cause for concern that the town could lose a substantial part of its business and the town council called a meeting to discuss having their own railway to Llangynog.

Advertisement calling the meeting to discuss the desirability of a light railway between Oswestry and Llangynog, *Montgomeryshire Times*, 9 May 1896.

OSWESTRY AND LLANGYNOG RAILWAY.

IN compliance with a request of a number of the inhabitants of Oswestry, Llanrhaiadr, Penybontfawr, Llangynog and Llansilin, asking me to call a PUBLIC MEETING for the purpose of considering the desirability of constructing a Line of Railway from Oswestry to Llanrhaiadr and Llangynog, I therefore convene a PUBLIC MEETING to be held in the GUILDHALL, OSWESTRY, on MONDAY, the 18th day of MAY, at 2 p.m.

Dated this 1st day of May, 1896.

CHAS. E. WILLIAMS, Mayor.

Llansilin.

Petter's series.

As first discussed, the light railway would have gone through Llansilin, a village just inside the Welsh border, 5 miles from Oswestry. The author is unaware of the existence of any plan showing this route. (*Petter's Series*)

The centre of Llanfyllin at the turn of the twentieth century. (Park, Newtown)

Cadwaladr Richard Jones (1829-1902), the farmer who had asked for the meeting, said that their town would be left aside if a railway was built that ran to Oswestry, its markets and fairs would lose business and houses and land would lose value; he had been one of the promoters of the 1873 scheme for a narrow-gauge railway to Llangynog. Ellis Roberts (1842–1913), a solicitor, thought they would get the Cambrian Railways' support because it had more to gain from it if there was traffic for destinations like Welshpool and Shrewsbury as well as Oswestry. One speaker said that Llangynog residents were in favour of the Llanfyllin route, which seems to have been wishful thinking; the claim was repeated at the light railway order inquiry without any supporting evidence. A motion in favour was passed and a deputation appointed to meet the Cambrian Railways (*Montgomeryshire Express*, 3 November).

The deputation met C. S. Denniss, the Cambrian manager, on 23 December 1896, saying that it wished the Cambrian to contribute a substantial proportion of the capital. He replied that his company would consider favourably a request to construct and work the line if its promoters had obtained the necessary capital.

A vote taken at a meeting held in Llangynog to solicit support for the Llanfyllin route on 6 February 1897 was deemed to support a motion in its favour, but the rector pointed out that they had previously supported the Oswestry route. The *Shrewsbury Chronicle*'s 12 February report said 'several hands were held up in favour', which hardly sounds like overwhelming support.

Owen, the Cambrian engineer, had been consulted and confirmed that his 1873 route was still the best available (*Shrewsbury Chronicle*, 29 January 1897). On 23 February Llanfyllin Town Council was informed of a recommendation that it contribute £3,000 to be borrowed and repaid over sixty years, to the railway, and £200 towards the preliminary expenses, but deferred making a decision (*Montgomery County Times*, 27 February).

Llanfyllin Rural District Council had four light railway proposals to consider on 16 March, two to Llanfair Caereinion and two to Llangynog. Hearing representations from all of them, it decided that any advances would be by way of loans and that the amounts requested would be made available to any of the schemes that obtained powers, £5,000 in the case of Llanfyllin and £3,000 for Oswestry.

On 27 March Oswestry Town Council agreed to give notice of its wish to loan £5,000, while Llangynog Parish Council resolved to ask its representative on Montgomeryshire County Council to give his support to the Oswestry line in preference to the Llanfyllin. At Hirnant, between Penybontfawr and Vyrnwy, a parish meeting heard the case for the Llanfyllin line, which it might have benefited from, and pledged to support the Oswestry route (*Montgomery County Times*, 3 April).

This case was cited by Joseph Parry Jones (1843–1915) at a County Council meeting on 6 April, when he pointed out that none of the parish councils supported the Llanfyllin route (*Montgomery County Times*, 10 April). Jones was a solicitor who had attended a meeting held in support of W. H. Spaull's scheme for a narrow-gauge railway to Llangynog in 1878 and who became very influential in the promotion of the Light Railway. As well as owning property in the Tanat valley, he was also the Cambrian Railways' solicitor, Oswestry's town clerk, a town councillor and served one term as mayor.

Undeterred by the lack of support, the Llanfyllin promoters appointed Everard Richard Calthrop (1857–1927) and Frederick Darwent Ward (1866–1935) as engineers to produce a narrow-gauge route (*Montgomery County Times*, 17 April 1897). Calthrop was the engineer of the 2ft 6in gauge Barsi Light Railway in India and went on to be the engineer of the Leek & Manifold Light Railway in Staffordshire. A Mancunian, Ward was the Powis estate's architect and surveyor. Both of them were then also working on what became the Welshpool & Llanfair Light Railway.

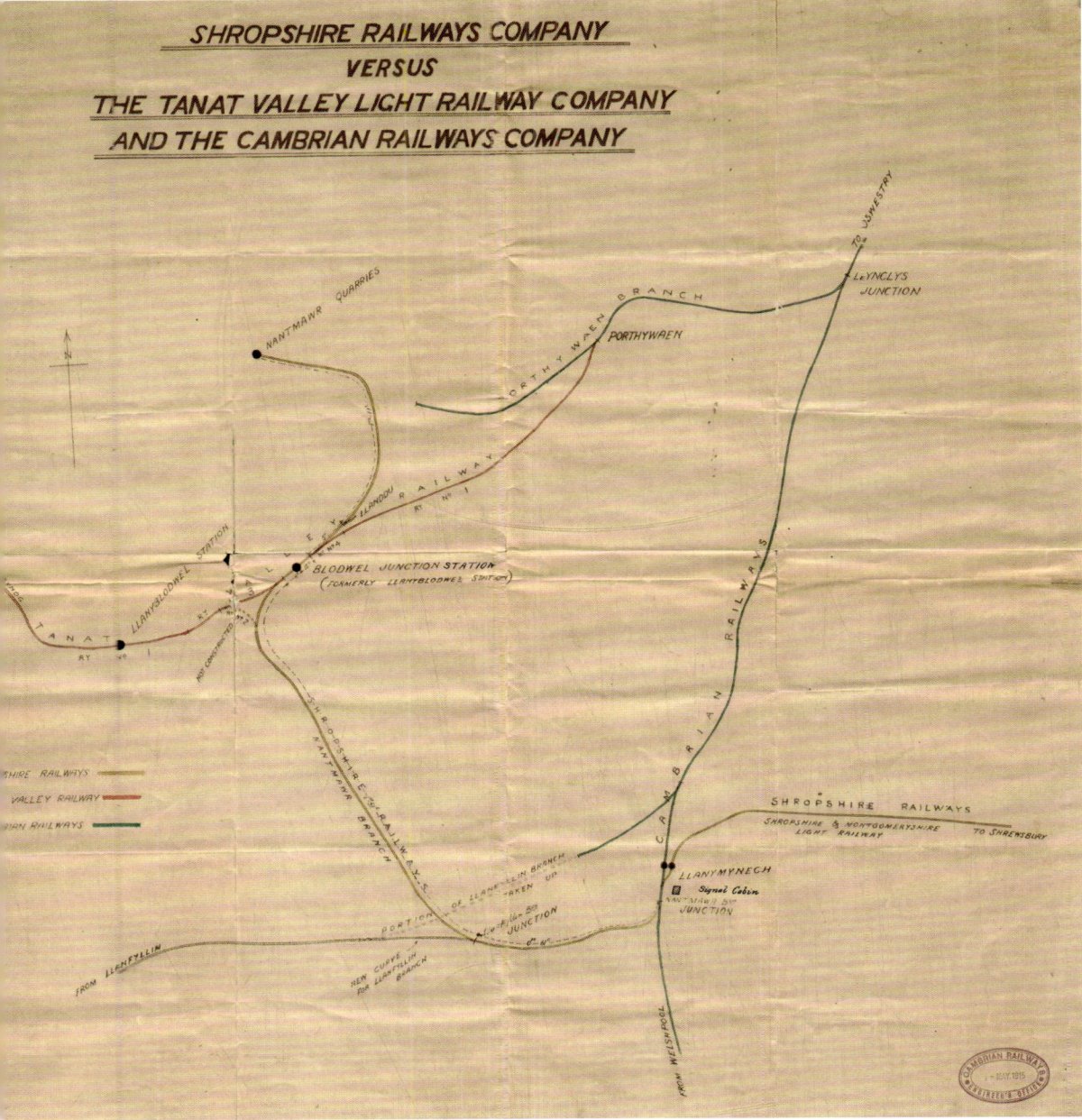

Produced in 1915, this plan shows the contentious areas around Llanyblodwel. (National Archives)

By the time the Oswestry Rural District Council met in May, the Oswestry route was being referred to as the Tanat Valley Railway, forming a junction with the Cambrian Railways at Porthywaen, the Llansilin route having been abandoned without comment (*Montgomery County Times*, 8 May). When the Light Railway Order application was submitted the railway had an independent route between Porthywaen and Llanyblodwel but at some point this was altered to make use of a short section of the Shropshire Railways' Nantmawr tramway, probably on the grounds of cost, as it would save need for a separate formation at the expense of some additional trackwork and signalling and making the section of the Shropshire Railways fit for passenger trains (Page 40).

Llanfyllin was not the only small town concerned about the effect of the Tanat valley line on its commercial feature, Llanymynech Parish Council passing a motion that complained of the 'serious and unnecessary' expenditure that could be avoided if the railway was routed via

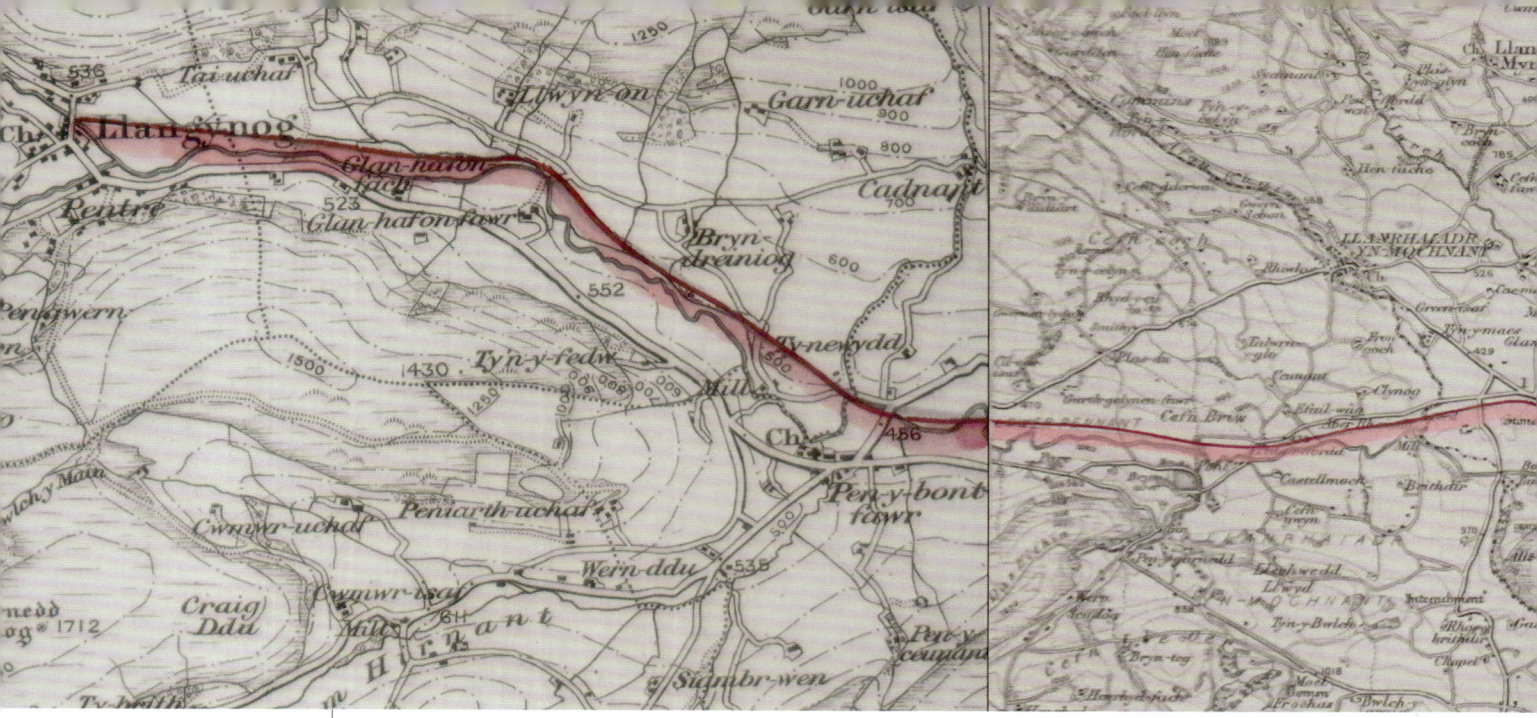

The deposited plan for the light railway showing it taking its own alignment between Porthywaen and Llanyblodwel and pencilled lines connecting it to a part of the Shropshire Railways' Nantmawr line. (National Archives)

the Shropshire Railways' Llanyblodwel branch to their town. Oswestry traffic would only have to travel 2 miles further, while there would be a reduction in distance for Buttington and Aberystwyth traffic. It was not clear to whom the motion was addressed (*Montgomery County Times*, 29 May 1897).

Light Railway Order applications for both routes were submitted in May and the Light Railway Commissioners held an inquiry in Oswestry on 3 August. There was a lot of interest, the room was 'uncomfortably full', and some could not gain admittance.

In his opening remarks, the Tanat Valley's barrister said that objections from the Bradford and Powis estates had been overcome by the promise to construct a loop line at Llanyblodwel, to enable trains to run directly to and from Llanymynech. Shrewsbury Town Council objected because the railway would divert any traffic that might be routed via the Shropshire Railways if it were reopened, which raised a laugh from the audience. Denbigh and Montgomery County Councils, Llanfyllin and Llanrhaiadr Rural District Councils and Oswestry Town Council had promised to advance, by loan, a total of £14,500 of the £45,000 capital. A total of 525 people had signed a petition in favour of the scheme, while 100 ratepayers in Llangynog had signed another petition in favour.

Forty-nine out of fifty-eight landowners affected agreed to their land being taken, five had offered no opinion and only four objected.

Charles Sherwood Denniss (1868–1917), the Cambrian Railways' manager, said that his company was prepared to work the line for 60% of receipts. The company did not object to the Llanfyllin scheme but felt that the Tanat valley offered greater advantages in developing resources and would open up a richer district.

Parry Jones explained that subscriptions had been obtained for £8,889 of share capital from 551 persons, 161 of them being Llangynog residents, but that the failure of earlier schemes meant that some would-be subscribers were waiting until the Order was made before committing themselves.

The strategy of the Llanfyllin scheme's barrister was not to promote 'his' railway but to criticise the Tanat Valley proposal. It would cost more, because by going via Llanfyllin half of the route was already made. Llanfyllin was the natural centre, he claimed; county and magistrates' courts sat there, its town council and rural district council were based there, an intermediate school was to be built there. The Tanat proposal would cut the town off and not improve its communications, which was also against the intention of the Act. The Llanfyllin promoters only wanted £6,550 from the Treasury, while

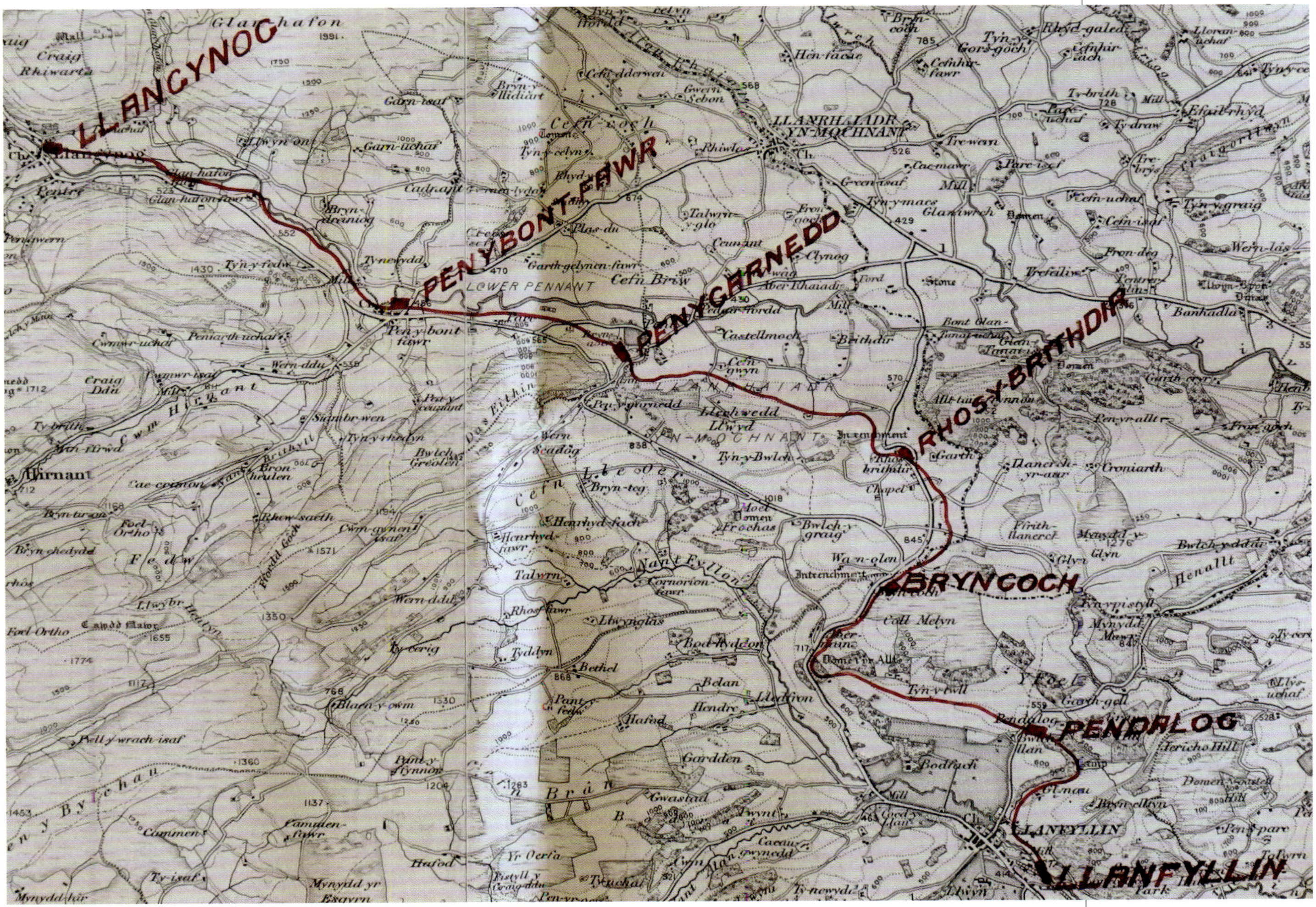

The deposited plan for the narrow-gauge Llanfyllin & Llangynog Light Railway. (National Archives)

the Tanat Valley wanted £23,000. If the commissioners made a paper assessment of the two proposals, they would 'instantly reject' the Tanat scheme. Unless there were strong and overwhelming reasons in its favour, the commissioners should not sanction it as the Llanfyllin line was the more economical. If the

Llanfyllin in 1955, the branch line terminus in the centre foreground. (James Valentine Ltd)

The Llanfyllin & Llangynog Light Railway's book of reference. Required to list the owners and occupiers of land through which a railway intended to pass, books of reference are not usually as well presented as this one. (National Archives)

decision was not for the Llanfyllin route then the town would suffer very much indeed.

Giving evidence, Calthrop said that the Llanfyllin railway would not have stationmasters and that tickets would be issued on the trains. Apart from stations at the termini, trains would stop wherever there was traffic; waiting sheds would be placed at ten locations. So far as Llangynog was concerned, the traffic would be the same by either route, but he thought the Tanat estimate of 20,000 passengers a year was excessive, half that was more reasonable. His system of carrying standard-gauge wagons on narrow-gauge transportation vehicles would be used to carry goods.

Horace Bell (1840–1903), a civil engineer who had worked in India so had probably known Calthrop from there, said that he thought the Tanat Valley estimates were inadequate and that the Llanfyllin line could be worked more cheaply. He disagreed with Calthrop over the use of transportation wagons, though, as he thought transhipment by hand would be more satisfactory, although nothing was made of this point.

Llanfyllin's mayor, J. Marshall Dugdale (1852–1918), said they were contemplating building an intermediate school in the town but if the Tanat Valley scheme went ahead the school would not pay, because some children who might attend would go to Oswestry. Only two of the seventeen quarries in Llangynog were working. The good that the Tanat Valley line would do on its own route would not outweigh the damage it would do to Llanfyllin. (The intermediate school was opened in temporary premises later in 1897 and moved to its own site in 1900. The building was listed Grade II by Cadw, the Welsh heritage agency, in 2005. After a period of use as a community centre it is presently out of use, its frontage completely obscured by bushes.)

Having heard eight hours of evidence, the commissioners then closed the inquiry, deferring their decision (*Montgomery County Times*, 7 August 1897).

Their report compared the two routes, noting that the journey from Llangynog to Oswestry would be 5 miles longer via Llanfyllin and that that route had a climb of 375ft out of the Tanat valley before falling 466ft to Llanfyllin. In contrast, with no steep gradients, the Tanat line had the advantage over the Llanfyllin route in every respect except the first cost, but it would be cheaper to run, they thought. Its steepest gradient was a short section of 1 in 64 and no curve was sharper than ten chains. It would require 71½ acres, 4¾ acres per mile with a 40ft formation, which was rather low, they felt. Construction costs, estimated at £3,100 a mile, were also low, and soon found to be an issue.

The decision in favour of the Tanat Valley Light Railway was announced in September (*South Wales Daily News*, 10 September 1897). In their report to the Board of Trade the commissioners observed that copies of the proposed order had been sent to all affected parties. Points raised that were not included in the Order included the following:

> Llanrhaeadr Parish Council got its wish for 'small stations' to be provided at Pentrefelin and Pedairfordd, but they were not specified in the Order. Requests for any local authority lending £2,000 or more to be entitled to representation on the company board were refused. The Commissioners thought that privilege should be reserved for authorities that had invested in shares, the logic being that the investors were taking a risk, while the lenders would expect to receive interest and, eventually, reimbursement. Authorities that made loans without borrowing could charge 3% interest.

Lord Bradford (1819–98, the 3rd) had made several requests, chiefly that the train service from Llangynog to Llanymynech should be as efficient as from Llangynog to Llynclys. Although the commissioners understood that the company intended to give his lordship an acceptable service, they did not make provision for it in the Order as matters relating to the train service were for the Railway Commissioners to deal with.

On 15 November the promoters met in Oswestry to be updated on progress. Parry Jones said that he had met the commissioners several times and they had told him that as the procedure was a new one, they had not yet decided exactly how to proceed but expected the order to be ready in January 1898.

The application for the Treasury free grant had been made and additional information requested. Before the grant could be made, though, the share subscriptions needed to be increased from £8,900 to £11,500; to make sure there would be no delay Jones had given a personal guarantee for the difference, a bold and generous gesture. So far as the local authorities went, Shropshire County Council had agreed to advance £2,000, bringing their contribution up to £16,500. Liverpool Corporation was also keen for the railway to be built, because it would reduce the cost of increasing the capacity of its Vyrnwy aqueduct; the corporation's water engineer, Joseph Parry (1844–1933), had given evidence at the public inquiry (*Shrewsbury Chronicle*, 19 November 1897).

Working for the Corporation on the Vyrnwy dam and subsequently on the pipeline was W. H. Bickerton, the engineer who had worked for France on the construction of the Potteries Railway (*Shrewsbury Chronicle*, 13 September 1907). The reservoir and first pipeline had been opened formally in 1892.

The Treasury notified the company of its grant decision on 22 December 1897, saying that it would make a free grant of £18,000 subject to the Order being issued by the Commissioners and confirmed by the Board of Trade. The grant would not become payable, however, until it had received a certificate from the Board of Trade saying that the line was complete and open for traffic and that a sum of not less than twice the amount of the grant had been spent, exclusive of the value of the land donated by landowners. It was also a condition that for a period of ten years after the order had been confirmed, none of the land occupied by the railway could have its rateable value increased (*Liverpool Mercury*, 30 December 1897). Not paying the grant until the railway was complete and open for traffic would leave the promoters with an £18,000 funding shortfall during construction that would have to be overcome by borrowing and incurring additional expense.

The grant was the first awarded under the terms of the Light Railways Act, the *Shrewsbury Chronicle* noted, also on 30 December, adding, 'Oswestry people are to be congratulated on the success which has so far rewarded their enterprise.'

Parry Jones was motivated by the award to suggest to Denniss, the Cambrian manager, on 17 January 1898, that when the Order was made the Tanat Valley line, and its £18,000 grant, should be absorbed into the Cambrian, for it to finance and manage the whole scheme, saving the cost of separate management, directorship and staff. He had not mentioned this to the promoters, he said, but if the Cambrian directors were interested, he would do so 'without delay'. Denniss saw Parry Jones to tell him that his company had no capital available and would require fresh powers to obtain authorisation for more. Some twenty years later the Cambrian saw that it would be in its interest to absorb the Tanat Valley line and did so.

At Llanfyllin on 18 January the town council marked the New Year with a special meeting to justify and approve the expenditure of £400 (£35,000 in 2021) on its Llangynog railway scheme and its opposition to the Tanat valley railway (*Montgomery County Times*, 22 January). Some of the members, if not all, must have known that in the circumstances their own railway venture was futile.

On the railway whose future would be linked to the Tanat Valley, derailment of a wagon at Nantmawr in March caused Alfred Jones Collin (1862–1916), the Cambrian's newly appointed engineer, to inspect the branch to assess the work needed to put it into 'decent order', writing to Denniss on 22 March that it needed 3,000 sleepers at a cost of £320, re-piling the river bridge, £150, and fencing, £40. As it generated so very little traffic – the engine only went up twice a week – he could not understand why consideration was being given to spending so much on it. Only the fencing was essential, and the bridge should be repaired if the branch was to remain open. Denniss's reply has not been found but obviously the work was done.

The Cambrian Railways' management records reveal that between July and September 1898 there had been an extensive correspondence between Denniss and Parry Jones over a guarantee for a minimum number of trains to be run to and from Oswestry, which the Cambrian was not willing to give. Jones was obviously determined to prevail, saying that as a guarantee had been given for a minimum of two trains to be run to Llanymynech, under pressure from Lord Bradford, Oswestry residents would see it as a betrayal if they did not get the same or better service. If they thought there was a risk that Tanat Valley traffic and business could be diverted to Shrewsbury, they would withdraw their support for the railway and the application would collapse when they found out, he threatened. Denniss eventually gave way but so far as the Order was concerned it was irrelevant because, as already noted, the Board of Trade thought that it was not a matter for it to legislate on.

In the spring of 1899, there was still a £2,000 shortfall on share subscriptions. On 7 March the Mayor of Oswestry told the council and tradesmen that only £800 had been subscribed from the town, despite the expectation that it would be the chief beneficiary of the railway, and called on townsmen to subscribe liberally and ensure that construction could be started soon. In May the 4th Earl of Powis (1862–1952) said that he would subscribe another £250 if the balance was subscribed within two months (*Montgomery County Times*, 12 March/14 May).

The Tanat Valley Light Railway Order was sealed by the Board of Trade on 4 January 1899. It comprised seventy-seven clauses and two schedules. The Tanat Valley Light Railway Company was incorporated, and the first directors were named as C. E. Williams, William Hopkins Thomas, Owen Roberts, John Kenrick Jones, David Davies and Charles Drew plus any appointed by the subscribing local authorities.

A land agent and accountant, Williams had been the mayor of Oswestry who called the town meeting in support of a railway in 1896. Thomas (1849–1922) was an Oswestry builder and contractor; he died of heart failure while on a partridge shoot (*Birmingham Daily Gazette*, 4 September 1922). Roberts was the Rhiwarth quarry manager who had initiated the 1890 scheme; he did not attend board meetings after 1899. Jones (1859–1920) was the Llanrhaeadr GP. Davies (1838–1913) was a Liverpool property owner who did not attend board meetings after 1906; he is buried in Liverpool's Toxteth Park cemetery. Drew (1841–1917) ran Oswestry's

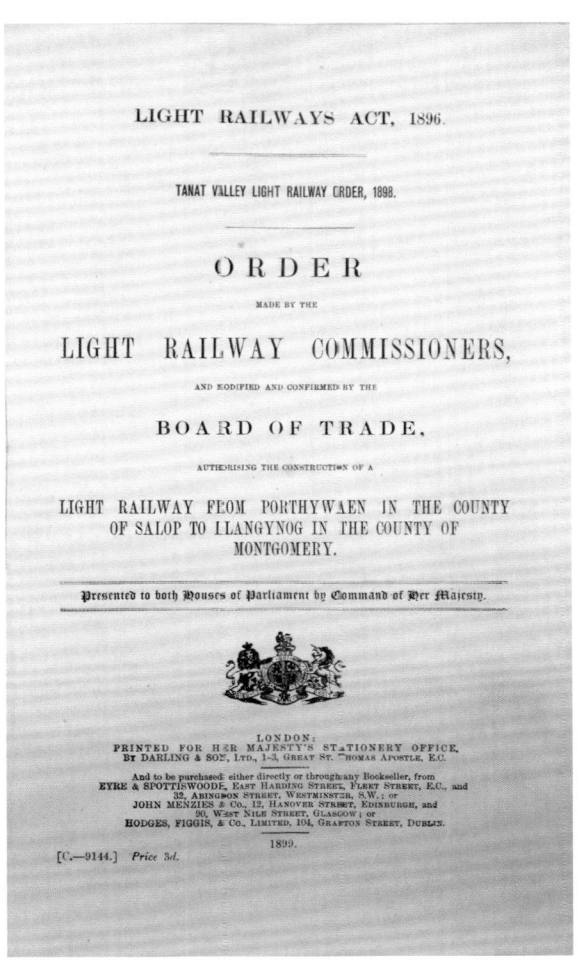

The Tanat Valley Light Railway Order, 1899. The date in the title is incorrect.

Wynnstay Hotel; he did not attend board meetings after 1907.

Legally, the railway comprised four lines. No 1, 14 miles 7 furlongs long, was the 'main line', from a junction with the Porthywaen branch to Llangynog. Unusually, it was split into two, separated by a short section of the Shropshire Railways' Nantmawr tramway, which it was empowered to use. Railway No 2 was to give access from the Tanat valley to Llanymynech. No 3 connected the main line at a point to the west of the Tanat with the Shropshire Railways at Llanyblodwel (Blodwel Junction) station, and No 4 connected the line from Porthywaen with the Shropshire Railways east of the station.

Five years were allowed for construction. Gates were to be provided at five specified level crossings and at any level crossing of a public road where the company

Charles Drew, one of the light railway company's founding directors, is buried in Oswestry's public cemetery. His estate was valued at £21,875 13s 4d, £1,198,702 in 2022.

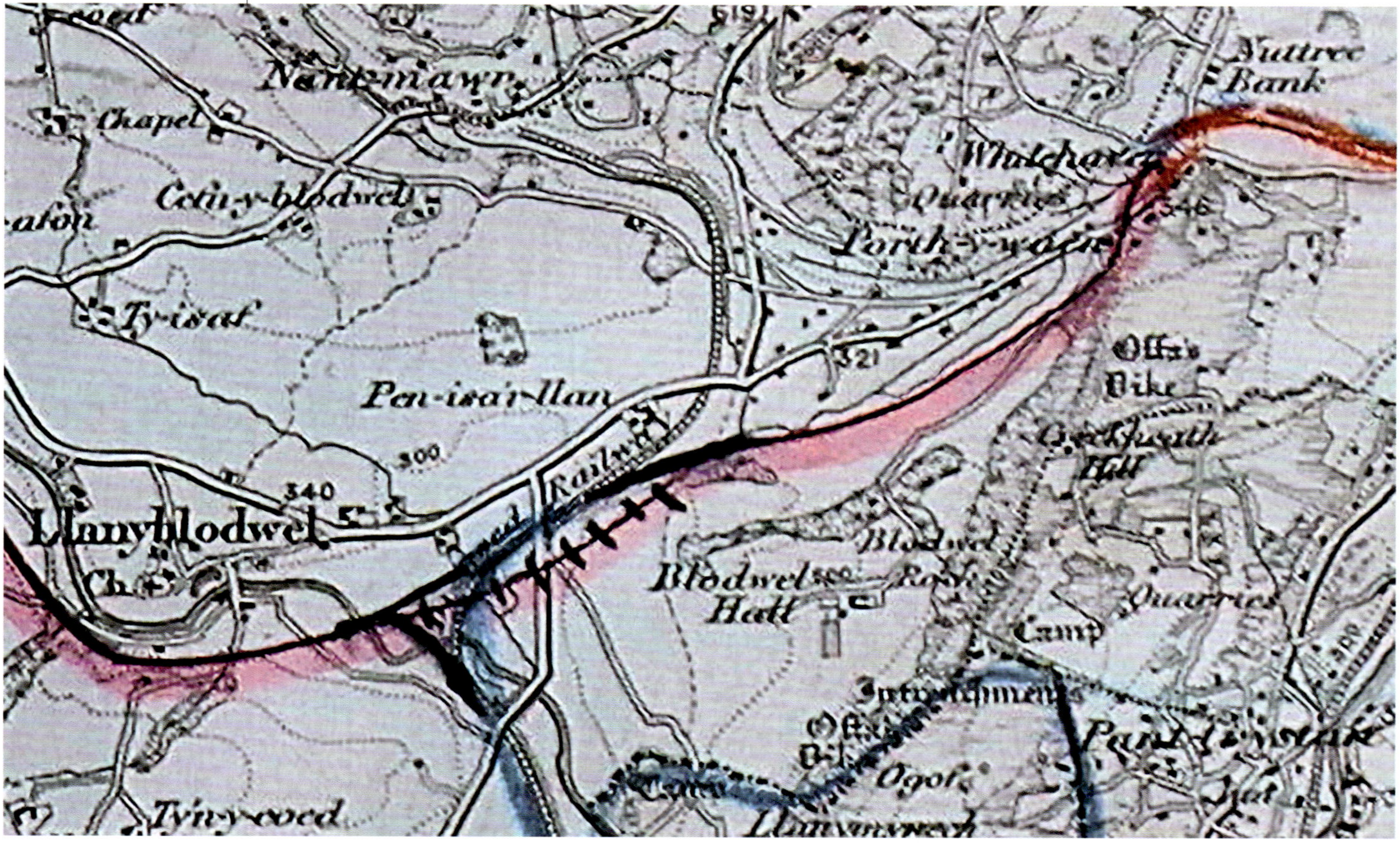

Extract from another copy of the light railway's deposited plan showing the route altered at Llanyblodwel. (National Archives)

determined to erect and maintain gates, and at any public road crossing where the Board of Trade required the company to erect and maintain gates. As noted earlier, the company was to employ 'a proper person' to open and close the gates at each crossing.

At Llanrhaeadr, Liverpool Corporation's Vyrnwy aqueduct was to be protected by the construction of a walled passage, with all accesses, where the railway crossed the existing aqueduct, with provision being made for a further pipe intended to be laid by the corporation, the passage to be extended 6ft beyond the foot of each side of the embankment.

At least six stopping places were to be provided, those designated being at Llanyblodwel, Penybont Mill, Llangedwyn, Llanrhaeadr, Penybontfawr, and Llangynog.

If the rails used weighed at least 60lb per yard, then the maximum axle load was 14 tons on any pair of wheels. Rails should weigh at least 56lb per yard.

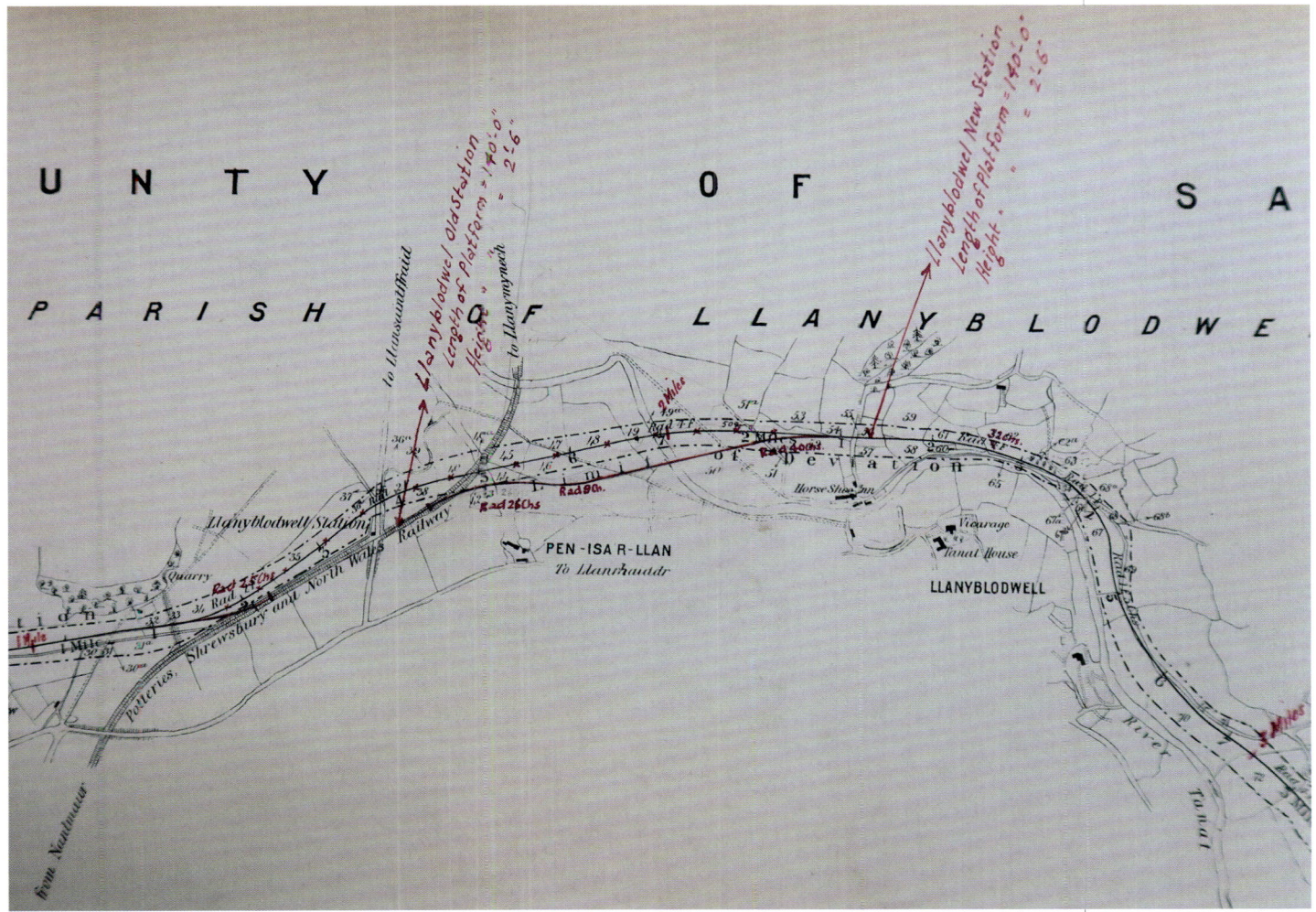

Construction plan of the Llanyblodwel area. North is towards the bottom of the image. (National Archives)

No train should exceed a speed of 25mph, or 10mph on curves with radii of less than 9 chains. Within 300 yards of ungated crossings of public roads speed should be reduced to 10mph unless the Board of Trade specified a lower speed. No tender engine running tender first should run at any speed greater than 15mph.

By agreement with the Cambrian Railways the company was authorised to repair, maintain and run over the Cambrian's mineral branch railway between the commencement of Railway No 1 and Llynclys station.

The Porthywaen Lime Company's rights for the reasonable enjoyment of its (4ft-gauge) canal tramway were protected.

The share capital was £15,000. In addition to any money advanced by loan by any local authority, the company could borrow up to £5,000 at the rate of £50 for each £150 of capital providing at least £11,500 of capital had been issued and half of it was paid up.

Providing two thirds of the capital had been issued and a certificate to that effect was obtained from the Board of Trade then up to 3% interest could be paid on the shares during construction.

The first schedule specified the permanent way, the (non) provision of turntables, electrical communication, signalling and platforms to be provided. It also absolved the company from any obligation of providing any shelter or convenience at any station. The second schedule related to the provision of a sinking fund.

THE LIGHT RAILWAY ORDER • 41

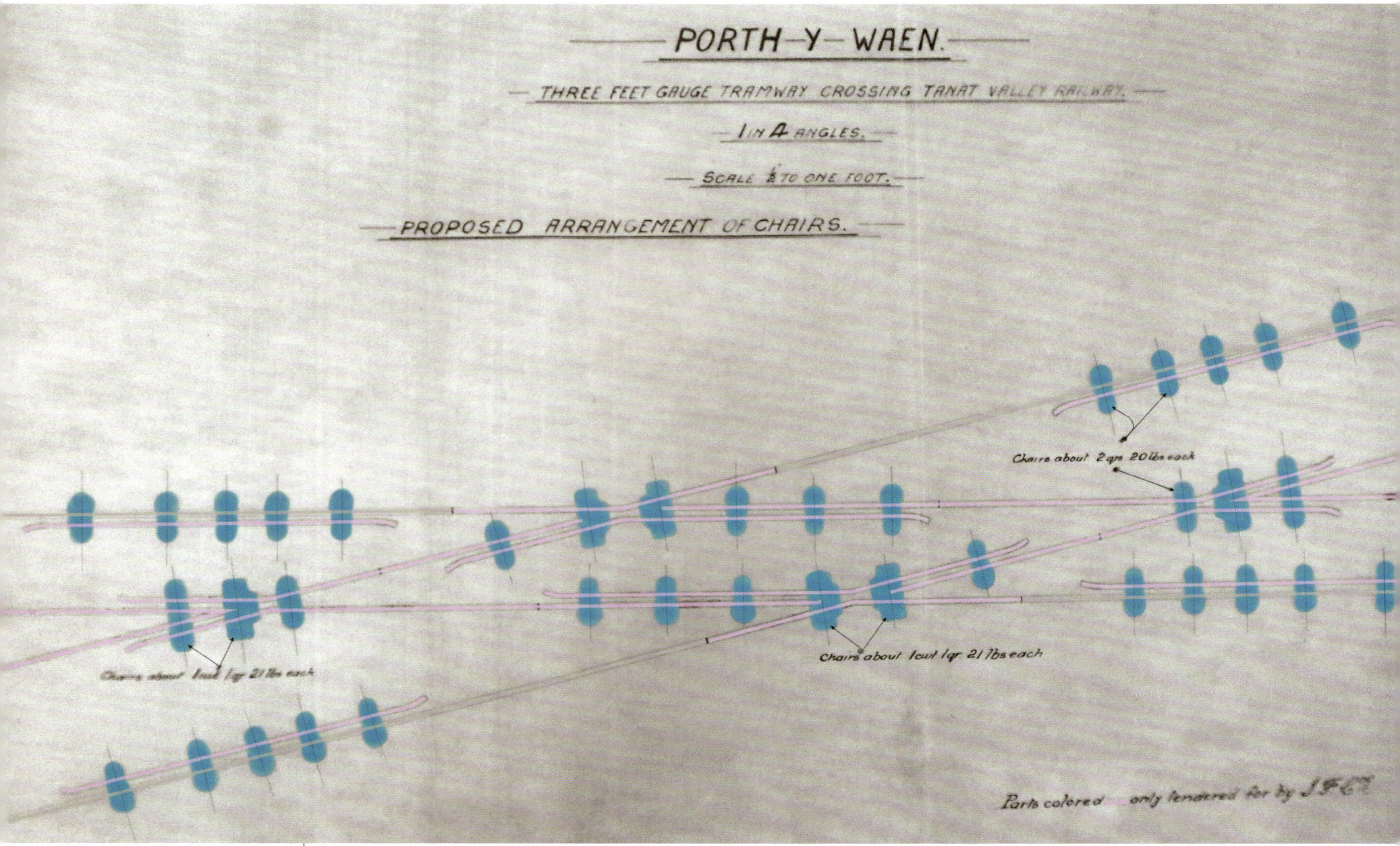

Diagram for the mixed-gauge crossing at Porthywaen. (National Archives)

One of the Whitehaven Quarry's two 4ft-gauge Bagnall 0-4-0STs in action during the winter of 1949. Although the cab has no back sheet, the extension of the side sheets would have provided some slight improvement to conditions for the crew. The locomotives were new in 1931 and 1933 and scrapped about two years after the quarry railway had been closed in 1951. (J. I. C. Boyd)

CHAPTER 3
BUILDING THE RAILWAY

Despite having overcome the obstacles that had lain in the path of obtaining the Light Railway Order, there would be more obstacles before a contractor could be appointed and yet more before the railway could be constructed and opened for traffic.

The directors met for the first time on 16 January 1899, electing C. E. Williams as chairman and John Williams (1850–1927) as secretary. A member of the committee formed to promote Owen Roberts' 1890 Oswestry–Llangynog scheme, the latter was a clerk in Parry Jones' office; in 1901 he told the census enumerator that his occupation was railway company secretary, which he was, but not in an employed capacity.

A key decision was the appointment of A. J. Collin, the Cambrian's new engineer, to be the railway's engineer, instructed to make a survey and prepare the necessary plans and sections. This was supposed to be a freely made decision on the company's part, and the Cambrian always denied playing a part in it, but the

George Owen, the Cambrian and the light railway's engineer, had also been the engineer for the 1873 Llanfyllin & Llangynog proposal. He died on 5 May 1901 and is buried in Oswestry's public cemetery. His property was valued at £20,975 7s 11d, £2,044,396 in 2022.

author suspects that the larger company would have threatened to withdraw if the smaller one had tried to appoint another engineer.

Collin had replaced George Owen, whose resignation as engineer had been accepted by the Cambrian directors on 7 August 1897. Aged 70, he had been in post since 1864 and had produced plans for several of the earlier Tanat Valley schemes. Born in Liverpool, Collin had transferred from the North Eastern Railway.

The Tanat Valley Light Railway Company's seal.

On 30 January 1899 the directors resolved to advertise for contractors to construct the railway. They also decided that a clause in the construction contract that the Cambrian should not profit from the railway's construction, which had been removed by the Cambrian's solicitor, should be retained, and instructed the solicitor to draft an agreement with the local authorities concerning the advances.

This was required because one of the Treasury's conditions for making the free grant, which it would not make until the railway had been constructed and open for traffic, was that the company should guarantee that the local authorities would make their contributions, which meant that the company wanted a promise from them. Nothing more was said about the attempt to prevent the Cambrian from profiting from the contract.

For its own part, the Cambrian held a special meeting to enable its shareholders to approve the agreement between the companies on 25 February (*Montgomery County Times*, 1 February 1899).

For most of the authorities guaranteeing their commitment was not an issue but when Llanfyllin Rural District Council, which had promised £3,000, dealt with it on 9 March, the council's clerk, William Arthur Pughe (1871–1948), said that it would be necessary to obtain counsel's opinion on the agreement, which would be expensive, and that the company should therefore guarantee the council's expenses, which the council accepted (*Montgomery County Times*, 11 March).

At its meeting on 4 May, one of Llanfyllin's councillors asked if it was really necessary to have counsel's opinion on the loan as it was taking a long time, they were delaying the railway and other authorities did not think it was necessary. Pughe stood by his position, and 'strongly advised' the council to have the opinion (*Montgomery County Times*, 6 May).

So far as the council was concerned, the matter came to a head at its 1 June meeting, when Pughe produced the loan agreement and said that as it did not comply with a resolution made two years earlier, a new resolution would be required, which could not be put on that day as no notice had been given. He also said that he had obtained counsel's opinion and the opinion was that the security offered by the company was unsatisfactory but if the council felt that it had pledged to give the support, it could lend the money on the terms contained in the deed. One of the councillors said that as the other authorities were satisfied with the security, the council ought to be satisfied. His proposal that the deed be executed and a new resolution be put to the next meeting was accepted (*Montgomery County Times*, 3 June). This pragmatic solution was sufficient to ensure that all the agreements had been sealed by the time the directors met on 12 June.

The first shareholders' meeting was held on 3 July, its prime purpose being to elect the directors and the auditors. The existing directors were elected, and Robert Ellis Hughes, John Jones Roberts and James Stewart added to their number. All Oswestry residents, Hughes (1844–1922) was a draper and former member of the Town Council, Roberts (1855–1904) a grain merchant, and Stewart (1859–1940) a land agent.

The notice for a meeting of the Cambrian Railways' shareholders, the business including obtaining their approval for their company to engage with the Tanat Valley Light Railway, *Montgomery County Times*, 1 February 1899.

CAMBRIAN RAILWAYS COMPANY.

NOTICE IS HEREBY GIVEN that the Seventieth HALF-YEARLY ORDINARY MEETING of the Proprietors of the Cambrian Railways Company will be held at the Queen's Hotel, Manchester, on Saturday, the 25th day of February instant, at Twelve o'clock Noon, for the transaction of the General Business of the Company.

And NOTICE IS HEREBY FURTHER GIVEN that immediately after the termination of the business of such half-yearly meeting, a SPECIAL GENERAL MEETING of the Proprietors will be held at the same place for the purpose of sanctioning an Agreement between the Tanat Valley Light Railway Company and the Cambrian Railways Company, for the construction and use, working, maintenance, and management of the undertaking of the Tanat Valley Light Railway Company by the Cambrian Railways Company upon the terms therein mentioned.

The Books for the Registration of Transfers of Ordinary and Preference Stocks will be CLOSED from the 16th to the 25th instant, both days inclusive, and of Debenture Stocks from the 16th to the 28th instant, both days inclusive.

Dated this 7th day of February, 1899.

J. F. BUCKLEY, Chairman.
R. BRAYNE, Secretary.

General Offices, Oswestry.

TANAT VALLEY LIGHT RAILWAY COMPANY.

NOTICE is Hereby Given that the First (Statutory) Ordinary Meeting of the Proprietors of the Tanat Valley Light Railway Company will be held at the Guildhall, Oswestry, on Monday, the 3rd of July next, at 2-30 o'clock in the afternoon, for the election of three additional Directors and the Auditors of the Company, and for the transaction of the General Business of the Company.

And Notice is hereby further given that immediately after the termination of the business of such meeting, a Special General Meeting of the Proprietors will be held at the same place for the purpose of sanctioning an Agreement between the Tanat Valley Light Railway Company and the Cambrian Railways Company for the construction and use, working, maintenance and management of the undertaking of the Tanat Valley Light Railway Company by the Cambrian Railways Company upon the terms therein mentioned.

Dated this 12th day of June, 1899.

CHAS. E. WILLIAMS, Chairman,
JOHN WILLIAMS, Secretary.

Oswestry.

The Tanat Valley shareholders were invited to give their approval to their company making an agreement with the Cambrian on 3 July, *Montgomery County Times*, 1 June 1899.

The minutes only recording the statutory minimum, the *Montgomery County Times* (8 July) contained a much lengthier report. Parry Jones apologised for not attending because he had to attend the Cambrian directors' annual inspection of their railway. He also explained that the start of construction had been delayed by the Llanfyllin and Llansilin local authorities, who had most to benefit from the railway. However, they both employed W. A. Pughe as their clerk, who insisted on employing separate counsel to give their opinions on the loan agreement at the company's expense. As the counsel gave diametrically opposing opinions, the money was wasted, Jones declared, when the councils accepted the same terms as the others.

Chairman C. E. Williams explained that capital raised or committed stood at £55,663 of the £63,500 required, £18,500 from the councils, £18,000 from the Treasury, £12,000 borrowing and £7,163 subscribed locally, which included £2,000 from Lady Wynn at Llangedwyn and £1,250 from Lord Powis. Promises for contributions to the shortfall had been accompanied by conditions, when the first sod was cut or when the contractors started work.

Pughe was also responsible for having Llanfyllin Rural District Council obtain counsel's opinion on the Welshpool & Llanfair Light Railway's advance at the railway company's expense. Whether his actions were the result of inexperience, he was only 28 years old in 1899, and young to be running his own legal practice, or whether he saw an opportunity of boosting his income at the railway companies' expense, there is no way of telling. Getting Llanfyllin and Llansilin to have opinions from different counsel on the same document seems to be indicative of the latter.

The Countess of Powis (1865–1929) cut the first sod in a field next to the school at Porthywaen, now the site of the Porthywaen Silver Band's premises, on 12 September 1899. After a shower and an overcast sky, the weather was fine. The arrival of a train from Oswestry was greeted with the sound of detonators and rock cannon exploding, and coincided with the arrival of the Earl and Countess by road carriage accompanied by an outrider. After C. E. Williams had explained that the first sods would reveal the letters TVLR, he asked the Countess to expose the first letter and nine ladies to reveal the others between them. She used a spade designed and made by Alfred Charles Minshall (1863–1939), an Oswestry jeweller. It had a carved ebony handle, an inscribed silver blade and a barrow made of oak with plated mounts made by William Hughes (1869–1952), an employee of the director and builder, W. H. Thomas.

After the other ladies, the wives of landowners, MPs, directors and the engineer, had revealed the other letters, C. E. Williams acted as navvy to barrow the earth onto a platform and tip it back to the ground, removing his jacket to do so (*Border Counties Advertiser*, 13 September). The newspapers did not comment on the tools used for this stage of the proceedings.

After lunch in a nearby marquee, there were numerous speeches with much praise heaped on all the participants who had at last brought a scheme for a railway in the Tanat valley to a point where construction was about to start.

The advertisement giving notice of the first sod ceremony, *Montgomery County Times*, 9 September 1899.

TANAT VALLEY LIGHT RAILWAY.

THE CUTTING OF THE FIRST SOD

OF THE RAILWAY
BY THE
COUNTESS OF POWIS
WILL TAKE PLACE
AT PORTHYWAEN,
AT 1 30 P.M.,
ON TUESDAY, THE 12TH DAY OF SEPTEMBER, 1899.

J. WILLIAMS, Secretary.

The start of works was not imminent because the call for tenders could not be published until agreement had been made with the Shropshire Railways over the use of its property around Llanyblodwel, which was to take a few months longer. A. J. Collin, the engineer, provided his estimate of costs to the directors on 22 September.

Contract works	£27,139 12s
Accommodation works	£9,000
Permanent way materials	£11,400
Signalling	£2,000
Telegraphs and block working	£1,000
Alterations and repairs to existing lines	£3,000
	£53,540 12s
For rubble instead of cement concrete	£54,000
If no [pipeline] bridge required at Penybont	£53,000

The first sod ceremony at Porthywaen. The event was chaired by W. E. Williams, who is partially obscured by the post behind the right-hand barrow. Presumably the woman seated closest to him is the Countess of Powis, and one of the two seated women in dark attire will be the Dowager Lady Williams Wynn. There are at least four journalists to be seen. The two men standing facing the barrows are most likely to be John Strachan, the contractor, and A. J. Collin, the engineer who had replaced George Owen. Behind the invited audience is a man on horseback. Those in the field behind were probably in a good position to see what happened when the speeches finished.

CAMBRIAN RAILWAYS COMPANY.

NOTICE IS HEREBY GIVEN that a Special General Meeting of the Proprietors of the Cambrian Railways Company will be held at the Euston Hotel, London, on Thursday, the 10th day of May next, at half-past 12 o'clock in the afternoon, for the purpose of sanctioning an Agreement as to working the Nantmawr Branch of the Shropshire Railways, as to arrangement with the Tanat Valley Light Railway Company, and for other purposes.

Dated this 20th day of April, 1900.

J. F. BUCKLEY, Chairman.
R. BRAYNE, Secretary.

General Offices, Oswestry.

Collin's suggestion to divide the works into three contracts, rails, signalling and everything else, was accepted by the Tanat Valley directors on 22 September. This gave the company the opportunity of negotiating the best price for the rails and signalling for its own benefit, otherwise the contractor would add a profit margin for himself.

There was a boost to the scheme in November, when Lord Powis and Sir Watkin Williams-Wynn (1860–1944, 7th Baronet) said that they would donate their land to the railway (*Wrexham Advertiser*, 18 November / *Shrewsbury Chronicle*, 24 November 1899).

A satisfactory agreement with the Shropshire Railways was not concluded until the directors' meeting on 23 April 1900; it had been approved by the court by the time the directors met on 21 May. The agreement with the Cambrian Railways over the proportion of the rent paid for the use of the Llanyblodwel branch by the latter to be paid by the Tanat Valley company was also agreed. Liverpool Corporation's nomination of William James Burgess (1855–1929), a provisions merchant, as its representative director was accepted on the same occasion.

The Cambrian obtained its shareholders' approval on 10 May and published a notice with the details when it had been made (*Montgomery County Times*, 2 April / 2 June).

Despite the generosity of the larger landowners, some of the land purchases had not been settled, including that required for land managed by 'Lady Wynn's trustees', who had started by asking for £2,218 14s for an unspecified area. The directors obviously thought this was excessive because although it had been negotiated down to £1,700 the secretary was instructed to make a final offer of £1,600.

THE SHROPSHIRE RAILWAYS COMPANY
AND
THE CAMBRIAN RAILWAYS COMPANY.

NOTICE IS HEREBY GIVEN pursuant to the Provisions of the Railways Clauses Act 1863 and the Regulation of Railways Act 1873 and the Shropshire Railways Act 1891 and the Tanat Valley Light Railway Order 1898 that it is the intention of the Shropshire Railways Company and the Cambrian Railways Company to enter into an Agreement for the following purposes viz. (among other things) the cancelling of an Agreement dated the 24th day of July 1885 made between the Official Liquidator of the Potteries Shrewsbury and North Wales Railway Company and the Cambrian Railways Company according to the terms of which the Cambrian Railways Company run over and use for the purposes of mineral traffic only the Branch Railway then of the Potteries Company but now of the Shropshire Railways Company between Llanymynech Station and the Nantmawr Quarries hereinafter referred to as the Branch Railway under the terms of the said Agreement although the term thereof is expired and of the Agreement dated the 11th day of April 1894 and made between the Shropshire Railways Company and the Cambrian Railways Company whereby the Shropshire Railways Company granted an easement in perpetuity over certain land for the purposes of constructing a loop line connecting their Llanfyllin Branch with the Branch Railway and whereby the Cambrian Railways Company have the right for a period therein mentioned to run over and use such part of the Branch Railway as lies between the Junctions therewith of the said loop line and Llanymynech Station for traffic of all descriptions and in lieu thereof to give the Cambrian Railways Company the right to run over work and use for the purposes of all traffic the Branch Railway and the said loop line the Cambrian Railways Company maintaining the branch line in a fit condition for such traffic subjecting themselves to all the duties and liabilities binding or imposed upon the Shropshire Railways Company or the Potteries Shrewsbury and North Wales Railway Company by Statute or at Common Law for securing the safe and proper working management maintenance and reparation of the Branch Railway for such traffic and the apportioning of the tolls rates charges and revenues levied taken or arising in respect of the traffic over the said Railways and that any Company or person aggrieved by such proposed Agreement and desiring to object thereto may bring such objection before the Railway Commissioners by sending the same in writing addressed to the Railway Commissioners at their Office at Rooms 106 and 108 Royal Courts of Justice Strand London on or before the 23rd day of July 1900 in which Office a copy of the proposed Agreement can be seen.

Dated this 21st day of June, 1900.

J. PARRY JONES,
Solicitor to the Cambrian Railways Company.

The notice for the special meeting for Cambrian shareholders to give their approval to agreements with the Shropshire Railways and the Tanat Valley Company, *Montgomery County Times*, 2 April 1900.

A more detailed notice was published giving anyone considering themselves aggrieved by the agreements an opportunity to object, *Montgomery County Times*, 2 June 1900.

BUILDING THE RAILWAY • 47

The call for tenders having been advertised by the time of the 21 May meeting, with a deadline of 5 June, Collin was told to tell the appointed contractor that he could make use of the company's rails, when purchased, during construction for 10% of their cost. Six tenders received by the deadline were opened on 7 June, when the directors realised that they would not have enough money to build the railway. The list was:

Thomas Wrigley, Blackpool	£68,777 19s 9d
Cleveland Bridge Company	£61,366 18s
Peter Smith, Manchester	£60,002 1s 10d
Libster & Jones, Bala	£56,269 2s 6d
L. P. Nott, Bristol	£49,097 16s 4d
J. Strachan, Cardiff	£48,700

Founded in 1877, Cleveland Bridge remained in business until 2021, being put into administration by a combination of reduced business caused by the global pandemic and excessive debt.

In response to the prices being much higher than the estimates, a consequence of post-Boer War inflation, the directors decided that an application should be made to increase the capital by £25,000 and to ask the Board of Trade for the clause protecting Liverpool Corporation's Vyrnwy viaduct crossing to be varied, both of which would require the Light Railway Order to be amended.

The cost of the bridge over Liverpool Corporation's pipeline gave the directors cause for concern. The Corporation wanted a civic structure, carved stone, ornate features. The directors preferred the idea of using timber baulks. Two weeks later they sought the Corporation's approval to change it. They eventually settled for something in between ornate civic and basic railway.

The directors also decided to ask the Cambrian Railways to obtain Parliamentary powers to invest in the railway. Their request and details of the tenders were accompanied by details of other anticipated costs totalling £21,530 (Appendix 5), the funds available to meet them, and the 'necessary expenditure' based on the latest figures and totalling £81,730 (Appendix 6). The company's authorised capital totalled £63,500 and it had promises of £44,500. It had not taken advantage of its £12,000 authorised borrowing and expected to secure another £4,000 in share subscriptions and £3,000 from local authorities.

Meeting on 16 July, the shareholders were told that as all the tenders were considerably more than the estimates none of them could be accepted. The reason was that the cost of materials had increased, and the scarcity of skilled labour caused contractors to provide for all exigencies in their tenders. What had Thomas Wrigley included in his £68,000 tender that John Strachan had not included in his that was £20,000 lower, one wonders?

In his speech, the chairman, W. E. Williams, commented on the delay caused by the Shropshire Railways, which had wanted £1,200 a year for use of the Llanyblodwel branch and Nantmawr tramway by both the Cambrian and Tanat Valley. The Cambrian had negotiated it down to £550, which had been approved by Shropshire shareholders by a majority of one. As the rate had previously been £500 for the Cambrian alone, a £50 increase for the use of a small amount of track at Llanyblodwel seems to be more reasonable, although the Tanat Valley had to pay £250 for its use of that tiny portion of track, which made the deal even better value for the Cambrian. Some of the landowners were asking more for their land than anticipated, Williams said, and their claims would be taken to arbitration if settlements could not be reached.

When one of the shareholders, a Welshman who had lived for thirty years in Liverpool, asked to be allowed to speak in Welsh, Williams agreed but said that the speaker would need to provide a translator, as six of the directors did not understand the language adding that he was prepared to give way to a bi-lingual speaker. Notwithstanding the request for a translator, the shareholder did speak in Welsh, saying that more effort should be made to make the company's intentions known in the Llanrhaeadr district, by means of Welsh, he implied (*Montgomery County Times*, 21 July).

A correspondent to the *Montgomery County Times* published on 25 August appeared to be rather pleased by the company's discomfiture over the tender prices, saying that routing via Llynclys was a folly, short-sighted and selfish, and half of the overspend could be avoided by using the existing railway to Llanymynech.

The notice of intention to apply to amend the Light Railway Order was published on 13 November. Power was sought to extend the time to purchase land, to complete the works and to empower the company to raise additional capital. It was also sought to enable the local authorities to make further advances and to permit the Cambrian Railways to subscribe towards the capital (*London Gazette*, 23 November).

In Llanfyllin, Town Clerk W. A. Pughe, now also an elected council member, saw an opportunity to object to the entire scheme in favour of the Llanfyllin railway, claiming that as the Tanat Valley promoters had got their estimates so badly wrong the Order must be invalid, pointing out that if the council did object there would be risk and cost. A committee was appointed (*Montgomery County Times*, 1 December). Pughe was obviously unaware that other light railways were also having to increase their capital because of increased costs and that his own favoured scheme would have faced the same problem.

A special meeting was called to discuss the committee's report on 8 December. It had recommended that the council circulate the other authorities with a view to getting them all to refuse to give further support to the company. After a letter was read out from the previous mayor, saying that no more support should be given, Pughe said that he thought it advisable to take steps to oppose the railway as much as possible. But then other councillors spoke against making further objections, on the basis that they could not be successful, they had no scheme available to replace the Tanat Valley line, the valley was the natural route from Llangynog, and they had spent enough money opposing the Tanat Valley scheme. A motion that it was not advisable to oppose the application was countered by Pughe proposing an amendment that the council should oppose it, but he failed to get a seconder and the motion was carried (*Shrewsbury Chronicle*, 14 December).

The company ended the year with the news that the Treasury would increase its free grant by £10,000, to £28,000, a third of the capital (*Herapath's Railway Journal*, 21 December 1900), a welcome boost as it went cap in hand to the investing authorities to ask for more money. The £10,000 was subsequently modified to be £4,000 free grant and £6,000 interest-free loan.

The local authority responses varied. When Oswestry Town Council agreed to advance a further £2,000, the town clerk pointed out that Welshpool Town Council, with a rateable value of less than £40,000, had advanced £9,000 to the Welshpool & Llanfair Light Railway, whereas Oswestry's rateable value was £63,000 (*Shrewsbury Chronicle*, 8 March 1901). When Shropshire County Council discussed it in May some of the councillors were unaware that the matter had been discussed, and a commitment made, previously (*Shrewsbury Chronicle*, 10 May). In the event, only Llansilin refused to make a further advance (Appendix 4).

When the directors met on 18 March Parry Jones reported that the Treasury had agreed to pay half of the grant when a portion of the line had been completed, which would help the cash flow. They declined the 4th Lord Bradford's (1845–1915) offer to subscribe £1,000 in shares and donate his land at Llanyblodwel if the Porthywaen route was abandoned, paying him £950 in July.

In an attempt to reduce costs further, the directors had asked Collin if he would construct the railway himself, without a contractor. He thought that by letting the earthworks in several portions to a local man and by buying the materials and sub-letting the labour for other aspects of the construction he could save the contractor's profit, which he estimated to be about £6,000. On this basis, he had obtained the Cambrian directors' approval to proceed on 23 January 1901. The Tanat Valley directors, however, thought that his terms for doing the work were too high so he withdrew, leaving them dependent on the terms offered by the contractors.

Regarding the tenders, they decided that separate contracts should be issued for rails, signalling and telegraph, fencing and gates, station buildings and 'general'. The call for construction tenders was advertised with a deadline of 23 April, the would-be contractors being shown over the route on 12 April (*Railway News*, 30 March).

Seventeen tenders were received for the two contracts by the deadline, seven for Contract No 1, for fencing and gates, and ten for Contracts Nos 1 and 2 (Appendix 8).

Of the contractors, Holme & King had built the Snowdon Mountain Railway and other railway works; they had also tendered for the Welshpool & Llanfair Light Railway, as had H. M. Nowell and J. Strachan. Pethick Brothers were building the Vale of Rheidol Railway, so getting the Tanat Valley would have been a useful job for them to move on to.

Meeting on 29 April, the directors decided to award the contract to Samuel Ernest Lucas (1860–1923) subject to his financial position, references and sureties being satisfactory. He had worked on many railway contracts, including the Manchester, Sheffield & Lincolnshire Railway's London Extension, as an engineer and had only recently started to tender on his own account but no details have been found of any contracts that he was awarded.

Within a month, however, he had revoked the contract because his partner had withdrawn (*Shrewsbury Chronicle*, 23 August), resulting in a special directors' meeting being called. Holme & King and John Strachan having intimated that they were prepared to discuss their tenders, the directors decided to ask them if they would be prepared to take £2,000 in shares, accepting Strachan's tender (Appendix 9) on 5 June. Reluctant to take £2,000 in shares, he had agreed to take half in shares and half in debentures. For reasons unknown, the contract was not for a fixed price but was based on a schedule of prices, which gave him plenty of scope for adding extras. Signed on 8 July, Strachan was contracted to complete the railway by 1 August 1903.

John Strachan (1848–1909) had recently started on the Welshpool & Llanfair Light Railway contract; having two in close proximity would be a benefit for him being able to transfer labour and equipment from one to the other if required. Born in Brechin, Angus, he had wide-ranging experience on public works. While working in South Wales he had married a Welsh woman and settled in Cardiff, where he worked on the Cardiff & Caerphilly Railway, the Rhymney Railway, Roath and Bute docks and the GWR's new station buildings at Cardiff in 1894. Buried in Forfar cemetery, his grave is unmarked.

Shropshire County Council's earlier decision in favour of its additional loan did not comply with standing orders, because no prior notice had been given, so it needed to be confirmed after notice. That resulted in further objection and two councillors having a row that spilled into the local media, the *Shrewsbury Chronicle* (21 June 1901) headlining 'A warm discussion on the Tanat Valley Railway: Mr Payne and Mr Jones at loggerheads'.

The meeting had taken place on 15 June. After the motion was proposed Major Algernon Heber Percy (1845–1911) said that although he knew it would make no difference to the loan, he objected to the council advancing money to a railway. He was supported by Alfred Ernest Payne (1850–1927), who owned land that would benefit from the Shropshire Railways being reopened and who wanted an assurance that the Tanat Valley would not be antagonistic towards any attempt to reopen that line. He also wanted to know why the promise to run trains to Llanymynech was not contained in the Light Railway Order or the draft of the amendment Order and going on at some length about the railway's strategy of insisting on having the Llynclys connection constructed.

Parry Jones made a robust defence of the company's position, which showed how some of Payne's claims were unfounded, and the motion to make the extra loan was carried. The paper's editorial gave the best response to Percy's objection, saying that the Light Railways Act would not have been passed if the legislators had not intended local authorities to exercise the powers given to them.

Payne took up the issue of the agreement with Lord Bradford in the *Shrewsbury Chronicle* (28 June), regretting that he had not consulted Parry Jones before the meeting and accepting that an agreement concerning the running of trains to Llanymynech was contained in the agreement for the sale of Bradford's land to the company, which he claimed he had not been told. But as the agreement was in the public interest then it should be in a public document, the Light Railway Order, he added.

The following week Parry Jones replied with evidence that Payne had been told what form the agreement had taken, and saying that it was unreasonable of Payne to expect the order to be changed to meet his view when it had been aired at a public inquiry, that Payne could have attended, three years before. Further, the 'elaborate provisions' that it contained for the protection of the Shropshire Railways had been drawn up by that company's solicitors and was deemed adequate by them, and the arrangements had been approved by the shareholders of three railway companies at statutory public meetings and by the Board of Trade, the Light Railway Commissioners and the Railway Commissioners.

This was not enough for Payne, who (*Shrewsbury Chronicle*, 12 July) remained insistent that the agreement should be contained in the Order. Parry Jones had the last word, saying (19 July) that Payne had been told that his interpretation of the Order was misleading and that by his actions he had done more to hinder the reopening of the Shropshire Railways than to help it. Obviously, Payne was unaware that the Board of Trade had refused to allow any clause about the number of trains to be included in the order but as a promoter Parry Jones should have known.

Strachan had started to get his plant on the ground by 19 July (*Shrewsbury Chronicle*) and soon had a gang laying out the centre line in the Llanyblodwel area.

Meeting on 22 July, the directors heard that Sir Watkin had offered 2 acres of land at Llangedwyn for a nominal 10 shillings but required to have authority to stop all trains at the station. The directors agreed, but the Cambrian might not be so amenable to the notion. They also learned that Cambrian director William Bailey Hawkins (1835–1922) had negotiated to buy 1,600 tons of rail from Guest, Keen & Company, for £5 1s per ton, £8,080, and fishplates and chairs at £6 10s per ton, loaded at Dowlais. A director of several railway companies and the National Bank, Hawkins performed the same service for the Welshpool Railway (*Shrewsbury Chronicle*, 23 August). Collin had estimated £7–8 per ton for the rail.

After Parrs' Bank and the North & South Wales Bank had refused facilities for a temporary overdraft, C. S. Denniss, the Cambrian manager, had suggested an approach to Lloyds Bank, which was accepted. The overdraft was not to exceed £9,000, with 4% interest and one sixteenth commission payable.

The Cambrian had asked for representation on the board, nominating Lord Powis, but was told that if a vacancy occurred the matter would be favourably considered, which smacks of the company striking a pose for its independence.

On 13 August a reporter from the *Shrewsbury Chronicle* (16 August) visited the construction site and was taken over the route by Strachan's engineer, Norman Robinson (1879–1943). Much had been achieved he wrote, a temporary bridge had been built across the river and within a few days a ballast train was expected to reach the meadow opposite Llanyblodwel church, about three quarters of a mile. Farmers were being recruited to carry timber from Llanyblodwel to the sites where it was needed. Collin, the engineer, had told him that providing the winter was

Llangedwyn Hall, one of the homes of the Williams Wynn family, who had a big influence on the development of a railway in the Tanat valley. Although the right-hand (east) wing was demolished in the late 1940s, the house is listed Grade II and the gardens are listed Grade II* in Cadw's Register of Landscapes, Parks and Gardens of Special Historic Interest in Wales. (William Charles Burns/Park, Newtown)

Sir Herbert Lloyd Watkin Williams Wynn, the 7th Baronet, is buried in St Cedwyn's churchyard, opposite Llangedwyn Hall. His personal property was valued at £386,150 2s 9d, £13,578,971 in 2022.

mild then Llangedwyn should be reached by February 1902.

For Robinson, the Tanat Valley was his first contract after completing his apprenticeship; after working on LNWR and Lancashire & Yorkshire Railway contracts he worked in Russia before managing Vickers Ltd's foreign department. Strachan was also supported by his son, George Lewis (1879–1929). The resident engineer, working for Collin, was Frederick Lawrence Triffitt (1876–1955) who ended his working life as the LNER's docks engineer at Hull.

A total of £3,592 19s 2d had been spent by the time the shareholders met on 19 August. Some £9,000 of land claims had been settled for £6,250, just under the £6,500 it had been valued at in the estimates. There had been thirty-five landowners to deal with. Three of them, Lord Powis, Sir Watkin Williams Wynn and John Morris Hughes (1840–1927) of Penybont Hall, had donated theirs. The claims of two who were holding out for more would go to arbitration. Strachan explained the work in progress and said that he thought the railway would be finished in two years (*Shropshire Chronicle*, 23 August).

had been made at Llanyblodwel, which allowed Strachan to take materials from the Cambrian with his own locomotive, and the junction with the Porthywaen branch was to be installed 'this week'. A 6ft-diameter culvert near Llanyblodwel had been completed and the bridge over the Tanat nearby was ready for its steel work. A cattle creep at 3 miles was nearly finished. With 282 tons of rail and 3,000 sleepers on the ground and rail fastenings in transit, track laying should be started shortly. Work had been hampered by stormy and frosty weather. A total of 125 men were employed, he said.

John Morris Hughes of Penybont Hall, who donated land for the railway, is buried in St Michael's churchyard at Llanyblodwel.

The Tanat Valley Light Railway (Amendment) Order, 1901 was made on 25 October. The 1898 Order was amended to increase the time allowed for construction by three years and to modify the sums allowed to be borrowed from the investing authorities. The company's additional borrowing was set at £5,000, at the ratio of £1,000 per £3,000 subscribed. The Cambrian was also allowed to subscribe up to £10,000. The company had asked for an additional four years to be allowed for construction, but the Light Railway Commissioners had decided that three years was enough. Meeting on the same day the Order was made, Denbighshire County Council resolved not to press for the extra ¼ per cent interest it had asked for earlier (*North Wales Weekly News*, 1 November).

On 25 November 1901 Collin reported that possession had been taken of 7 miles of the route. Four miles of fencing was practically complete, and posts awaited wires on another 2 miles. The junction

The 4th Earl of Powis, who also donated land, was buried in Welshpool's Christ Church churchyard. His personal effects were valued at £110,638 7s 6d, £2,542,110 in 2022.

BUILDING THE RAILWAY • 53

The Tanat Valley Light Railway (Amendment) Order, 1901.

```
                                                924

        LIGHT RAILWAYS ACT, 1896.

    TANAT VALLEY LIGHT RAILWAY (AMENDMENT) ORDER, 1901.

              ORDER
               MADE BY THE
    LIGHT RAILWAY COMMISSIONERS,
       AND MODIFIED AND CONFIRMED BY THE
           BOARD OF TRADE,
              AMENDING THE
    TANAT VALLEY LIGHT RAILWAY ORDER, 1898.

    Presented to both Houses of Parliament by Command of His Majesty.

                  LONDON:
     PRINTED FOR HIS MAJESTY'S STATIONERY OFFICE
        By DARLING & SON, LTD., 34-40, Bacon Street, E.
     And to be purchased, either directly or through any Bookseller, from
        EYRE & SPOTTISWOODE, EAST HARDING STREET, FLEET STREET, E.C.,
             and 32, ABINGDON STREET, WESTMINSTER, S.W.;
               or OLIVER & BOYD, EDINBURGH;
            or E. PONSONBY, 116, GRAFTON STREET, DUBLIN.
                      1902.
    [Cd. 865.]    Price 1d.
```

The bridge over the Tanat east of Llanyblodwel. The timbers in the river are the remains of Strachan's temporary bridge.

Regarding Strachan using his own locomotive to fetch materials from the Cambrian, traffic superintendent William Henry Gough (1853–1917) issued special instructions for working his train between the new railway and Whitehaven Rock siding on 14 February 1902, effective from 17 February. Scotch blocks had been placed on the Tanat Valley line and on the siding and the operation controlled by a pilotman. Strachan had agreed to cover any damage done by his men ignoring the pilotman's instructions.

Triffitt, the resident engineer, told the *Shrewsbury Chronicle* (18 March) that Strachan hoped to have half of the line completed by midsummer and to reach Llangynog before the summer was over. Fifty more men would be employed as soon as they could be found. Collin said that fencing was complete between Porthywaen and Penybont, about 4 miles. A total of 38,000 cubic yards of earth had been excavated to create cuttings and used to make embankments. Masonry work for bridges and cattle creeps had been delayed by frosts. The steel for three bridges was on site. Permanent track had been laid between Porthywaen and Llanyblodwel

One of Strachan's trains. The loco, his No 3, is a Manning, Wardle 0-4-0ST built in 1885. It was on the contract from 20 August 1901 until 31 July 1903.

and between the Tanat river bridge and 3 miles 50 chains, a total length of 3 miles, but this work had been stopped for want of rail; the secretary was instructed to write to Guest, Keen & Company to urge the delivery of more. Collin told the Cambrian directors that on 9 April he had travelled 4 miles on Strachan's engine.

Strachan actually used four locomotives on the contract, a Hunslet 0-4-0ST and three Manning, Wardle 0-6-0STs, the last two being new to this contract in 1903. In 1905 Herbert Edward Jones (1854-1926), the Cambrian's locomotive superintendent, recorded the dates they arrived and left. While he did not correlate the locomotives to the dates, it is reasonable to assume that the Hunslet arrived first, when its light weight would be an asset on temporary track, followed by the second-hand Manning, Wardle (Appendix 12).

In preparation for the forthcoming shareholders' meeting, on 17 July Strachan arranged an inspection visit for the directors and officers of both companies, travelling by train as far as they could. Near Llangedwyn, the cutting through a mound known as 'Spion Kop' being incomplete, the passengers disembarked while the train ascended the mound on temporary track. Stopping at Llangedwyn, where the engineering staff had their base and the permanent station buildings had already been erected, the party took lunch. Afterwards, the journey continued another 3 miles, progress beyond Maes Mochnant, just short of the Llanrhaeadr station site, prevented by an incomplete river bridge. The remainder of the construction sites were surveyed by road (*Shrewsbury Chronicle*, 18 July).

The shareholders met on 21 July, where, as well as a report on progress and the accounts, they were encouraged to take up, or to encourage their friends to take up, more of the unsubscribed shares (*Shrewsbury Chronicle*, 25 July).

The land arbitration cases were heard at Llanfyllin on 25 July. Each party put up two valuers to argue their case, the railway company paying for all of them. In response to his claim for £747 for 3 acres 3 roods of land, Evan Evans (born 1862) of the Railway Inn, Penybontfawr, had

BUILDING THE RAILWAY • 55

been offered £275. He had paid £70 an acre eight years before and used it for fattening bullocks; his claim included an allowance for severance. He denied making improvements since receiving the company's notice to treat. His valuers put the value at £754 and £655, while the company's put it at £309 and £272. (The Railway Inn, incidentally was built, with that name, in 1881, its builder obviously expecting that the railway proposed that year would be built (*Liverpool Mercury*, 22 October 1881).)

William Taylor (1839–1912) of Llangynog wanted £183 for 1 rood 28 perches, 2,000 square yards; he had been offered £30. It had no direct access. One of the valuers said that an ash tree that would have to be cut down was valued at £2 and its shade at £10, which caused some comment. His land was valued at £152 and £114 by his valuers and £23 and £37 by the company's (*Shrewsbury Chronicle*, 1 August 1902).

The arbitrator's decision was announced later, awarding £416 15s to Evans and £56 to Taylor, so no party got what they wanted. The company had to pay the costs. (*Liverpool Daily Post*, 20 August).

In Oswestry, the Town Council nominated Thomas Whitfield (1836–1913) as its representative on the Tanat Valley board on 10 August. Accepting the nomination, he said he 'felt sure that in a few years the large amount of money the Council had invested in the railway would yield a fairly good dividend'. He was an auctioneer and estate agent.

Tribute was paid to director Owen Roberts, who had died aged 66 on 20 September, when the directors met on 20 October. The Rhiwarth quarry owner whose letter-writing campaign had been the impetus for the 1890 attempts to build a railway to Llangynog, he had been born in Ffestiniog and had worked in the Llanfair slate quarry, near Harlech, before moving to Llangynog; he had died of spinal sclerosis. To replace him the directors resolved to ascertain whether Lord Powis would be willing, as the Cambrian had previously proposed, but when Parry Jones saw the Earl, he did not get a definite answer and Powis eventually refused.

The directors also noted that the engineer, A. J. Collin, had agreed to take 100 shares in part payment of his commission. On 1 November he told the Cambrian directors that 99,112 cubic yards of soil and 4,000 cubic yards of rock had been excavated, that except for one cutting the railway was practically complete to Llangedwyn, 6 miles 30 chains, eleven bridges were finished and five approaching completion, five cattle creeps were nearly finished and five stream diversions were finished. Track was laid from Porthywaen to beyond Penybontfawr, nearly 13 miles, 4 miles had been ballasted, and embankments were being left until they had consolidated. The girders for the second Tanat river bridge would be in position in a few days. A total of 130 men were employed.

To certify that half of the railway had been built, and half of the capital spent, for the Treasury, the Board of Trade sent

Owen Roberts, proprietor of the Rhiwarth slate quarry, who tried to promote a railway in 1890 and became a Light Railway Company director, was buried in Llangynog's Methodist chapel's cemetery in 1902. His property was valued at £2,006 6s 5d, £195,521 in 2022.

Major Edward Druitt (1860–1922) to make an inspection on 26 November. Rails had been laid for 13 miles 40 chains and 6in of bottom ballast for about 4½ miles. The river bridge near Llanyblodwel was finished and four others had their girders in position. Collin provided a certificate showing that £36,486 17s 2 had been spent on the works, £46,292 9s 3d including land and preliminary expenses (Appendix 10). A cheque for £14,000 was received in time for Christmas (*Shrewsbury Chronicle*, 28 November/26 December).

Collin's report on the same date was brief. Two thirds of the earthworks were complete, rail had been laid within a quarter of a mile of Llangynog and the fencing within half a mile. All bridges were complete except for their parapets and several cattle creeps were finished. Unsettled weather and a sharp spell of frost had interfered with the work.

He refused to help when the directors asked him to sound out the Bradford estate on the possibility of not operating the loop connecting with the Shropshire Railways that became known as 'Lord Bradford's curve'. Designed to facilitate access to and from Llanymynech, it existed at Bradford's insistence, to secure the withdrawal of his objection to the 1898 Order. In a letter dated 30 December 1902, Collin argued that as the agreement regarding the curve had been made by the directors then they should deal with any matters relating to its operation, it was not a construction matter. The chairman and secretary were deputed to see Bradford's agent and on 16 February 1903 Collin reported that the Cambrian was prepared to put on a through carriage for Llanymynech on trains from Llangynog. By 20 April, however, Bradford had agreed not to ask for the loop to be worked during the first two years.

Towards the end of 1902 the railway was sufficiently complete for the *Shrewsbury Chronicle* (2 January 1903) to report that Strachan had been delivering coal and lime to farms along the line, no doubt charging a fee for the service. On 17 November 1902 Jesse Huxley (1853–1931), an Oswestry coal merchant with depots in Llynclys, Llanyblodwel and Four Crosses, had complained to Denniss about Strachan running wagons loaded with coal into the valley and taking his business. He did not think that it was honourable or just and thought Denniss should know; Denniss's response was not preserved.

On 19 January 1903 Collin reported that works had been 'seriously interfered with due to excessive rain and frost' but no damage was done when the Tanat overflowed its banks after heavy rain on 7 January. Fencing and trackwork had both reached Llangynog, and with the exception of four small occupation bridges, all the bridges and cattle creeps were complete.

Two of the directors reported flooding after the 7 January rain, in the cutting at Pentrefelin and on the Llangedwyn estate. Triffitt, the resident engineer, said that the issue at Pentrefelin would be resolved when the cutting was opened out to its full width and that flood relief channels would be made to resolve the problem at Llangedwyn.

Details of the design for the Vyrnwy pipeline crossing had not been finalised with Liverpool Corporation. Collin said it could be made of concrete for £940 but the Corporation wanted ornamentation incorporating ashlar that would cost £1,581 3s 11d. The Corporation's water engineer was asked to reconsider, and an agreement was reached by 20 April. Given that the structure was below track level and would be seen by very few people, making a feature of it would have been pointless.

On the railway, meanwhile, one of Strachan's labourers, 22-year-old William Michael, had been run over by 'some wagons' at an unspecified location on 27 January, sustaining injuries that required one of his legs to be amputated at Oswestry cottage hospital (*Shrewsbury Chronicle*, 6 February 1903). This was the only accident reported during the railway's construction. By the time of the 1911 census, Michael was out of work, married with an adopted daughter; no trace has been found of him thereafter.

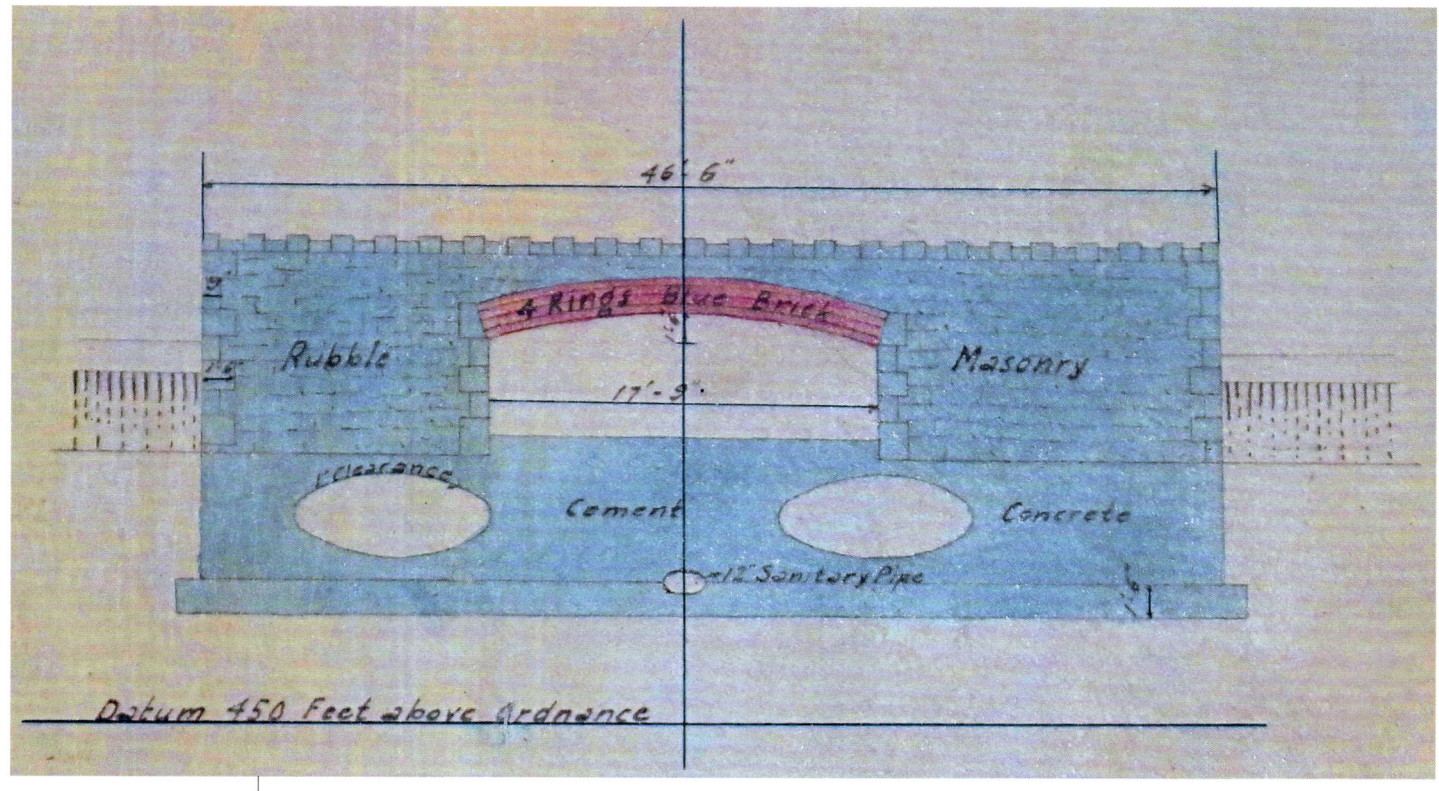

A drawing of Liverpool Corporation's pipeline bridge as built.

Better weather enabled more men to be employed on the contract, Collin reported when the directors met on 16 February 1903. Half the cuttings had been completed, the remainder well in hand. All cattle creeps and bridges were 'practically complete'. Two retaining walls near the 12-mile milepost were complete.

The question of liability for damage to any pipes transported on the railway before it was completed was discussed by the directors on 16 March. Strachan agreed to be responsible for the wagons used and to return them to the Cambrian, and he and the company agreed to be jointly responsible for any damage done to the loads unless it were caused by the negligence of Strachan or his employees. No date for the start of the pipe traffic has been found. Although the report of the directors' inspection on 27 July (*Shrewsbury Chronicle*, 31 July) said that it had started, when the directors met on 31 August it appeared to be an outstanding matter that was being dealt with by the Cambrian.

A free ride to Oswestry market on 18 March must have been a red-letter day for the valley's inhabitants, and would have been quite exhilarating if they had ridden in Strachan's ballast wagons as claimed in the *Manchester Guardian* (19 March). The paper also said that the contractor had announced his intention to run free trains to Oswestry on Wednesdays and Saturdays until the line was opened.

Investigating at Denniss's request, Gough found no evidence of passengers being carried in wagons and said that they travelled in an old carriage that the railway had sold to Strachan, the train being timed to give enough time to walk to Llynclys to catch the 11.10am to Oswestry. On receipt of a free ticket, passengers had to sign a book accepting the risk. Gough understood that about forty passengers had travelled. Later, he managed to acquire one of the tickets. The Cambrian had charged £45 for the carriage, plus £8 7s siding rent for stabling it at Blodwel Junction.

During March, some work was done on Sundays, presumably to avoid inconvenience to the public if it were done on other days, but some residents were sufficiently offended by this despoiling of

Both sides of a ticket issued by Strachan for travel on his trains. (National Archives)

the Sabbath to circulate what the *Liverpool Daily Post* (20 March) called a 'remarkable manifesto' that asked those responsible to put a stop to it, and if they did not then the men involved should abstain from accepting the request to work. When the directors asked Collin about it at their 20 April meeting, he said that there was some work that could only be done on Sundays.

On the same occasion, Collin said that the earthworks were in an advanced state and pointing bridges and fixing their copings and timber floors was bringing them to completion.

The construction was responsible for a ceremony that took place in Westminster on 21 April, when Strachan's engineer, Norman Robinson, married Rose Mary Leslie (1865–1944) of Bryn Tanat, Llansantffraid, an event that escaped the attention of the local press. The bride's mother had participated in the first sod ceremony

The question of identifying locomotives suitable for the railway tasked the Cambrian during 1903. On 30 April Herbert Jones, the locomotive superintendent, told Denniss that as three were required the only suitable ones were the 'Seaham' class of 2-4-0Ts, Nos 57–9, built in 1866 by Sharp, Stewart, but they were allocated to the Llanfyllin and Llanyblodwel branches and Birmingham Corporation's Elan Valley reservoir construction railway and alternatives had to be found for them there. Substitutes for the Llanfyllin and Llanyblodwel services were soon found but it took longer to find one for the Elan Valley; the outcome was not recorded in the papers preserved.

Cambrian Railways 2-4-0T No 58, one of three 'Seaham'-class locomotives initially designated for use on the light railway. It had been built by Sharp, Stewart in 1866 and rebuilt at Oswestry.

BUILDING THE RAILWAY • 59

A tank installed by Strachan to supply water to his locomotives.

The line had been engineered to accommodate four-wheel rolling stock, of which the Cambrian had a supply that was out of use. On 5 August Jones told Denniss that he required instructions if he was to have it ready in time for the opening. He also said that he could convert four-wheeled carriages into brake vans for £30 each, although with a tare weight of only 9½ tons they would not be the equal of new-build vehicles. In later years six-wheeled carriages were used.

On 27 June 1903 the Cambrian directors had inspected the line in their saloon carriages, inviting chairman C. E. Williams and Parry Jones to accompany them. At Porthywaen, Strachan's engine took over the train for the run to Llangynog, making only a water stop in each direction (*Shrewsbury Chronicle*, 3 July).

At the Tanat Valley directors' meeting two days later, Collin reported that the three river bridges, two over the Tanat and one over the Iwrch, a Tanat tributary east of Llanrheaedr, and all the cattle creeps and culverts were complete. Excavation of the cuttings was nearly complete. Strachan was pushing on with ballasting.

The shareholders' annual meeting took place on the same date. Up to 31 December 1902 £47,660 5s 5d had been spent, with a further £2,592 4s 7d spent since. It was hoped that the railway would be ready to be opened in September (*Shrewsbury Chronicle*, 3 July 1903).

The Tanat Valley directors had their own inspection train on 27 July, travelling from Oswestry in 'wet and disagreeable' weather, the journey taking seventy-five minutes. Strachan provided a champagne lunch in a marquee at Llangynog. In addition to directors and officers, guests included the engineers, local authority representatives, landowners and shareholders. Among the guests was Clinton James Wilson Holme (1863–1931), representing Holme & King, the contractors laying the second Vyrnwy pipeline for Liverpool Corporation. A nephew of Arthur Hill Holme (1841–1912), one of the partners of Holme & King, who had also tendered to build the railway; he had worked on the Snowdon Mountain Railway contract in 1895 (*Liverpool Daily Post*, 7 July / *Shrewsbury Chronicle*, 31 July).

In the boardroom, tenders for signalling, telegraph and station buildings were

The Cambrian directors' inspection train on 27 June 1903. Making an impression to go with the Cambrian's saloons, Strachan put his newest engine on the train, a Manning, Wardle, No 7 in his fleet, which had been delivered in January.

Construction of the new Blodwel Junction (formerly Llanyblodwel) approaching completion in 1903. A new station building has been erected on the site of the former Potteries building.

approved when the directors met on 31 August, Tyer & Company for the signalling (£2,326), Saunders & Company for the telegraphs (£1,435 19s 6d), and Strachan for the buildings (£960, Appendix 18).

A request from landowner John Lawton Parry Hamer (1880–1939) for a flag station near his house at Glanyrafon, Llanyblodwel, was accepted provided he contributed two thirds of the cost; a mile of the railway passed through his land. He seemed not to like the idea of having to make a financial contribution and made the request several times, receiving the same answer each time.

Station names approved were: Porthywaen, Blodwel Junction, Llanyblodwel, Llansilin Road, Llangedwyn, Pentrefelin, Llanrhaiadr Mochnant, Pedairffordd, Penybont Fawr and Llangynog. Llansilin Road was at Penybont, 4 miles from the village it purported to serve. Weighbridges were to be installed at Llansilin Road, Llangedwyn, Llanrhaiadr Mochnant and Penybont Fawr. The omission of Llangynog, considering that it was expected to be a major source of traffic, appears to have been an oversight.

Denniss asked Collin about running a test train on 16 September 1903, but was told that it should be delayed as long as possible to enable Strachan to have the formation in the best condition. Collin also said that the locomotive superintendent had told him he wished to try six-wheeled stock. He, however, had understood that four-wheeled stock was to be used but if the larger stock was used the Board of Trade would not allow it to run at 25mph on 9 chain radius curves.

Meeting on 26 October 1903, the directors approved Strachan's tenders of £325 for an engine shed and £115 for a water tank, both at Llangynog, and agreed with Collin's proposal to extend the retaining wall near Penybontfawr because the river was encroaching on the site. They had no suggestions to make to the Cambrian's enquiry about the provision of refreshment rooms at stations and asked that company to defer making unspecified alterations to the Shropshire Railways line at Llanymynech, presumably to accommodate the Tanat Valley service in some way.

Transportation of Liverpool Corporation's pipe traffic, which had started in May 1903, had been stopped because the pipeline contractors, Holme & King, had not been removing the pipes from railway premises, hindering Strachan's work, which resulted in the Corporation issuing a writ against the company in a claim for damages for non-compliance with a contract made in 1900 and calling for specified performance. Parry Jones advised that the company was not responsible as the agreement did not come into effect until the line had been approved by the Board of Trade but W. J. Burgess, the council's director, disagreed.

Denniss explained the background to his directors on 28 October. After the Corporation's water engineer had asked

J. L. P. Hamer, the Glanyrafon landowner who wanted a platform but who did not want to make a contribution towards its cost, is buried in the churchyard of St Michael in Llanyblodwel. A platform was provided when the line opened.

Penybontfawr, looking eastwards. Lying on the ground, lower right, is a line of pipes for the Vyrnwy pipeline waiting to be buried. (William Charles Burns/E. C. Burns)

about having the pipes hauled over the incomplete railway he had consulted with Collin and said, verbally, that they 'should' be able to arrange for Strachan to haul the pipes from May, which had been used as the basis for a contract requiring the delivery of eighty pipes per week from 1 May. The Corporation took umbrage with the stoppage and issued the writ despite an extended correspondence with Denniss.

A meeting with all the parties took place in Denniss's office on 26 October 1903, after the Tanat Valley directors' meeting, during which A. H. Holme said that his firm could not remove the pipes until the railway yards had been made accessible to his traction engine. The meeting ended with agreements for Holme & King to build the access roads, and for the Corporation to pay the loaded-wagon demurrage that had been accruing and withdrawing the writ. As the railway was still in the contractor's possession, surely the company could not have been legally responsible for providing any service. On at least one occasion the pipes were taken to Llanfyllin, making their onward journey by road.

Accommodating the pipe traffic before the railway was complete was more trouble than it was worth. In a letter to Liverpool Corporation on 18 April 1904, Denniss was clearly frustrated by it. The Cambrian had, he wrote, incurred expense and inconvenience to obtain the traffic and it had caused annoyance and difficulty with Strachan. Its proportion of the through rate from Staveley was £1,177. If it had hauled the pipes to Penybontfawr itself, it would have paid the Tanat Valley £143, but it had paid Strachan £780 and he was claiming more. It was also being charged demurrage by the Great Central and Midland Railway for retained wagons that it had been unable to recoup. Had Denniss foreseen the difficulties he would have refused to have moved a single pipe until the line had been completed, he concluded.

No public explanation was offered for the opening being postponed until 1904 but when the Cambrian directors had visited the railway on 27 June 1903, they found that Strachan's workforce had been discharged, with no explanation offered. Collin had not commented on the lack of activity, which appeared to be extended, and did not do so subsequently. The Cambrian directors instructed Denniss to expedite the line's completion.

On 28 October 1903 he reported that he had consulted Parry Jones, who had recommended that Collin be asked if he thought that Strachan was in breach of the contract by failing to have the line completed by 1 August. Collin replied that he could not say that Strachan had not exercised due diligence and had made such progress as he should have done, which was hardly the case if the workforce had been laid off, but Denniss noted that exceptionally wet weather in the last two months had hindered progress and it was still impossible to say when the line would be finished. The bad weather continued until the end of the year.

With the opening approaching, the Cambrian asked the Tanat Valley to pay £132 13s 6d to equip the stations with ticket racks, dating and copying presses and other items but the directors, meeting on 16 November, thought that article 4 of the working agreement required the Cambrian to supply these items and replied to that effect.

Article 4 specified what the Cambrian should provide, including locomotives, rolling stock and personnel, after the railway had been constructed, inspected by the Board of Trade and authorised to be open for public traffic. It did not specify station equipment, which Denniss argued needed to be provided before the inspection and was therefore part of construction, capital expenditure. In an extended correspondence between him and Parry Jones this view eventually prevailed because Jones thought it advisable to avoid friction between the companies. The Tanat Valley directors grudgingly agreed, but not unanimously, when they met on 21 December.

In the end the amount claimed was reduced to £121 1s 2d by the removal of some 'first issue' consumables and staff uniforms after Denniss had sought advice from the London & South Western Railway, which told him that in its view furniture, platform barrows and appliances should be charged to capital but not uniforms and small stores.

A few days before, in preparation for Druitt's inspection on 18–19 December, a trial run had been made over the line with a Cambrian loco and carriages on 15 December, with Collin, traffic superintendent Gough and locomotive superintendent Jones in attendance (*Shrewsbury Chronicle*, 18 December 1903).

Those three, with Strachan, accompanied Druitt, who submitted his report on 21 December. The surviving copy comprises carbon flimsies, some of which are illegible. The line was, he said, single track with passing places at Llangedwyn and Llanrhaeadr. The track comprised 63lb per yard flat-bottom rail double spiked to fir sleepers with a sole plate on each side of the joints; it was in good order and had already carried a certain amount of goods traffic. The steepest gradient was 1 in 63, the sharpest curve of 9 chain radius, the deepest cutting was 24ft and the highest embankment 15ft.

At seven places embankments were supported by retaining walls, the highest being 12ft. The passing places had two platforms, the remaining stations, one. All were 2ft 3in high and provided with shelters. There were twenty-nine

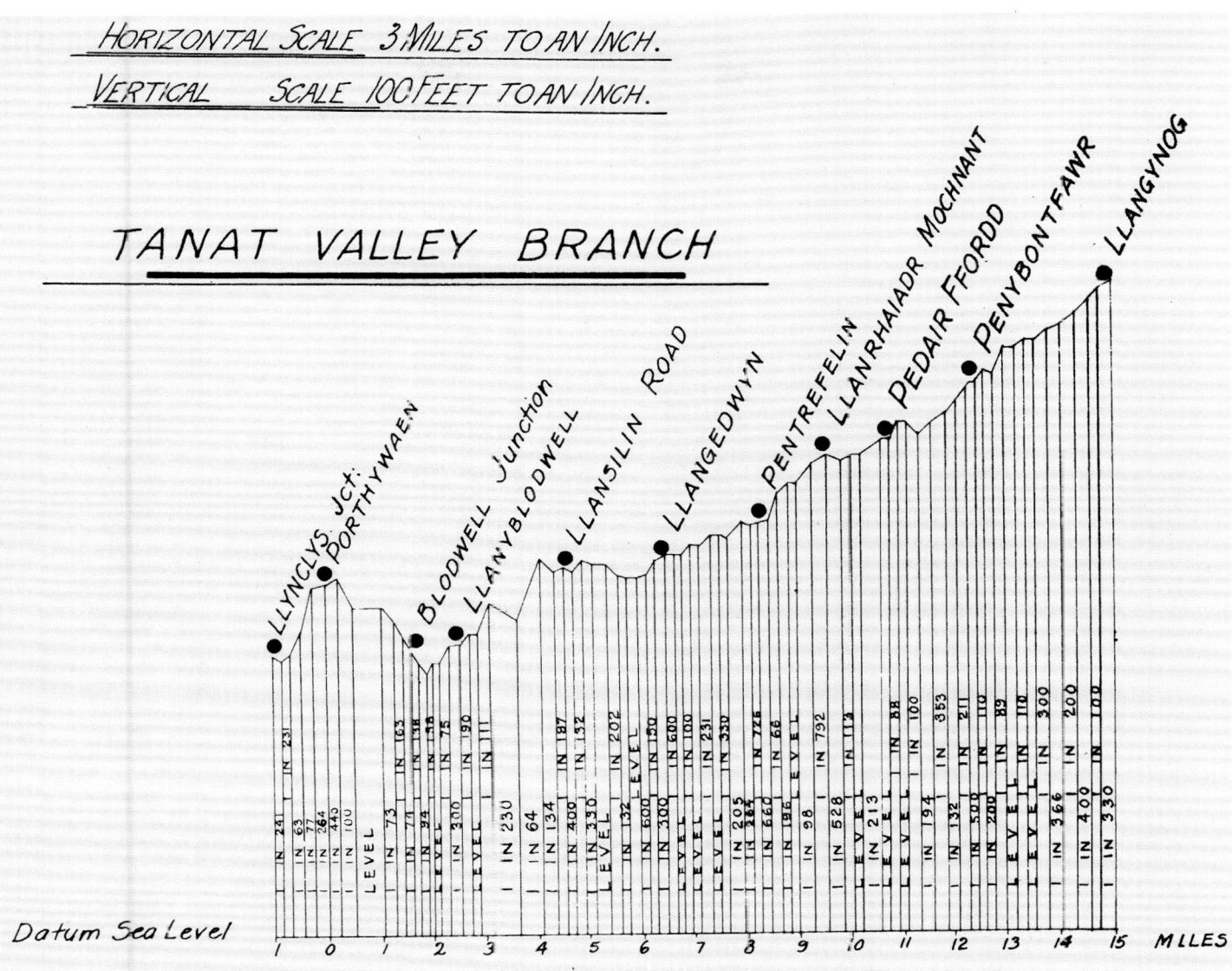

Tanat Valley Light Railway gradient diagram.

underbridges, mostly formed of timber baulks under each rail mounted on masonry embankments. Three were formed of brick arches, six of rolled steel joists under each rail and two with plate girders carried on masonry embankments. Two river viaducts of three and two spans were made using steel girders, cross girders and rail bearers with masonry abutments and piers, the largest spans being 59ft and 54ft. There were three culverts of 3ft or greater diameter.

All girders, joists and beams of the underbridges had sufficient theoretical strength and deflected moderately under load but the joists at one side of the bridge at 7 miles 15 chains, just west of Llangedwyn, were not well bedded and needed attention.

Druitt described the ground frames installed at sidings and loops, saying that they were not connected. Collin later told the directors that this was to give Strachan access to them with his engine; they were connected before the railway was opened.

On the Shropshire Railways no change had been made at Llanymynech, while at Nantmawr Junction a new signal box had been installed. Ballasting on both the Cambrian (Porthywaen branch) and the

Cambrian Railways 4-4-0 No 21 was decorated when it was rostered to haul the Tanat Valley Light Railway's inaugural train on 3 January 1904. This nugget of information was contained in the 'fashion and function' section of the *Wellington Journal*'s 9 January report of the day's activities. Bylined 'Sabrina', it also, as might be expected, described the ladies' attire.

Shropshire Railways' sections required improving.

Druitt expressed himself satisfied with the work and the opening ceremony was set for 5 January 1904 although the goods service started on 28 December 1903 (*Shrewsbury Chronicle*, 25 December / 1 January 1904).

On the appointed day, a train hauled by a decorated locomotive and loaded with about 300 passengers left Oswestry just before noon. At Porthywaen it was halted by a gate closed across the line, secured by a silver chain and padlock. There, close to the spot where the Countess of Powis had cut the first sod in 1899, the Dowager Lady Williams Wynn (1827–1905) performed the opening ceremony, opening the gate with a gold key provided by Strachan.

As the train passed along the line it was greeted by crowds at decorated stations. At Llangynog, lunch was taken in the schoolroom. During the congratulatory and self-congratulatory speeches that followed, it was noted that Lady Williams Wynn had also cut the first sod for the Oswestry & Newtown Railway at Welshpool on 4 August 1857. In his reply to the toast to his employers, C. S. Dennis, the Cambrian manager, said that working the Tanat Valley line for 60% of the gross receipts meant that it would be worked at a loss to his company, its expenses being about 65% of its receipts.

Saying that the railway had cost more than expected, chairman C. E. Williams appealed for the unsubscribed shares to be taken up and for the shareholders who had not paid their calls to do so. In

66 • THE TANAT VALLEY LIGHT RAILWAY

of the pipeline contractors, Holme & King, again, and W. H. Spaull, who had launched the 1878 scheme for a narrow-gauge railway from Oswestry (*Shrewsbury Chronicle*, 8 January 1904).

the final reckoning, there were thirty-one shareholders with more than £100 invested in the railway, while eighty-nine had invested £1. Of the directors, only Davies and Stewart had more than the £150 that qualified them to be directors, £300 and £250 respectively.

Parry Jones, who had done so much to have a railway made in the Tanat valley, was unwell and had been forbidden by his doctor from travelling to Llangynog, although he had been allowed to observe the ceremony at Porthywaen. No photographs of the opening day ceremonies and train have been found.

Among the guests, the usual mix of local dignitaries, landowners, directors, officers, mayors, councillors and council officers, and shareholders, were C. J. W. Holme,

Far left: Marie Emily, the dowager Lady Williams Wynn (1827–1905), who performed the railway's opening ceremony, was buried alongside her husband in St Cedwyn's churchyard, Llangedwyn.

Left: Joseph Parry Jones, the solicitor, town clerk and mayor whose enthusiastic support for the railway made a substantial contribution towards ensuring that it was built, is buried in Oswestry's public cemetery. His estate was valued at £16,999 14s 7d, £1,380,325 in 2022.

W. H. Spaull, who attempted to promote a railway to Llangynog in 1878 and who supported the light railway, is buried with his brother in this plot in Oswestry's public cemetery but his name was not recorded on the stone. His £3,221 9s 10d estate would be worth £262,572 in 2022. One of his executors was William Henry Bickerton, son of the engineer of the same name who had worked for R. S. France on the construction of the Potteries Railway.

BUILDING THE RAILWAY • 67

CHAPTER 4

THE TANAT VALLEY LIGHT RAILWAY

The poster announcing the railway's opening. (National Archives)

Timetable poster for 1904. (National Archives)

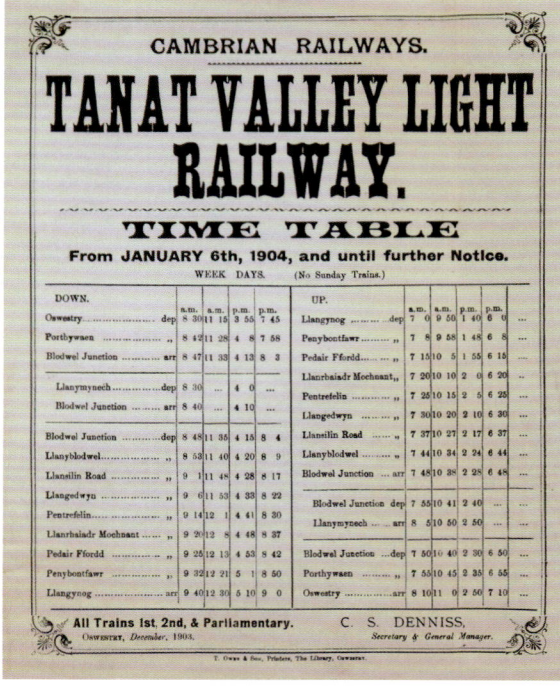

A poster issued in December 1903 advertised the start of passenger services on 6 January 1904, when about 150 passengers used the railway to visit Oswestry market. The Cambrian also ran an extra train from Penybontfawr to Llangynog carrying schoolchildren for free. These then joined children from Llangynog for a commemorative tea provided by J. Parry Jones. (*Shrewsbury Chronicle*, 8 January). On 20 January Cambrian general manager C. S. Denniss told his directors that until the water tank was installed at Llangynog, trains had been subject to delay. It appears that the tank's absence had not been brought to his attention until just before the opening ceremony.

The timetable comprised four trains a day with no Sunday service. With services centred on Llangynog, the first train left at 7.00 and the last arrived back at 9.00pm, the train crew must have lodged in the village, which would have done little to contain operating expenses. There were two trains from Llanymynech and three in the opposite direction.

Any expectation that the Cambrian might have had that the agreement with Lord Bradford for the through running of carriages between Llangynog and Llanymynech would not be closely supervised was soon disabused when his Lordship wrote, on 15 January, to press for its compliance.

Passenger loadings between Blodwel Junction and Llanymynech

Date	Ex-Llanymynech		Ex-Blodwel Junction		
	8.30am	4.00pm	7.55am	10.41am	2.40pm
8 January	2	2			
9 January	2	1			
11 January	2	4	3	3	
12 January	2	3			1
13 January		1		2	2
14 January	2	2		1	
15 January	8	1			
16 January	2	2		2	8

Suggesting that a compartment in a second-class carriage be converted to provide third-class accommodation for the Llanymynech service, traffic superintendent Gough helpfully supplied a table of loadings, shown above.

Denniss agreeing to Gough's proposal, the resulting composite vehicle entered service on 4 February.

Four stationmaster positions were created for the railway, men being transferred from other positions on the Cambrian system. At Llangynog, J. Edmunds, formerly booking clerk at Machynlleth, was also responsible for Penybontfawr; at Llanrhaeadr, Charles Watkin Davies (1876–1942), formerly stationmaster at Fairbourne, was also responsible for Pedairffordd and Pentrefelin; at Llangedwyn, Levi Cooper (1879–1957), formerly stationmaster at Boughrood, was also responsible for Llansilin Road; and at Blodwel Junction, George Edward Davies (1864–1957) was also responsible for Llanyblodwel. Thomas James Goodwill (1875–1930), the stationmaster at Llynclys, was given responsibility for Porthywaen and Thomas Pryce (1851–1934), stationmaster at Llanymynech, had Nantmawr Junction added to his brief (*Wellington Journal*, 9 January 1904). Davies later emigrated to Canada and died there.

A typical passenger train with a 'Seaham'-class locomotive and four-wheeled carriages passing Blodwel Junction soon after opening.

A local postcard publisher soon decided that the railway was worthy of mockery in the style of Cynicus. (Park, Newtown)

Reviewing the first month's operations on 16 February (Appendix 19), Denniss reported to his directors that the average earning of £7 6s 8d per mile per week would equate to £381 per mile per annum if maintained, compared with £1,318 per mile per annum on the Cambrian in 1902. Anticipating lower costs on the railway, he forecast a fair margin of profit from operating it.

Liverpool Corporation soon made arrangements to install the extra sidings that it needed at Llanrhaeadr and Penybontfawr. Major Druitt visited twice, to examine a siding connected to the up line of the loop and controlled from the existing ground frame at the former, report on 11 February, and then on sidings made to the running lines at both, 16 July. They had points facing up trains worked from two-lever ground frames, controlled by the Llanrhaeadr–Llangedwyn electric tablet at Llanrhaeadr and the Llanrhaeadr–Llangynog tablet at Penybontfawr. He recommended that the Board of Trade sanction the use of all of them.

When the Lambourne Valley Railway, in Berkshire, put its three 0-6-0T locomotives on the market the Cambrian's locomotive superintendent thought they would suit the Tanat Valley. On 9 June he was authorised to offer not more than £2,200 of D debentures for them, £2,090 at the then current market price. One of the locomotives had been built by Hunslet, the others by Chapman & Furneaux.

In operation the railway did pretty much what the promoters wanted for it, except for paying interest and dividends. It carried passengers and goods to and from Oswestry market and stone from Llangynog, but none of them in any vast amounts. Withdrawal of one of the passenger train workings in 1909 brought an end to the costly practice of stabling

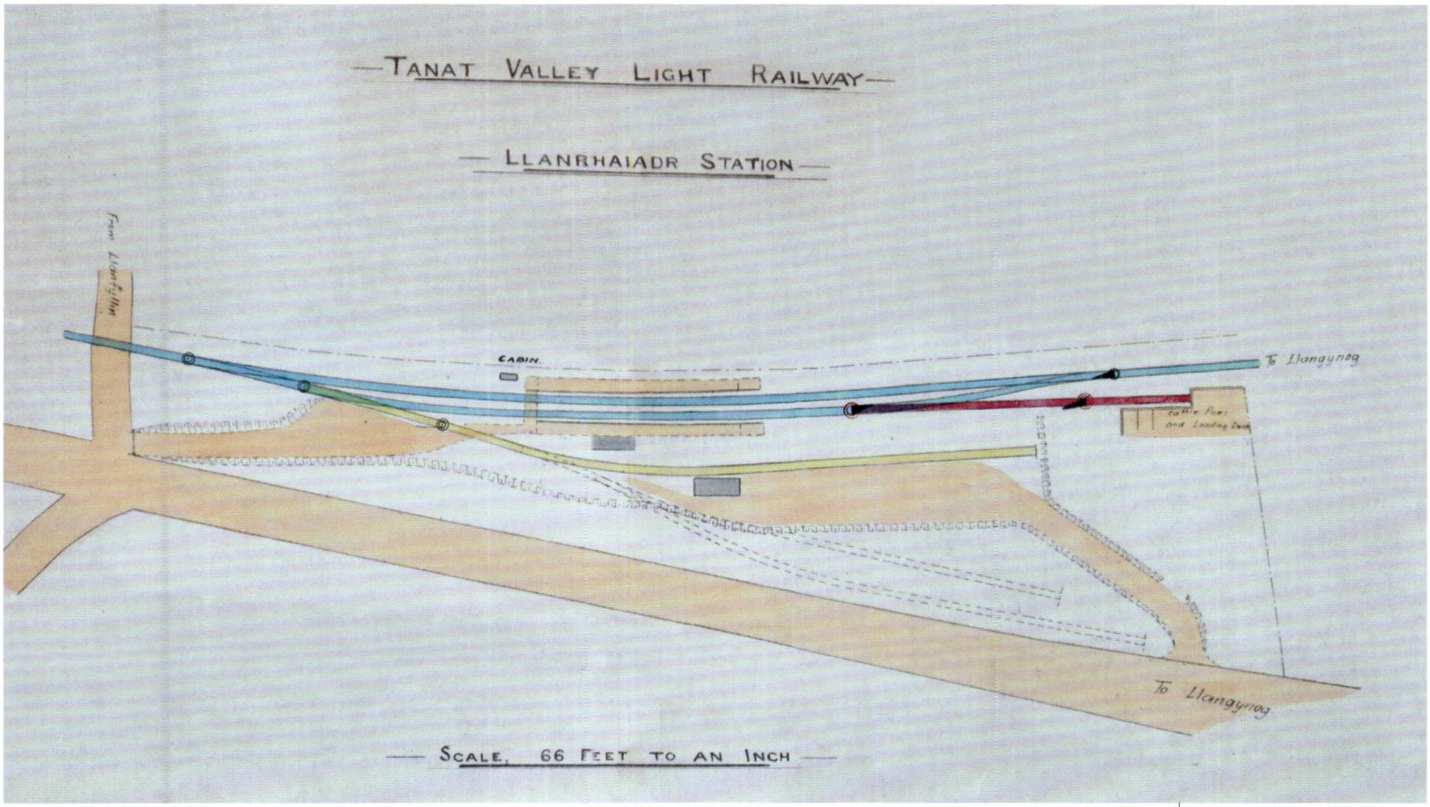

Plan of Llanrhaeadr showing the addition of a siding to serve the cattle pens. The sidings shown by broken lines were installed for Liverpool Corporation.

Seen in later years, one of the three Lambourne Valley Railway locomotives acquired by the Cambrian for the Tanat Valley in 1904.

a locomotive overnight at Llangynog; henceforth the trains ran mixed until the First World War.

A fatal accident had upset the routine at Llangedwyn station on 20 July 1904, when goods guard William Sandells Downes, aged 34, was crushed between the buffers of two wagons. He was buried in Oswestry's public cemetery. The *Welsh Coast Pioneer* (29 July) reported that it was

Penybontfawr from Station. Photo. by Burns.

A postcard view of a train at Penybontfawr. (William Charles Burns/Lloyd, Llanrhaeadr)

the railway's first fatal accident, as though it expected there to be more; it was actually the only recorded fatality of an employee in the railway's history.

But although the railway was open to traffic and there had been a joyous celebration of its opening, the directors could not rest on their laurels. The company was seriously in debt, Strachan had not been paid since 30 September 1903, and the overdraft exceeded the amount of the outstanding Treasury grant by nearly £3,000. Thanks to the shortage of funds, which was never resolved, the shareholders and investing authorities did not reap the rewards they expected. The following years were marked by disputes and litigation.

Apart from giving their approval to expenditure, any comments the directors made about the cost of works *vis-à-vis* the funds available were not recorded. A balance sheet produced for the Cambrian showing the position on 15 June 1903 (Appendix 13) attracted no attention either, but by the autumn there had been signs that the edifice was creaking a little.

No comment had been made when Strachan went unpaid. During the autumn of 1903 his tenders for installing the engine shed, water tank and weighbridges had been accepted but a few weeks later he had refused to do the work; it was taken on by Tanat Valley director W. H. Thomas, but the tank had not been functional when the railway was opened.

On 16 November, it was reported that the Cambrian was trying to get Strachan to agree to payment due to him being deferred with 5% interest being payable, and Saunders, the telegraph contractor, had already agreed to the payment of £1,200 being deferred for three months for 5% interest.

Tanat Valley chairman C. E. Williams mentioned on 21 December 1903 that the construction of the railway would cost considerably more than anticipated and suggested that it would be advisable to have instructions to apply to the Treasury for a further grant.

Denniss advised his directors about the Tanat Valley finances on 19 January 1904. Certificates dating from October and totalling £5,352 13s 6d remained unpaid and there was probably another £1,500 due. There were other amounts owing, including £700 to J. B. Saunders & Company for telegraphs, that the Cambrian was not responsible for.

Commenting on his attempt to get Strachan to agree to deferred payments, Denniss said that Strachan 'is an extremely awkward man to deal with' and the matter was deadlocked until Strachan passed it to his solicitors. They said that they would only accept an agreement if the Cambrian was a party to it. In February, though, Strachan demanded immediate payment for the oldest outstanding certificate before he would make an agreement.

Deciding that it would be better not to argue about the inclusion of £490 for station buildings, which was not part of the construction contract, the Cambrian paid £2,000 'on account', which raised the issue about how much of the Tanat Valley's 40% of gross earnings it could retain as a contribution towards any debt incurred on the company's behalf. It ignored the question about the arrangements it was going to make to ensure that the full amount was paid by the June deadline that Strachan had set. The £2,000 payment, and a further one of £1,460 5s 6d, were not enough to deter Strachan from acting, and by 6 April he had issued three writs against the Cambrian. The only case reported, concerning a certificate for £2,437 10s issued on 15 February, was heard in the King's Bench Division on 23 April, a Saturday. The Cambrian's barrister argued that as the certificate was for half of the retention money, it was not due until the final certificate was issued. The judge agreed and gave judgment to the Cambrian with costs (*Evening Express*, 25 April). During his evidence Strachan said that he expected to receive £20,000 for extras on the contract. Denniss, who attended, asked Collin what Strachan meant by this but Collin could not answer because, he said, the extra work would be itemised in the final certificate, which he had not completed.

There were also problems with Collin, which were probably related to his health. He had stopped attending the directors'

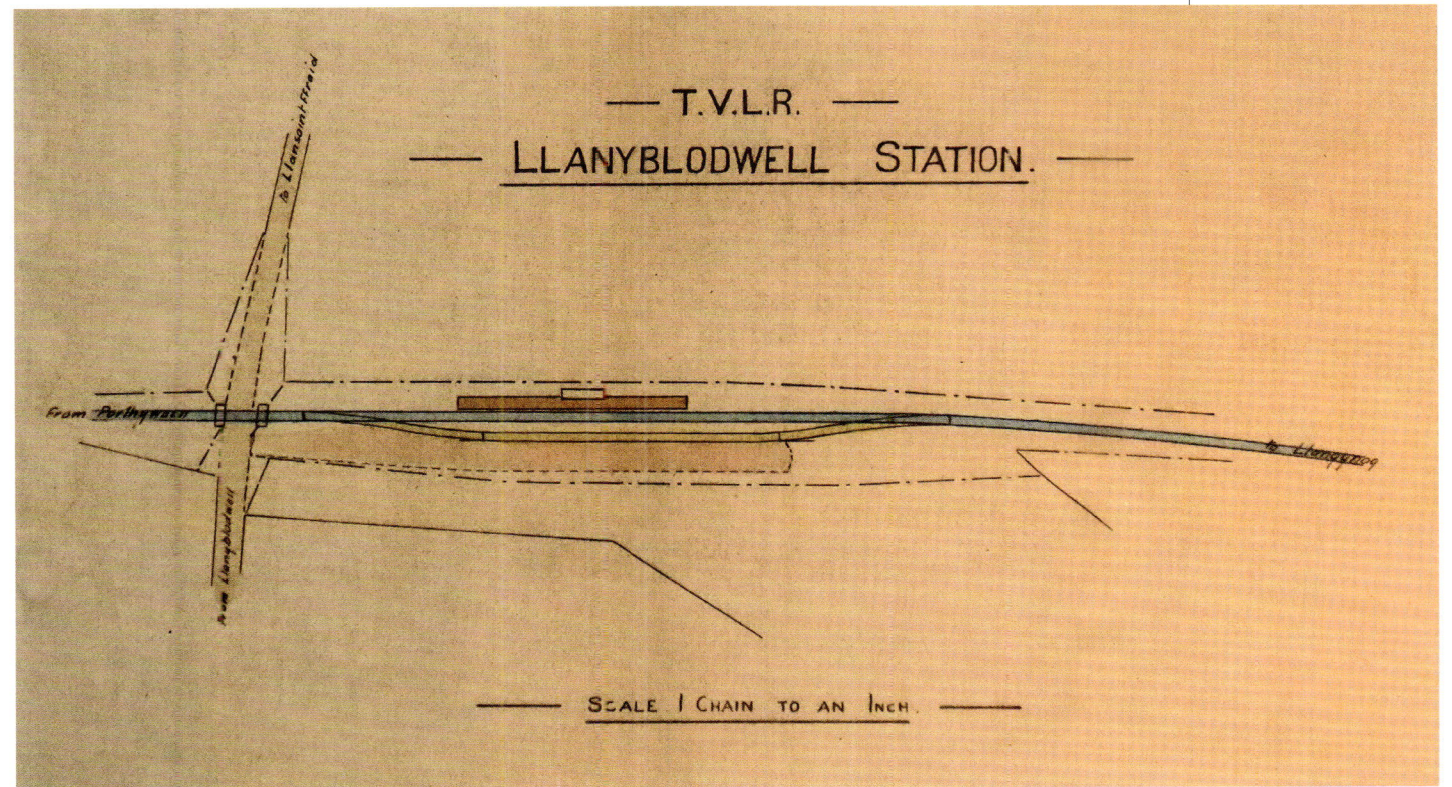

An engineer's plan of Llanyblodwel. This set of plans was produced to show how the stations should be laid out when constructed. Except for Llanyblodwel, which had capacity for 15 wagons, they also show the wagon capacities of sidings. (National Archives)

meetings and had to be asked more than once to supply a statement of the railway's costs. In November 1903 Strachan had complained to him, copied to secretary John Williams, about the 'want of instructions'.

The directors' first meeting after the railway had been opened was held on 29 January 1904. They had received Collin's statement of costs (Appendix 15), which the chairman explained, adding that he had arranged a meeting with the Light Railway Commissioners. Collin had again sent his apologies.

They had a special meeting on 15 February and resolved to tell Denniss that there was no money available to pay Strachan. Another special meeting, on 1 March, dealt with the Cambrian's request for a £2,500 mortgage as security for the £2,000 payment to Strachan. Wait for the Treasury decision on the grant application, they replied.

A. J. Collin resigned as the Cambrian's engineer, citing ill health, on 13 February, standing down from the light railways at the same time. Acting for three companies, two of them under construction, had probably not done his health any favours. He obtained work for J. B. Saunders but in 1906 he was noted to have gone to Torquay 'for his health'. He died in East Sheen on 5 February 1916, his effects valued at £64 5s, and was buried in East Sheen public cemetery, Richmond.

George Champion McDonald (1867–1937) replaced Collin as engineer from 7 April. Since completing his three-year pupil-ship in 1888 he had worked for the Midland Railway, latterly as resident engineer for new lines and works.

The remainder of the Treasury grant had been paid on 7 March, reducing the overdraft to £2,459 18s 4d. The bank was asked if it could be increased to permit payments due to Llanfyllin and Llansilin councils and for land purchases, about £1,500, not knowing that Denniss had recommended that the facility be refused.

One of the matters dealt with when the directors met on 11 April was Strachan's complaint to the Cambrian that he had been refused a pass to travel over the line; they declined to act, there was nothing they could do about it. Strachan had wanted the pass in order to inspect the Corporation's bridge and had to pay his own fare. Liverpool Corporation was told that no objection would be made if it installed another siding at Penybontfawr at its own expense.

Still on 11 April, the directors also dealt with two writs, one from the Cambrian for £4,074 17s 6d paid to Strachan, and one from Strachan for £1,066 for the station buildings. They decided to take no action over the first, except to ask Denniss not to apply for the appointment of a receiver until it 'became necessary', whenever that was, and to defend the second.

John Jones Roberts, one of the Oswestry directors, died on 22 April, aged 49. The directors' condolences were recorded in the minutes and a copy was sent to his widow. He was buried in St Oswald's churchyard in Oswestry, where, following a landscaping scheme, his grave is unmarked.

The Cambrian had one of its auditors, James Fraser (1854–1942), appointed receiver on 30 April (*Shrewsbury Chronicle*, 6 May). He would not run the railway but would receive the 40% of gross revenues. Strachan's application to appoint a joint receiver had been refused.

Denniss's report, to his directors, about a meeting with the Secretaries of State to the Treasury, the Board of Trade, the Board of Agriculture and the undersecretary for Scotland, at the Treasury on 18 April indicated that they were unhappy about the amount paid for land, which to comply with the Light Railways Act's ethos was supposed to be either donated or sold cheaply, and the law costs. They thought that the railway had been equipped as a branch of the Cambrian, rather than as a light railway, so it is probably no surprise that the application for a further grant was refused on 20 May.

While the company had got some of the land without charge, some of the remainder was vested in trustees and

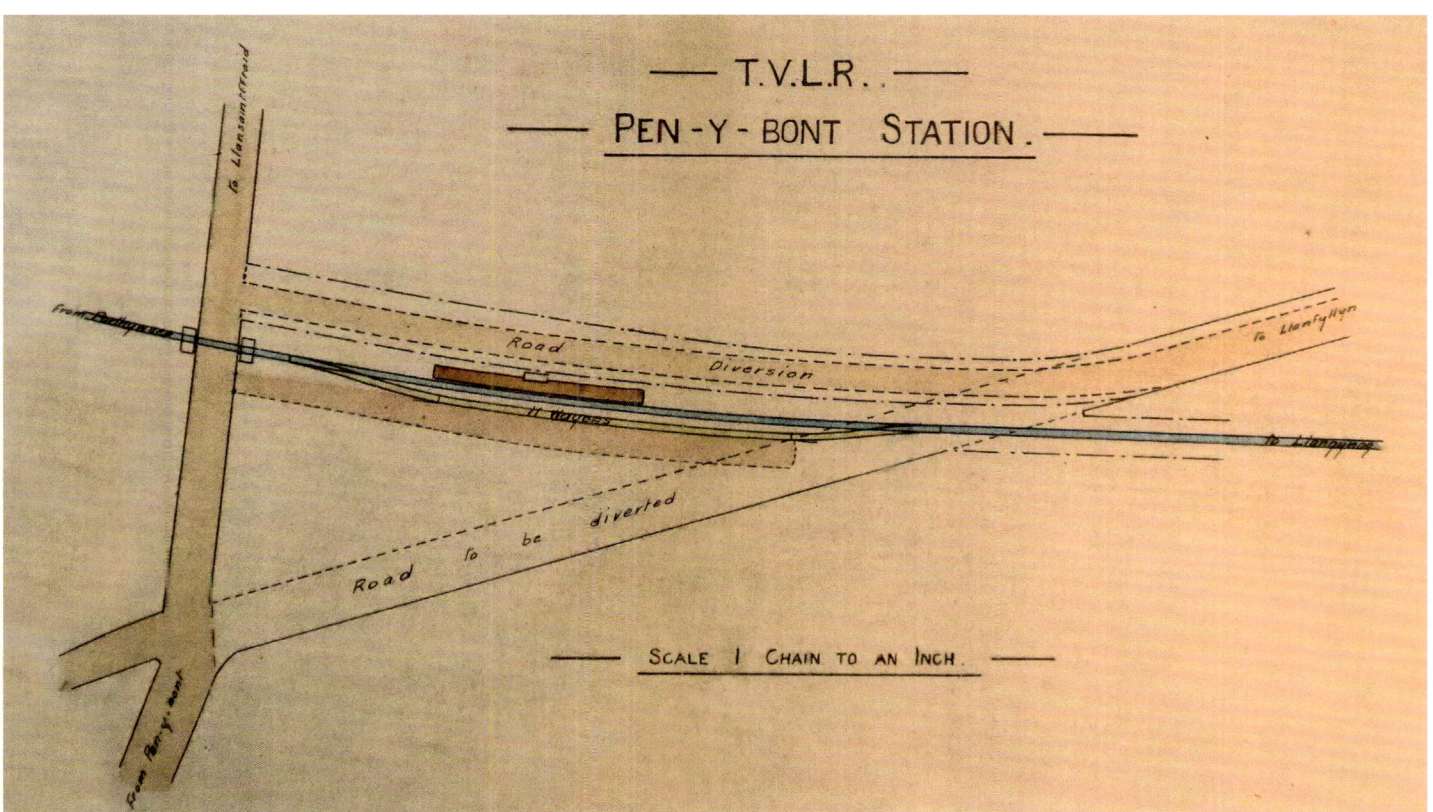

Penybont, Llansilin Road in operation. (National Archives)

mortgagees who would have insisted on receiving its full value, and the legal expenses included the costs of the land arbitration cases (Appendix 15). As to the way the railway had been equipped, this was the responsibility of the Cambrian and Collin; the directors were not railwaymen and would have deferred to any advice they were given. It is worth pointing out that the Treasury's policy of not paying half of the advance until the railway had been approved for public operation had resulted in the payment of £959 15s 3d interest on a short-term bank loan.

The directors had obviously made no plans for the grant being refused and did not know what to do. In his 8 June report to the Cambrian directors Denniss said he was surprised when Williams had told him that they had done nothing since being told that there would be no grant. Advising Williams to call a special meeting to discuss the situation, he told him that the Cambrian would retain the 40% of receipts until the debts had been cleared, which surprised Williams, who said that he had expected the Cambrian to pay the investing authorities to prevent them from taking action. The railway's gross receipts for the three months to 31 March had been £1,499 14s 10d, 40% of which was £599 17s 11d. If that turned out to be typical it would take several years to pay off the debt, and much longer if the investing authorities were paid.

Denniss was of the opinion, he told his directors, that the Tanat Valley directors' strategy was to let the matter drift in anticipation that the Cambrian would sort things out for them. The author thinks that he was crediting them with too much intelligence. They were small-town businessmen and professionals who were out of their depth.

Denniss also told his directors about letters received from J. B. Saunders and Company, claiming £1,950 10s 5d, Tyer & Company, £2,480 11s 3d, and Isca Foundry & Engineering Company, £119 10s 0d, saying, in different ways, that they had taken Tanat Valley contracts because they thought that the Cambrian's involvement protected them, and claiming payment.

Saunders was particularly aggrieved because Collin had put the company under pressure to complete the work, including over Christmas, in order for the railway to be opened; writs were issued to both the Cambrian and the Tanat Valley later. Told that its order had nothing to do with the Cambrian, Tyer issued a writ against it. Isca said that its orders had come from Collin at his Oswestry office on Cambrian letterheads, with nothing to indicate that they were being made at the behest of another company, to which Denniss replied that previous orders had been paid for by the Tanat Valley company.

Strachan, meanwhile, was entitled to claim for half of the retention money from 31 May, so Denniss deposited a cheque for £2,430 1s 10d with his company's solicitors. Instead of claiming, though, Strachan issued a writ for £2,516. Rather than disputing the difference, the solicitors deposited £2,479 8s 10d, which their examination of the accounts told them was the amount due, into court.

The recently departed A. J. Collin had also written to Denniss about money owed to him by the Tanat Valley company, hoping that as his former employers had been covering the money owed to Strachan it would look kindly on him, but he was disappointed.

Meeting on 18 July, the Tanat Valley directors decided to postpone the shareholders' meeting and not to circulate the statement of accounts for the year ending 31 December 1903. On 24 October they were informed that the Cambrian had submitted a bill for £3,100 10s 3d for the work done to adapt the Porthywaen and Nantmawr branches to accommodate the railway. The Cambrian also asked for a set of plans, and was told that the company had none. No explanation was offered for the delay in submitting the bill and surely one party or the other could have asked Collin for plans.

During the summer the investing authorities discussed the railway's situation and what they could do to protect their investments, appointing a joint committee that on 10 October decided to petition the court for an order appointing their own receiver (*Shrewsbury Chronicle*, 14 October). Liverpool Corporation took

Llangedwyn. (National Archives)

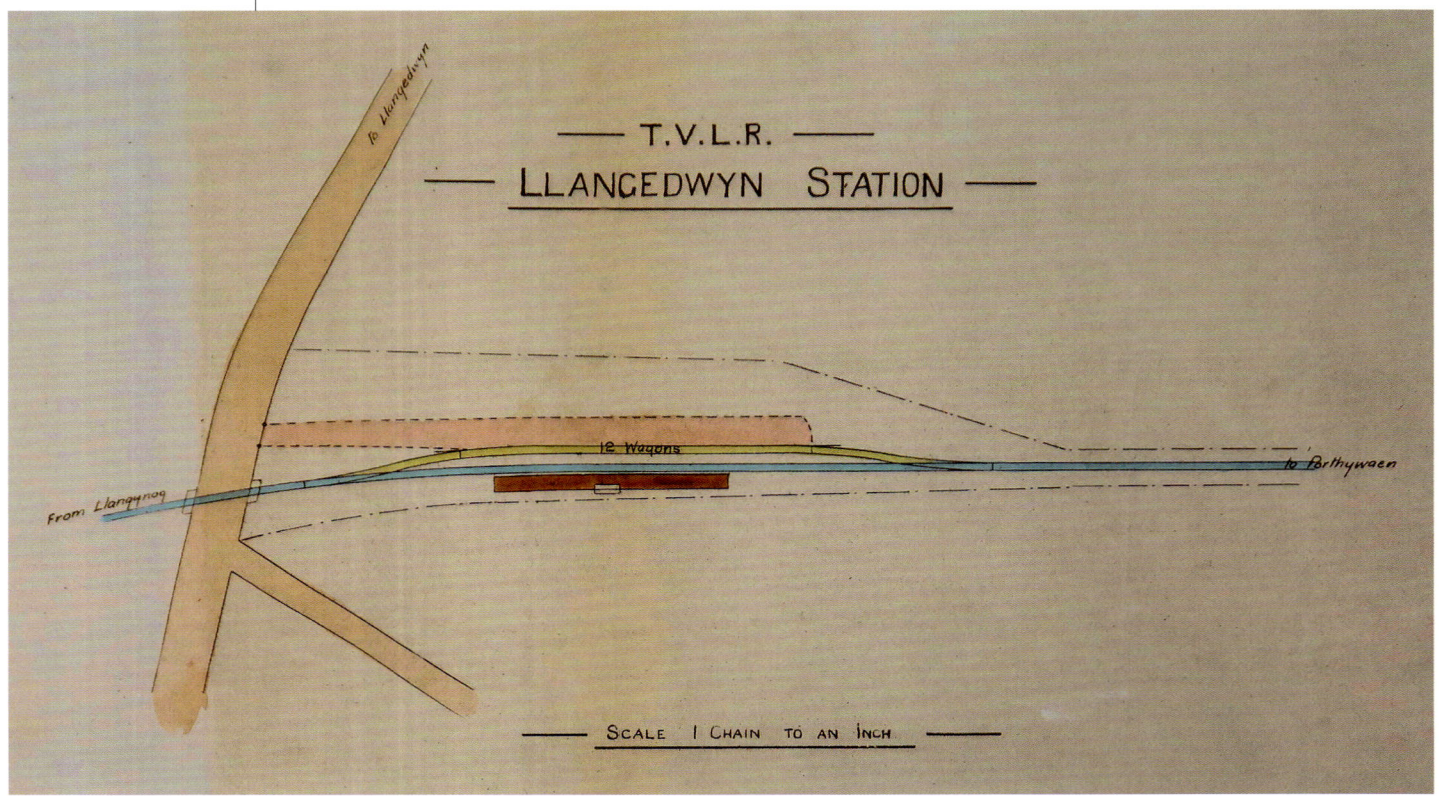

the lead in issuing a writ against the Tanat Valley and Cambrian companies, and their co-investors, seeking a ruling on the priority to be accorded to the parties. It took a while to achieve a resolution.

On 10 October Denniss informed his directors that from 5 January until 30 June the railway had earned £3,048 3s 3d, 40% of which, £1,219 5s 4d, had been credited against the company's debt; later he added that the receipts included the pipe traffic, which would not be maintained although it would be reasonable to expect traffic from other sources to increase. He had received no information, he said, about the company's intentions but had told chairman C. E. Williams that with reasonable care the company would have no difficulty in making arrangements to relieve the situation and to get the receivership cancelled. He saw no reason why the company could not issue the £5,000 debentures that remained unissued and arrange for further capital powers from the Light Railway Commissioners.

In the autumn there had been a glimmer of hope with the belief that the railway would unlock developments in the valley when the newly equipped Llwm Bar granite quarry started producing stone at Llangynog in September; its new machines had been delivered by rail, too. Reporting the development on 29 September, the *Merioneth County Times* commented that the expectation of the railway causing the opening of new works and the development of existing ones 'had not been realised to any large extent'.

On 3 November the Cambrian agreed to the installation of a new siding and wharf for this traffic at Llangynog, charging half the £177 expenditure to the Tanat Valley company's account; the quarry owner would pay the other half. An extension to the existing siding and loading dock for the Rhiwarth Slate Company was approved at the same time, cost £10.

By the end of the year Denniss was really frustrated by the behaviour of the Tanat Valley directors, their failure to act and poor communications. He was annoyed that he had not been consulted when they decided to apply for powers to increase their company's capital. The first he knew about it was the publication of a notice in the *London Gazette* on 29 November,

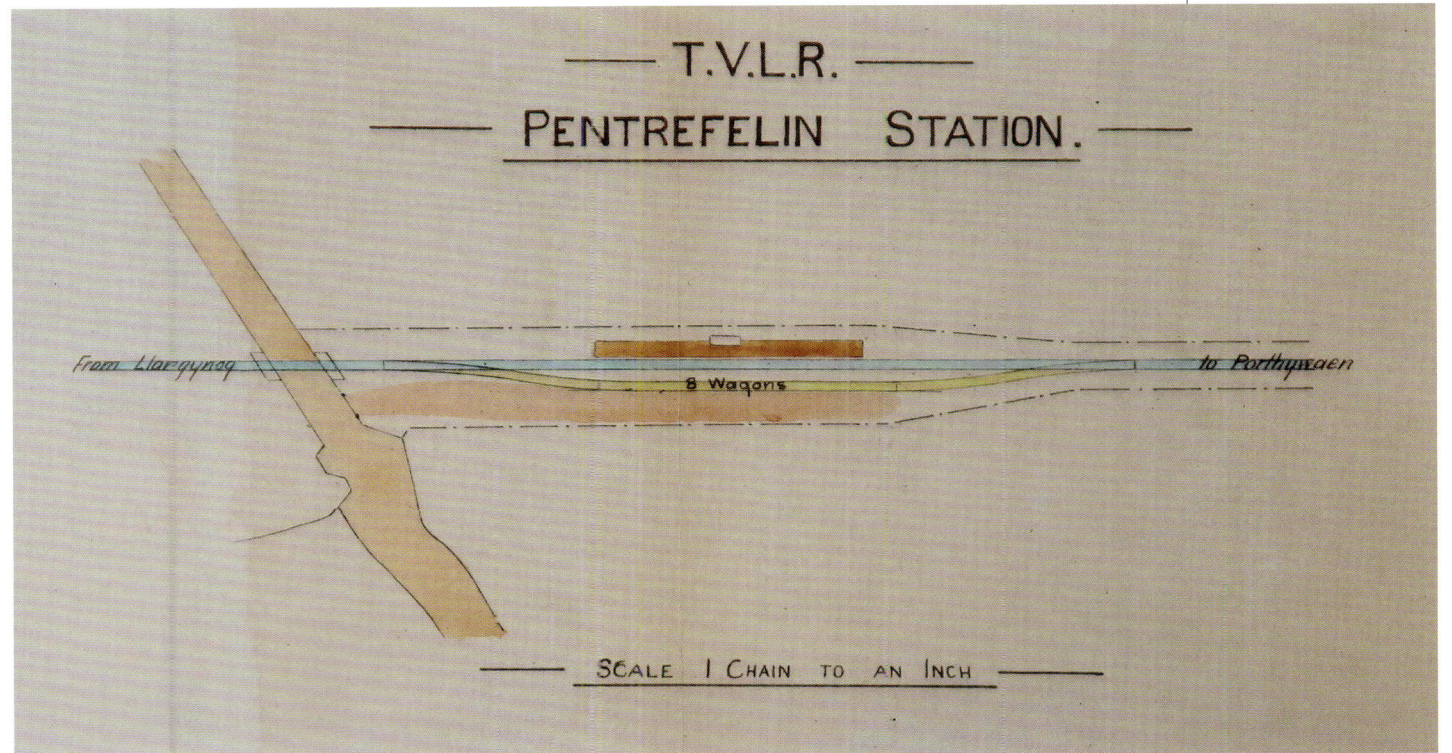

Pentrefelin. (National Archives)

which he thought had been drafted in such a way that it would annoy the investing authorities. Going behind their backs, he established a rapport with Liverpool Corporation, where his new friends were quite relaxed about the application, saying the Tanat Valley was within its rights to seek additional capital if it wanted to.

C. E. Williams told Denniss that the notice had not been properly considered before publication and that it was his intention to have it withdrawn and to call a special meeting of shareholders to review the situation and to obtain authority to dispose of the undertaking. However, the Tanat Valley directors decided to proceed with the application, hoping that the traffic figures would encourage the Treasury to look favourably on a fresh loan application.

As well as quoting extensively from his correspondence with the Tanat Valley in his 7 December 1904 report to his directors, twelve typed pages, Denniss thought he should tell them something about Strachan's character, as revealed in correspondence about the pipeline bridge that had been passed to him by C. E. Williams.

A man named Davidson had been employed on the Tanat Valley contract as an inspector and after his contract had ended Strachan employed him on another contract as a clerk of works. In September 1904, when Strachan received a complaint about the 'disgraceful' condition of the pipeline bridge when it was handed over, he asked his son to get Davidson to say that he had been satisfied with it on completion and that Holme & King's men had 'knocked it about' when they put the pipes through, but Davidson replied that the bridge was incomplete, and the pipes had not crossed the river, when he left, so Strachan sacked him with a week's notice.

As Denniss had forecast, the investing authorities objected to a clause in the draft Order that would have given proposed new debentures priority over those existing, which led to the clause being withdrawn on 13 March 1905.

The investing authorities formed a joint committee and appointed a Liverpool accountant, Henry Douglas Eshelby (1846–1905), to investigate the railway's finances (*Shrewsbury Chronicle*, 2 December 1904). He reported on 20 March 1905.

As well as describing the company's legal, contractual and financial position, his twenty-four-page printed report reproduced a letter from Collin explaining the background to the various estimates and giving reasons for the increased costs from his perspective. When appointed, he said, he had visited several light railways then completed or under construction, although his four years' experience on 'up country' railways in the colonies, which were effectively light railways, was also relevant. The information gained informed his first estimate of £53,540 in September 1899, when prices had been low. Station accommodation was limited, to be expanded to meet traffic requirements. Trains would be run using the (cheap) train staff system.

The February 1901 estimate was based on the prices in the June 1900 tenders, which had been unaffordable, and was more detailed. The Tanat Valley directors decided it would be more economical in the long term to take more land at stations and the Cambrian added further expense with its demand for an engine shed at Llangynog, for five stations to be equipped with weighbridges and three of them with warehouses, and wanting the line to be worked using the electric train staff.

Having a locomotive based at Llangynog and running a timetable that required two locomotives to work would have a considerable impact on operating costs. Station staffing levels also suggest that the Cambrian did not understand how a light railway was intended to be run and had treated the railway the same as it did the nearby Llanfyllin branch, which also had a locomotive based at the terminus.

During construction it had become obvious that retaining walls were required in two locations to protect the railway from

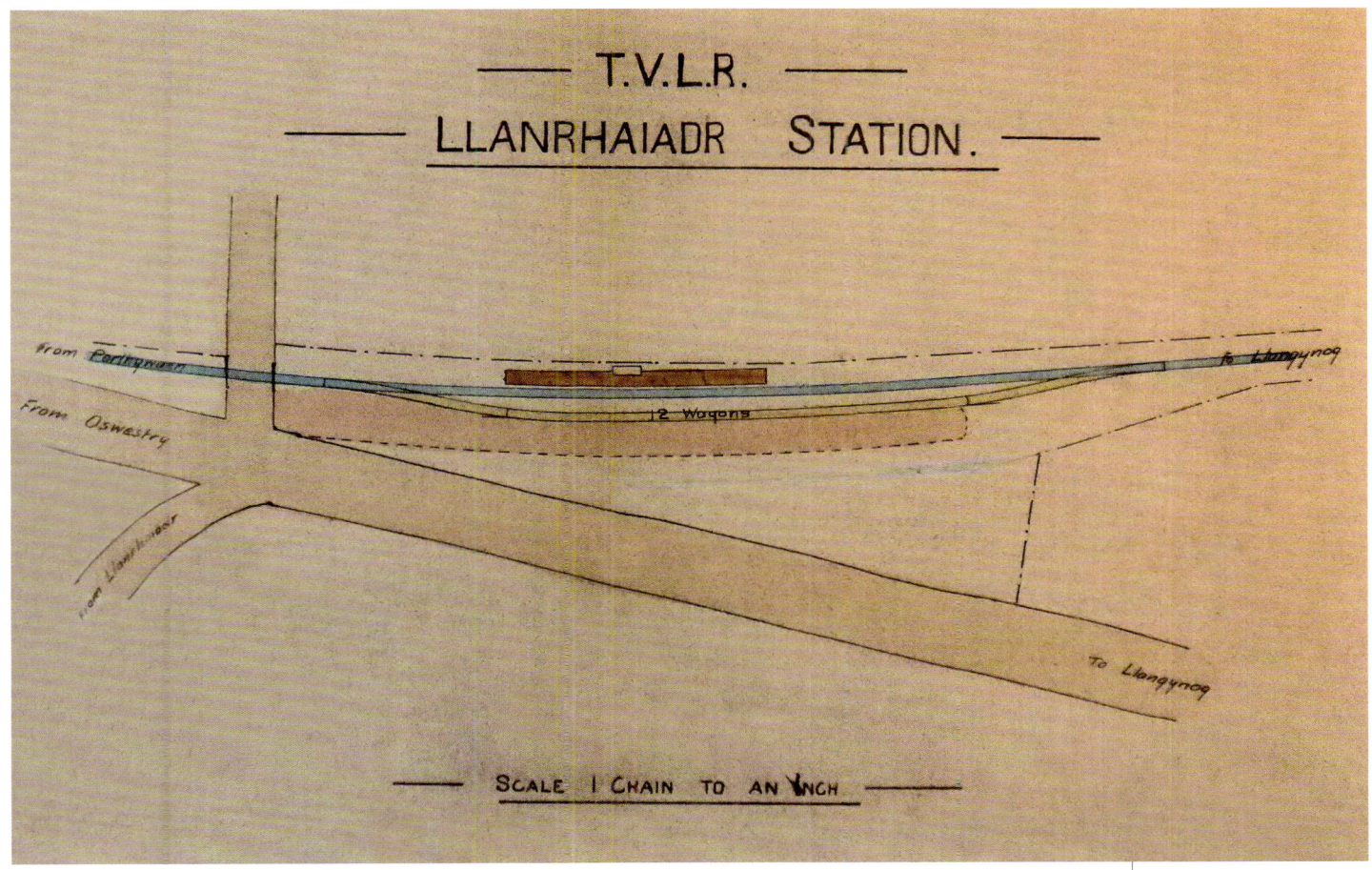

Llanrhaeadr. (National Archives)

the Tanat when it flooded. The need for flood relief channels near Llangedwyn had also not been anticipated. The estimated and actual costs are shown in Appendix 17.

Eshelby concluded his report by saying that the company needed to raise £27,000 to stabilise its position, which would cost £1,360 per annum to service if borrowed at 4% over forty years, and suggesting that the existing loans be adjusted to bring their interest rates and terms in line and making arrangements with the creditors for settling the existing debts.

Given that the railway had only two passing places, and probably neither of them seeing much use, train control could have been simpler than by using the electric train staff. Insisting on five weighbridges on a railway that was unlikely to have any station-to-station traffic seems like overkill; a weighbridge at Llansilin Road to weigh wagons as they entered and left the railway would have been enough, at least until regular traffic patterns had developed and were understood.

The first shareholders' meeting since the railway had been opened was held on 3 April 1905. Chairman C. E. Williams explained that the railway had cost £92,000 and needed £25,000 to settle its debts. The gross receipts for 1904 were £6,267, with £2,506 due to the company, and 99,000 passengers had been carried.

Under the terms of the contract, the arbitration for Strachan's claims for extras should have been dealt with by Collin or the (Cambrian's) 'engineer for the time being' but Collin refused to act, both because he had resigned and because the Tanat Valley was indebted to him. Strachan refused to accept McDonald's substitution, however, which led to a hearing in the High Court before the GWR's Walter Young Armstrong (1853–1934) was appointed.

Collin, the Cambrian's solicitor noted before the hearings, was a willing witness but would be justifying his own decisions and actions; that he had not managed Strachan effectively was implied, particularly with regard to extras. Having a full-time job with the Cambrian and supervising both the Tanat Valley and the Welshpool & Llanfair contracts simultaneously would not be a good position for him to have been in.

Just two of the disputed items will be mentioned. Under the contract Strachan was allowed to use excavated materials suitable for ballast. If more was required, it would be provided at his expense, but by excavating more from the cuttings than required there was sufficient stone for all the ballast needed. Therefore, the Cambrian objected to paying for the additional excavation, for which Strachan claimed £210 10s 6d. He also wanted paying £47 2s 3d for taking Druitt over the line during his inspections.

The arbitration started on 18 April 1905 but was not completed in a timely manner, either because Strachan's erratic behaviour caused hearings to be adjourned or because of time wasting by his legal team. He claimed £25,980 for the Tanat Valley work. The respective engineers examined the claims and agreed on some items on 30 May 1905, leaving £12,451 to be dealt with by the arbitrator.

On 19 February 1906, three days before a resumed hearing, Strachan submitted a new claim for £16,081 including interest and damages and the arbitration proceeded on that basis. His counsel spent more than two weeks reading and commenting on correspondence, much of which was irrelevant to the case, his objective seemingly to force the Cambrian to settle the claim to limit the costs he was incurring at a rate of £150 a day.

The Cambrian submitted a counterclaim of £2,844 8s 2d, £1,025 in respect of the £50 a week penalty due because the railway had not been completed before the 1 August 1903 contract date and the remainder for various charges, including demurrage on the pipe traffic, hire of a locomotive in 1904 (£6 5s 3d) and a £513 charge for using the rail for twenty-five months.

In its evidence the Cambrian wanted to make something of the use Strachan

Penybontfawr. (National Archives)

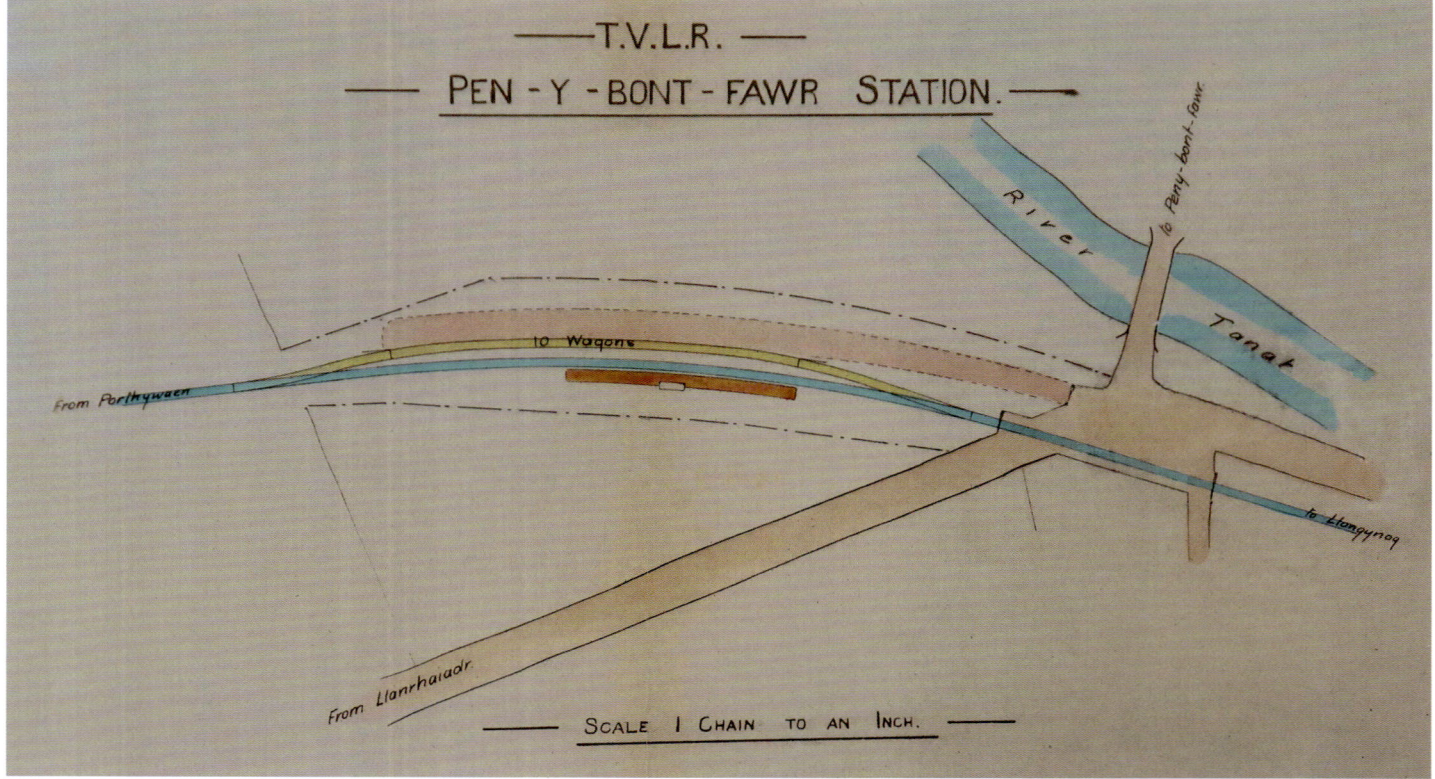

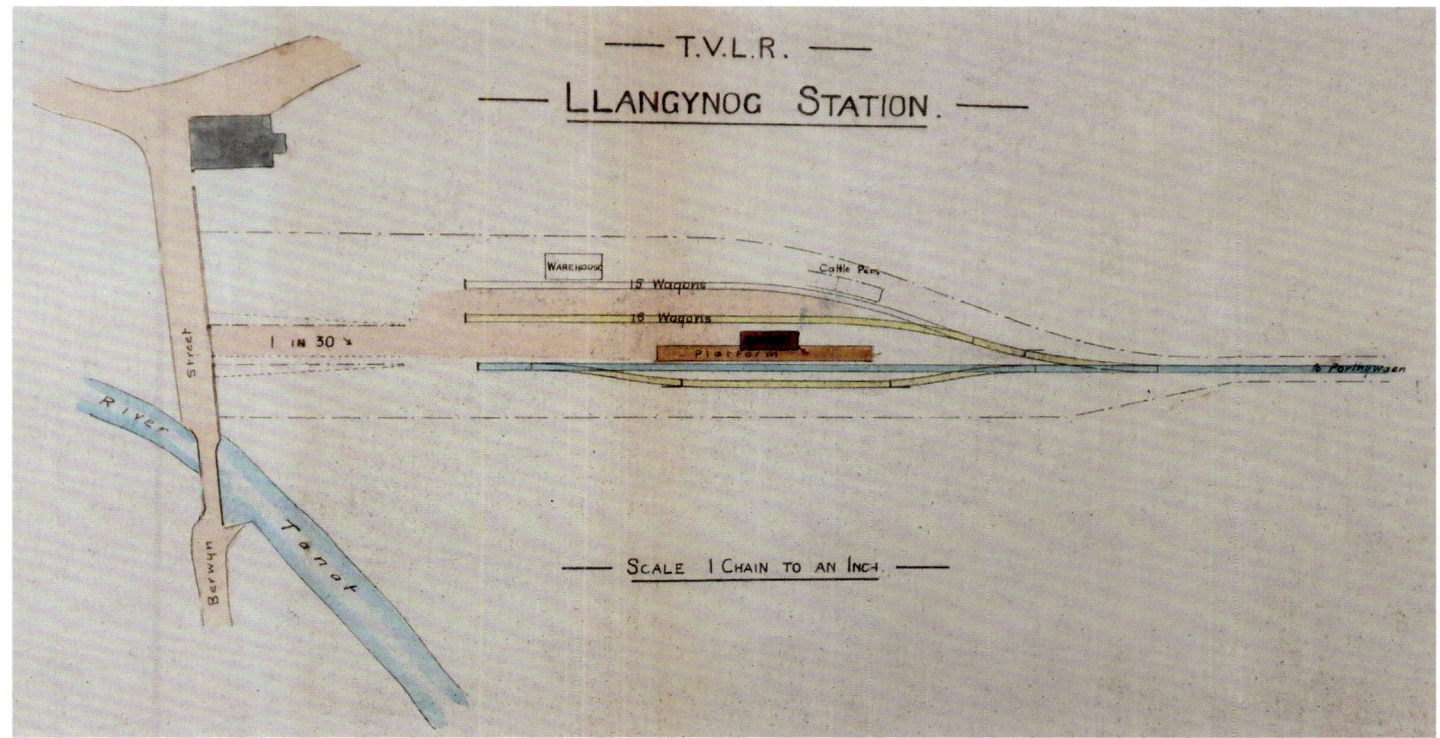

Llangynog. (National Archives)

had made of the railway to carry coal and lime during the twelve months before it opened. Denniss told the Cambrian's London solicitors that Strachan's son had established a business as a coal and lime merchant at Llanrhaeadr and that father and son were more interested in developing this while there was no competition than they were in finishing the railway. The arbitration was settled for £5,750 on 20 March 1906, bringing the total paid to Strachan to £57,236 8s 6d.

The two-year extension allowed by Lord Bradford for not using the Blodwel loop line expiring, his lordship pushed for the agreement to be honoured. In April 1906 a twelve-month extension was offered, with a proviso that the Cambrian agreed that on its expiration the loop would be worked in accordance with the original agreement and without any attempt being made to obtain further delay. This rather concerned Denniss, because the trains from Llanymynech usually carried only three or four passengers and in the return direction they were usually empty and he obviously did not want to spend money on installing the loop that was not going to be recouped.

In June an estimate was obtained for the loop line, £1,200 for signalling and £400 for track. The signalling included two signal boxes, which would have required the employment of two under-employed signalmen if they had been built. However, Bradford started to change his stance, saying that he would consider a further extension if the Cambrian installed a siding to serve his Flascerrig brickworks, at Llanymynech, which he had asked for in 1896. It had not been installed because Bradford had not wanted to contribute £50 towards its £79 5s 11d cost. Now, Denniss obviously thought that installing it would be a good bargain and the directors agreed with him. It was not mentioned, however, when Bradford's solicitor wrote to say that his lordship was willing to defer the working of the loop for a further year, until 5 January 1908.

With the Treasury making it clear that there would be no more grant or loan, and investing authorities taking action against the company, on 5 June 1905 the directors resolved to see if the Cambrian would be

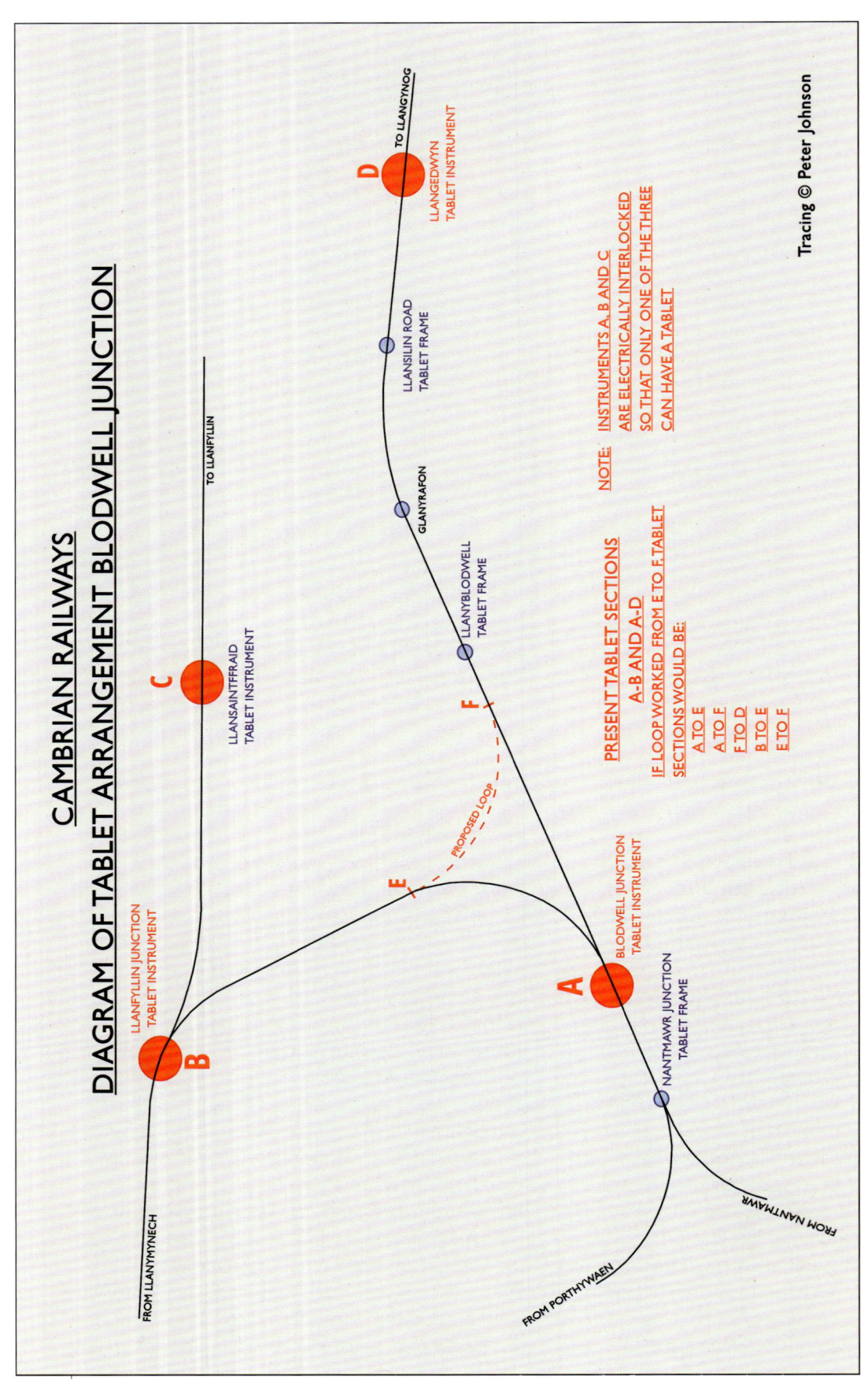

Proposed train control arrangements if the Blodwel loop line (Lord Bradford's loop) was installed. (National Archives)

willing to purchase the railway and take over its liabilities. Denniss took some time to produce a report for his directors, on 3 January 1906 offering them two schemes that included issuing Cambrian D debentures to produce the equivalent of 3% interest on the investing authorities' loans, clear the debt and make provision for settling the Treasury's £5,000 interest-free loan.

Neither of the schemes were adopted but on 12 February Denniss met representatives of the investing authorities, except Montgomeryshire County Council and Llansilin and Llanfyllin Rural District Councils, and obtained their approval for a scheme that reduced the interest rates by ½% and deferred repayments of principal until 1912. He also agreed that his company would pay £300 for expenses incurred by the joint committee. Afterwards Llansilin and Llanfyllin agreed to participate on payment of £50 costs. Montgomeryshire wanted £150, which Denniss thought was excessive, and agreed to settle for £100, which he also thought was too much; £75 was paid.

Saunders, the telegraph supplier, billed the Cambrian for the work done between Llynclys and Porthywaen, which led to a back-and-forth correspondence between the companies in March 1906. The telegraph company said that as Denniss had instructed Collin to have the work done to Cambrian requirements, it was reasonable to think that the work was being done for the Cambrian and that that company would pay.

Denniss replied that the work was required in compliance with the 1898 Light Railway Order and therefore it was a Tanat Valley responsibility. Collin was not authorised, he said, to order work to be done on the Cambrian's behalf without receiving a board instruction. But he was the company's engineer, Saunders replied, and under their prior agreement with the Cambrian any instruction given by him was in order and acted upon. The company was prepared to settle for a proportion of its claim.

The sum of £232 0s 4d was paid to Saunders 'without prejudice' on 23 April, the Cambrian making it clear that it did not admit that the liability for the Llynclys–Porthywaen section was any different from that done elsewhere on the light railway and the Tanat Valley was the liable party, on whose behalf the payment was now made. Some further negotiation ensued on how the debt could be settled and an offer of £1,800 in D debentures became £1,400 in cash, which was paid on 28 December.

Embedded in the correspondence with Saunders was also a dispute with Collin, Denniss accusing him of not co-operating with requests for information, while the former engineer said that he had provided a great deal of information. Denniss based his assertion on Collin's claim for £150 for his expenses, which he thought was exorbitant, and alleged that he had removed all Tanat Valley documents when he left.

During these legal actions against the Cambrian, Dennis became annoyed by the actions of Tanat Valley secretary John Williams, who was obstructive, refusing to make documents available when requested and in the Tyer case making it clear that his sympathies lay with the plaintiff. On 24 July 1906 Denniss referred to Williams' 'hostile attitude' in his report to his directors. He had previously discussed his manner with C. E. Williams, the Tanat Valley chairman, and been told that most of the directors were under his influence and would not do anything to 'interfere with his position'.

Opening Tyer's claim for £2,480 on 1 February, the company's barrister complained of the difficulty in obtaining documents from the Tanat Valley and had obtained a copy of the agreement between the Cambrian and the light railway from Liverpool Corporation (*Liverpool Courier*, 2 February). After three days of evidence, during which Tyer argued that the Tanat Valley had issued contracts as the Cambrian's agent, the jury found in Tyer's favour, the judge awarding costs but issuing a stay of execution until the Cambrian's appeal could be heard (*Lancashire Evening Post*, 8 February).

Acquired when it took over the Liskeard & Looe Railway in 1909, the GWR transferred Barclay 2-4-0T *Lady Margaret*, numbered 1308, to the Tanat Valley, where it was photographed shunting at Porthywaen. The Tanat Valley line was to the left of the signal box, the centre line of rails was the 4ft-gauge Whitehaven Quarries' track.

The Whitehaven line, which closed in 1951, passed through the left-hand portal seen here.

The appeal was heard over two days a week apart, the adjournment required 'for the production of certain documents'. The Cambrian argued for the judgment to be overturned or for a new trial on the basis that the judge had misdirected the jury but on 12 July the appeal was dismissed with costs, the Lord Chancellor saying that the jury was entitled to draw the inference it did, and he would have done the same had he been in its place (*Wellington Journal*, 7 July / *Liverpool Courier*, 13 July). The result was that the Cambrian ceased to contest its liability for orders placed by Collin for the Tanat Valley.

This was not the only legal matter dealt with during 1906, for after several adjournments, the investing authorities' 1904 summons for the appointment of a receiver was heard on 23 July. An outline of the compromise reached between the authorities and the Cambrian earlier in the year were put before the judge with a request for the summons to stand over until the Tanat Valley had obtained the powers required. In addition to reducing the interest rates by ½% and deferring the repayment of principal until 1912, it was agreed that the mortgages and debentures would be deemed to be a first charge on the entire undertaking and its surplus land, not just on the 40% gross revenue. The Cambrian also agreed to guarantee the interest. The judge agreed, and the summons was stood over until 31 December 1907 (*Liverpool Daily Post*, 24 July).

An ongoing issue for Denniss during 1906 was the Tanat Valley overdraft with Lloyds Bank, which was getting restless about the lack of action to clear it. He had encouraged the bank to give the company facilities in the first place and the local manager said that the bank had only allowed the overdraft because it looked upon the Cambrian as being the company's virtual parent. In September Denniss suggested that the bank put pressure on the Tanat Valley, to let the directors know they were responsible for clearing things up.

Discussing the bank's solicitor's letter on 17 September, the Tanat Valley directors resolved to remind the bank that a receiver had been appointed and to ask for an explanation why no request for payment had been made previously.

Invited to attend a special meeting of the directors on 19 November 1906, Denniss reviewed the company's position. His directors wanted to co-operate in getting the company out of its difficulties, he said, proposing the appointment of two Cambrian-nominated directors. Presumably this was seen as a device to circumvent the secretary's influence, as well as broadening the directors' experience, but they deferred a decision.

The Treasury might be induced to advance a further £10,000, Denniss and Minshall were told when they met one of the Light Railway Commissioners on 20 February 1907. Informed of this, Williams, the secretary, wrote to Denniss on 25 February to say that if £10,000 was obtained then he accepted the Cambrian's offer, that it should be used to settle the other liabilities apart from the Treasury loan, covering the debt with Tanat Valley debentures. On behalf of his directors, he wrote, he thanked Denniss for his active assistance and support.

Then, on 15 March, the Tanat Valley directors resolved to appoint Liverpool Corporation's deputy town clerk, Ernest Wilson Pierce (1865–1927), as the company's solicitor to act in the adjustment of its affairs with the Cambrian and in regard to any application that might be made for further Treasury funding. Pierce had been employed by the Corporation since 1891 and retired in 1922, after he had not been interviewed for the position of town clerk for the second time (*Liverpool Mercury*, 7 May 1891 / *Liverpool Echo*, 26 July 1922). Both the directors and Denniss had established a good rapport with him in trying to resolve the company's problems.

In its attempt to make the directors face up to the seriousness of the company's situation, the Cambrian submitted a claim for £32,360 10s 5d. Williams also reported that other creditors were owed another £4,292 7s 1d.

A deputation of directors and local MPs was expected to see the president of the Board of Trade, David Lloyd George, on 20 March to promote the award of another grant but the meeting was postponed (*Shrewsbury Chronicle*, 22 March) after the directors resolved to delay the application until they could present a better case, appointing a subcommittee to prepare a scheme for submission to the Treasury. They also resolved to ask the Cambrian to enter into an agreement to put the debt to arbitration, if agreement could not be reached, and for its agreement to support any further grant application. They also resolved that any grant be applied in payment of the company's debts, taking any balance due in 4% debentures that ranked after the local authority loans, and for it to have the right to appoint two directors.

The subcommittee decided that the case for more Treasury funding would be improved if the Cambrian reduced its claim to £20,000, Pierce writing on 9 July that while loath to take a hostile attitude it had instructed him to prepare a case against it. There were grounds, he said, for contending that the amount due from the railway did not exceed £17,300 and that if proceedings were started it would have to raise 'the larger question' of whether the Cambrian was acting as the railway's contractor and therefore liable for any negligence. As the original estimate, prepared by its engineer, was £53,540 but exceeded £100,000, there would seem, Pierce wrote, to be a prima facie case of negligence, either in producing the estimate or in the supervision of the work.

Furthermore, he continued, the railway would not have proceeded with the construction had it not been for the estimate; it had sustained a substantial injury for which it was entitled to hold the Cambrian responsible. Likewise, it was not until its funds were exhausted that it learned that costs had so much exceeded the estimate; in fact, its directors had been kept in the dark about the real situation, and had not been informed, for example, about Tyer's action until it was considerably advanced. This would have been right if the Cambrian was acting as contractor, as the light railway believed, but if the Cambrian was to contend that in the preparation of the estimate, the execution of the works and the dealings with the contractors they were acting under the instructions of the light railway then there ought to have been a fuller disclosure as matters proceeded.

Without prejudice, Pierce concluded, the light railway was prepared to settle the matter in an amicable way by agreeing that its liability to the Cambrian should be fixed at £20,000, but if this was rejected then there would be no alternative but to institute proceedings. The £100,000 cost appears to be an overstatement by about £10,000 even when taking land purchased and legal costs into account. While the Cambrian rejected Pierce's assertions they influenced its actions, insofar as it was determined to avoid an examination of the details of its claim against the light railway and a ruling on its status as a contractor.

The meeting with Lloyd George took place on an unknown date, the deputation being told that the Treasury took the view that the Light Railways Act contained no power to make advances to a light railway that had already been constructed, which rendered the previous negotiations and discussions futile.

Three and a half years after the railway had opened, in July Denniss compiled a report on the railway's gross traffic receipts (Appendix 20). Over the period, he noted, passenger and goods traffic had declined, while parcels, mineral and livestock traffic had increased steadily. He could not account for the reduction in passengers and goods but in 1904, he thought, travelling on the railway would have been a novelty for many and not repeated; there would also have been some passenger traffic attached to the pipe traffic, which had

The river bridge near Llangedwyn. The undermining of the right-hand abutment in 1960 brought about the end of the Llanrheaedr goods service.

The Iwrch bridge, near Pentrefelin, was of a different style to those over the Tanat. The postcard caption is incorrect. (William Charles Burns/Lloyd Llanrheaedr)

The Tanat River at Pentrefelin, Llanrhaiadr.

now ended. The increased mineral traffic was a consequence of slate and roadstone quarries being opened at Llangynog but he did not expect any further developments there, one of the quarry owners having told him that the cost of cartage from the quarry to the station almost put him out of the market. Llangynog slate was thicker and heavier than the Caernarfon equivalent and sold for less.

There had also been complaints of the inadequacy, or the absence, of accommodation for goods in transit, particularly at Penybontfawr, where farmers had to cart goods and stock to and from Llanrhaeadr, a loss of 2 miles carriage to the railway.

Since the railway had been opened visitors to Vyrnwy had transferred from using the 10-mile 'main' road from Llanfyllin to the 7-mile 'rough, narrow' 'district' road from Penybontfawr, and Llanfyllin Rural District Council had been petitioned to make the Penybontfawr route the main road (*Liverpool Daily Post*, 13 September 1906). The council must have been unenthusiastic about the idea because a year later Liverpool Corporation asked Montgomeryshire County Council to use its influence to improve the road, saying that its property in the area had a rateable value of £25,936 and it was not unreasonable for it to ask for the road to be made suitable for its traffic. It was intimated that Liverpool was prepared to make a financial contribution to the costs incurred (*Aberystwyth Observer*, 26 September 1907).

Led by solicitor Pierce, a subcommittee reported to the directors on 4 October 1907 that a settlement had been reached with the Cambrian reducing its claim from £32,362 to £20,000, to be paid as £5,000 in cash, £15,000 in 4% debentures and the allotment of the unissued Tanat Valley shares. The settlement was conditional on the Tanat Valley obtaining a grant of not less than £10,000. The £5,000 not paid to the Cambrian would be used to pay the other creditors, some of whom had agreed to accept 10s in the £1.

The Tanat Valley Light Railway (Additional Powers) Order was made on 8 September 1908, giving the company authority to increase its borrowing and gave legal effect to the agreement with the investing authorities for reducing the interest rates by ½%. It included a clause for the protection of the Postmaster General and required the costs of the Order to be met by the company, but only after it had discharged its liabilities to the Cambrian. This last, inserted at the Cambrian's insistence, diverted the costs onto the investing authorities.

There was no comment on the Order because the directors had not met since 7 November 1907 and did not meet again for ten years. They failed to call the statutory shareholders' meetings, too, and the annual reports. They had abandoned their railway.

With the Tanat Valley company inactive, there were two constants in the railway's history, as recorded in the Cambrian records: the payment of interest to the investing authorities and various requests for expenditure on Tanat Valley infrastructure.

One of these, of course, was the construction and bringing into use of 'Lord Bradford's curve', his lordship's extension having expired in January 1908. When, on 16 September, his lordship's agents informed the Cambrian that the work should be put in hand without delay, Denniss replied that the Tanat Valley had no money with which to do the work and that revenue was 'very seriously depressed', which seems to have been the last time that it was mentioned.

The state of the company's finances was the subject of a report submitted by the Cambrian's solicitor, William Kenrick Minshall (1870–1944), on 7 April 1909. The amount charged to the Tanat Valley in the Cambrian's accounts up to 31 December 1908 was £38,745 3s 11d, including 5% compound interest. Against this £9,196 15s 2d represented the 40% proportion of the

LIGHT RAILWAYS ACT, 1896

TANAT VALLEY LIGHT RAILWAY (ADDITIONAL POWERS) ORDER, 1908.

ORDER

MADE BY THE

LIGHT RAILWAY COMMISSIONERS,

AND MODIFIED AND CONFIRMED BY THE

BOARD OF TRADE,

CONFERRING ADDITIONAL POWERS UPON

THE TANAT VALLEY LIGHT RAILWAY COMPANY, INCORPORATED BY THE TANAT VALLEY LIGHT RAILWAY ORDER, 1898.

Presented to both Houses of Parliament by Command of His Majesty.

LONDON:
PRINTED FOR HIS MAJESTY'S STATIONERY OFFICE,
BY EYRE AND SPOTTISWOODE, LTD.,
PRINTERS TO THE KING'S MOST EXCELLENT MAJESTY.

And to be purchased, either directly or through any Bookseller, from
WYMAN AND SONS, LTD., FETTER LANE, E.C., and
32, ABINGDON STREET, WESTMINSTER, S.W.; or
OLIVER AND BOYD, TWEEDDALE COURT, EDINBURGH; or
E. PONSONBY, 116, GRAFTON STREET, DUBLIN.

1908.

[Cd. 4339.]   Price 2d.   EYRE AND SPOTTISWOODE, LTD. EAST HARDING STREET, E.C.

The Tanat Valley Light Railway (Additional Powers) Order, 1908.

gross earnings from 1904, to which, he wrote, should be added 5% interest. The Cambrian was also responsible for £2,888 0s 5d, which comprised the Lloyd's bank overdraft (£2,528 10s 8d) and money owed to Pooley & Son (£240), the weighbridge supplier and maintainer, and Isca Foundry (£119 10s 0d). There were other debts of about £2,500 that ranked after the Cambrian's.

For 1908 the Tanat Valley's 40% of the gross receipts was £1,695 13s 1d, from which was deducted £250 rent for use of part of the Shropshire Railways and £699 13s 9d interest to the investing authorities, leaving £745 19s 4d. When the principal became due for payment in 1912 a further £459 18s 6d would be payable, leaving, at the present rate of traffic, only a tiny amount for settling the debt to the Cambrian.

E. W. Pierce, the Tanat Valley solicitor, had been urging Denniss to advise the Cambrian directors to fix the debt at £20,000, which would have been done if the Treasury grant had been forthcoming, but he did not see any benefit to the Cambrian in doing this at the present time, even though he recognised that all the amounts claimed by the Cambrian would not be allowed if they were investigated.

In the long term, he thought the only solution would be for the Cambrian to take over the Tanat Valley entirely, but he also did not see any advantage in doing that at the present time. As owner, it would not earn any more, and it would have to make settlements with the other creditors.

With regard to the Lloyds bank overdraft, he had suggested to the bank that it obtain a judgment against the Tanat Valley to register its interest and to prevent the debt from being barred by the statute of limitations. The bank had done this, obtaining judgment for £3,013 7s 5d and £5 6s 0d costs on 31 March 1909. The bank subsequently assigned the benefit of the judgment to the Cambrian.

Denniss left the Cambrian to manage the Cardiff Railway in February 1910, being replaced by Samuel Williamson (born 1867), who had taken over Denniss's responsibilities as secretary in 1906. Producing a table of the receipts and working expenses between 1905 and 1919 (Appendix 21), Williamson remarked that the loss of £1,189 to the Cambrian in 1905 had reduced to £217 six years later but it turned out that it did not get any better.

The Treasury raised the state of the company's finances with regards to the repayment of the £6,000 interest-free loan with the Board of Trade in 1910. After commenting that the company had not applied to exercise its increased borrowing powers and that the Cambrian did not release separate accounts for the railway so it could not tell if its earning had increased, it concluded on 11 June that, 'The prospect of recovering the amounts advanced by the Treasury are not particularly good.'

In 1912 the Cambrian also took an interest in the loan's status because it was considering taking over the Tanat Valley and the loan was due to be repaid when the railway was in a position to do so.

Charles Sherwood Denniss, the Cambrian manager who dealt with the railway's construction, was buried in Handsworth (Birmingham) cemetery. His estate was valued at £10,332 15s 6d, £566,171 in 2022.

The Cambrian, therefore, wanted to know if an amalgamation would trigger a request for repayment by the Treasury. If it did then there would be no amalgamation but if the Treasury was prepared to forego any rights it might have, then it would consider the matter further. Asking the Treasury for its opinion on 16 February resulted in a merry-go-round of letters.

Saying that it had heard from the Cambrian, the Treasury asked the Tanat Valley for a statement showing its financial position. When secretary J. Williams asked for a copy of the Cambrian's letter so that he could inform his directors, he was told to ask the Cambrian. When he did that, he was referred back to the Treasury, which again refused his request.

Williams addressed the Treasury's request on 15 April, saying that he could not give a precise statement of the company's financial position because it was in receivership, adding that the Cambrian claimed to be owed more than £30,000, subject to verification and audit, and that the company was not in a position to repay the loan, which it had not expected to be asked to repay. He thought, he wrote, that the Cambrian was trying to 'get hold of' the Tanat Valley. While he did not know this for certain, he thought the shareholders should know what was happening. When the Cambrian had obtained the appointment of the receiver it was said to be for the railway's protection but now it appeared to him to be using the receiver to obtain control of the railway for the value of the debt, instead of its greater true value. He apologised for writing at length.

Williams was mistaken in saying that the receiver had been appointed to protect the light railway; he was appointed to give the Cambrian a prior claim over any that might be made by the local authorities or other creditors to the 40% gross receipts.

On 18 May the Treasury told the Cambrian, copy to Williams, that it would not waive its claim to repayment in the event of an amalgamation. The amalgamation proposal was abandoned.

The First World War had little direct impact on the railway, but wartime inflation considerably increased operating costs and the loss to the Cambrian (Appendix 21). When the operating loss in 1915 was almost triple what it had been the year before, Williamson was asked for an explanation. The figures he produced are given in the table:

	£	£	£
War Bonus			
Locomotive department	47		
Permanent way department	107		
Traffic department	94	248	
Increased price of locomotive coal		13	
Heavier locomotive repairs		35	
Renewal of station platforms		295	
Renewal of signals and drains		25	
Repairs to engine shed, cattle pens, weighing machines, &c		54	670

Two recorded accidents occurred during the war, the first being the result of a train from Oswestry running into a horse and cart being driven across an occupation farm crossing between Llynclys and Porthywaen on 12 January 1915. The horse was killed, and the cart driver sustained some slight injury to his hand (*Liverpool Daily Post*, 13 January 1915).

The second was a derailment between Llansilin Road and Llangedwyn on 13 July 1916, that although minor in itself, had consequences for future maintenance. In his report the next day, engineer G. C. McDonald said that although the track had spread, there were no injuries and little damage. He added that because of heavy recent stone traffic he had been concerned about the track and had replaced some sleepers, but the accident was evidence that a large amount would have to be spent on maintenance.

The problem, he continued, was with the dog spike fastenings that worked loose and pulled out on curves. The constant re-spiking required had split the sleepers

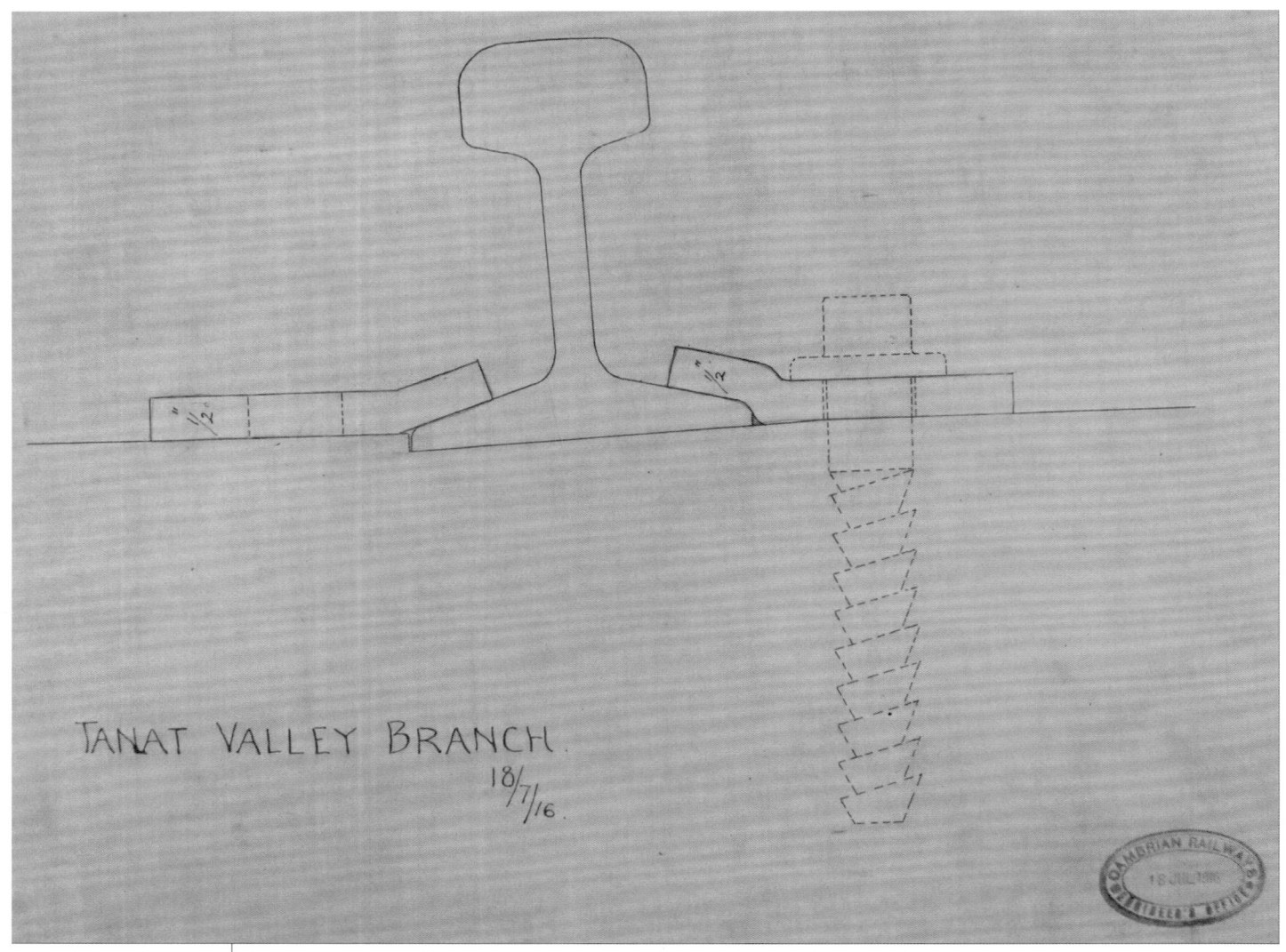

G. C. McDonald's drawing of fang bolts and coach screws to be used when the track was relayed with flat-bottom rail. (National Archives)

and thousands would be required to put the track in good order. He thought that fang bolts should be used, at least on curves, instead of spikes, and on 18 July produced drawings of the components he intended to use.

He continued by saying that despite being built as a light railway, apart from the engines ordinary rolling stock had been used, recommending that until the track had been fully overhauled, which would take some time, the stone traffic be run separately from the passenger trains. If there were a derailment with several loaded wagons behind the passenger carriages, he said, the consequences could be very serious.

A short extension to the railway at Llangynog was brought into use during the war, although it had been requested by the Llangynog Granite Company in 1913 and developed a considerable correspondence file before it was completed. The Granite Company wanted more space for loading wagons and proposed a 185-yard siding extension of the main line and crossing the road. For the Cambrian to provide the level crossing with gates either side, and all the track materials for the siding and loop, and laying it – the Granite Company providing the ballast – the cost would be £194. The siding would be shunted once daily for the sum of £1 annually.

With the layout altered to make two dead end tracks, McDonald made the siding available for traffic on 4 August 1914. The actual cost was £200 5s 4d, the

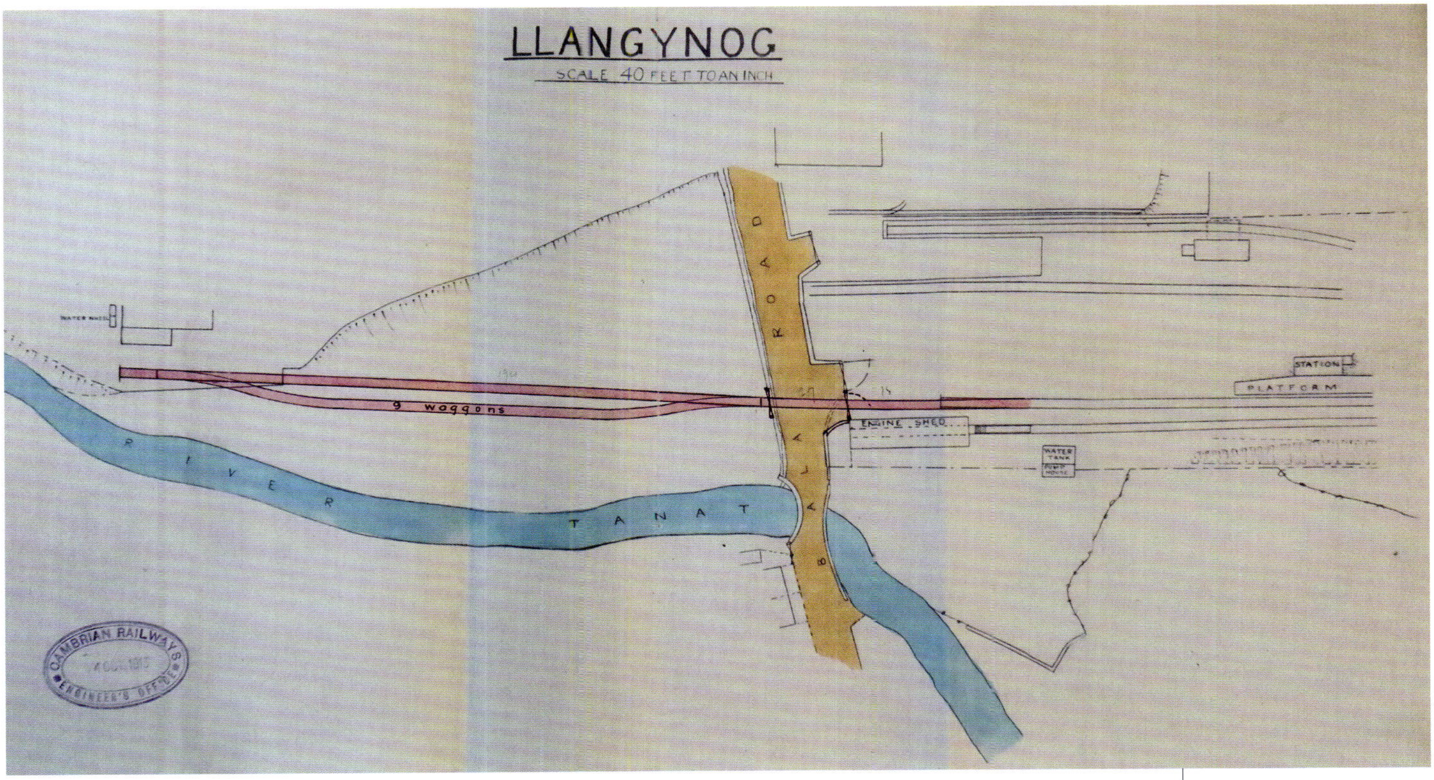

Proposed layout for the mineral extension at Llangynog. (National Archives)

A second proposal for the mineral extension. It appears to have been built as just a single siding. (National Archives)

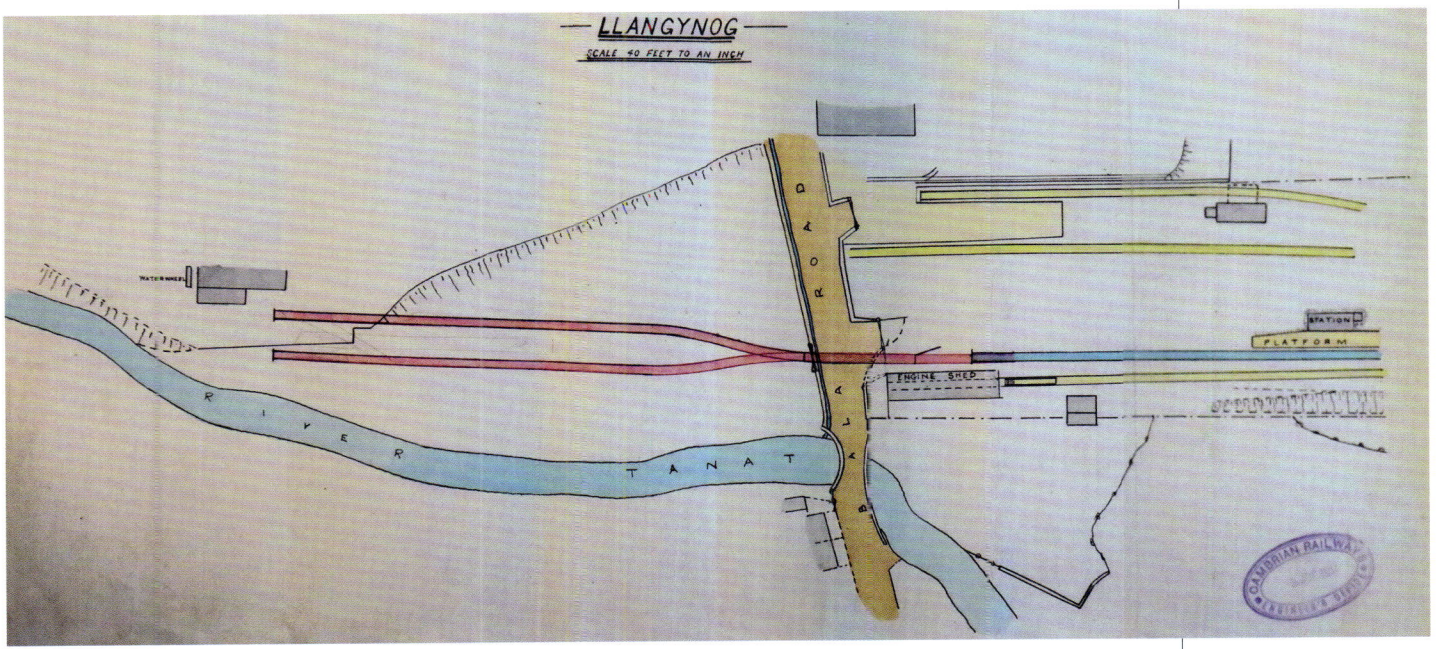

Granite Company paying the extra but recouping the £18 cost of the siding laid on Cambrian land by means of a 3d per ton rebate on traffic shipped. The Cambrian had to chase for the additional £6 5s 4d before it was paid on 20 January 1916.

James Fraser, the receiver, exhausted the funds available to him to pay small

A postcard view of Llangynog with the mineral extension in place, the engine shed removed and the original timber water tank replaced by a steel one. The mineral extension appears to have been removed by the time Ordnance Survey made its 1949 revisions of the area. Users of the road might like to note the chicane where it crosses the river. (RAP Co. Ltd)

bills, tithes and insurances in 1911, and had asked the Cambrian for further funds. The £25 sent being exhausted, on 10 February 1916 Williamson reported Fraser's request for further funding to the directors, saying the only money belonging to the Tanat Valley company, the remnant of the deposit made to the Board of Trade before construction started, was held by the Paymaster General by court order. If an application were made to release it, or some of it, it was possible the whole of the Tanat Valley accounts would be examined, he commented, presumably concerned about the number and value of items that would be disallowed if the Cambrian's claim was audited. Another £25 was approved to be sent to Fraser.

As the railway headed inexorably toward being absorbed into the Cambrian, there is nothing to be said about its operations, except that on 7 October 1920 the 4.20pm from Oswestry was derailed at Llansilin Road. There were no injuries and the passengers were ferried to their destinations by motor cars, which also collected those waiting to travel eastwards. Considerable damage was done to the track and it was not repaired until 'very late at night' (*Evening Express*, 9 October). The incident does not appear to have been reported to the Cambrian directors or the Ministry of Transport.

CHAPTER 5

CHANGES OF OWNERSHIP, AND CLOSURE

The Tanat Valley Light Railway's position in receivership and its relationship with the Cambrian Railways ought really to have been resolved in 1908, when the terms of the local authority loans and interest payments were altered, but matters were allowed to drift along, probably not helped by the First World War.

The events that led to the end of the company and the railway's nominal independence started with the Cambrian's solicitor's report on 4 April 1917. In 1911 he had obtained counsel's opinion on how the company's debt was affected by the statute of limitations and was advised that it would be well, at intervals of, say, every ten years, to require an acknowledgement of the debt, or failing that to obtain a judgment.

As the Tanat Company was not in a position to acknowledge the debt, which stood at £39,573 17s 7d, because it had not held any meetings since 1907 and had no qualified directors, then the only option was to obtain a judgment, which might open the situation to examination, possibly not a desirable contingency, he concluded. The directors referred the matter to Williamson and the solicitor, with authority to consult counsel.

The opinion received confirmed that obtained in 1911, that it would be advisable to obtain a judgment. Therefore, a writ for £40,676 16s 8d was issued on 12 November 1917. Four Tanat Valley directors, W. E. Williams, R. E. Hughes, J. K. Jones and W. H. Thomas, considered it on 20 November and resolved to take no action. Their status as directors was probably invalid in any event, as their appointments would have expired

C. E. Williams, the Oswestry mayor who called a town meeting in support of a light railway to Llangynog, and company chairman throughout its existence, was buried in Oswestry's public cemetery. His estate being valued at £3,920 17s 3d, £220,211 in 2022, low in comparison with his professional contemporaries, might have been affected by him fathering six children, four of them girls.

R. E. Hughes, a director throughout the company's existence, was buried in Oswestry's public cemetery. His estate was valued at £21,303 1s 1d, £956,177 in 2022.

CHANGES OF OWNERSHIP, AND CLOSURE • 95

three years after the last general meeting but this was overlooked.

While the directors resolved to take no action, someone, either the chairman, W. E. Williams, or the secretary, J. Williams, made contact with the local authorities' joint committee, explaining that the company had no funds to defend the action and suggesting that it would be undesirable for the Cambrian to obtain judgment until the issues had been investigated. With E. W. Pierce appointed secretary and solicitor, the joint committee was reconstituted on 26 September 1918.

Working in consultation with the railway companies, a plan was devised to ensure the railway's continued existence as a part of the Cambrian system. To protect the Cambrian from the risk of being requested to refund the Treasury's £6,000 interest-free loan, the first step required the Tanat Valley to ask the Treasury to forego it. If the application was successful, then the Tanat Valley would assign the railway and all associated property to the Cambrian. Agreeing to work the railway and charge normal fares and rates, the Cambrian would vest in each shareholder an equivalent value of Cambrian ordinary stock, take on responsibility for the local authority loans as provided for in the 1908 Order, pay the costs incurred by the company and the local authorities in defending its 1917 writ and obtain the necessary legislative approval at its own expense.

The necessary agreement was executed by all parties involved and completed on 20 February 1920. It should be noted that the exchange of Tanat Valley shares for Cambrian stock was not as generous as it might appear because the Cambrian Railways (No 1) Inland stock that the shareholders would receive was being traded at 1½–2½% of its face value so it was a purely nominal transaction.

On 30 November 1918 the Treasury was asked to forego the £6,000 loan to enable the Cambrian to take over the line and make improvements at the stations but this was refused on 1 May 1919.

The reason was explained in a report to Stanley Baldwin MP, then a junior minister in the Treasury but soon to be Prime Minister, which explained that if there were no prospect of the railway being taken over then there would be no objection to writing off the loan, because there was no likelihood of it ever being repaid, but if a nationalisation scheme came into being, a consequence of surrendering the claim could be that the government would have to pay £6,000 more to the Cambrian for the railway at a future date. Of course, there was then no nationalisation scheme, the railways being grouped instead.

Further representations made during a meeting at the Ministry of Transport, which had taken over the Board of Trade's transport responsibilities later in 1919, on 12 February 1920 produced a different result, though. On 3 May the Ministry advised that the government would waive its claim to the loan and accept £6,000 Ordinary (No 1) Inland stock in lieu, which was a way of writing it off because of the (No 1) Inland stock's low market value.

At a meeting of Tanat Valley shareholders to approve the transfer on 25 September 1918, a Liverpool Corporation representative said that if the transfer scheme were not approved then the railway would probably still pass to the Cambrian, which would then be in a position to close it if it wished. The motion was approved without dissent (*Oswestry Advertiser*, 2 October).

In an editorial, the same newspaper described the meeting as the funeral of an enterprise with a chequered career. Like many other such concerns, its cost exceeded the roseate estimate of its promoters and the result had been a financial embarrassment that could only end by the transfer of the line to its principal creditor. The only question remaining was why the Cambrian had not acted earlier. The meeting was the last recorded activity of the Tanat Valley company.

The Cambrian advertised its intention to apply for a transfer Order in the *London Gazette* on 22 June 1920. The only objections were from the Shropshire Railways and the Shropshire & Montgomeryshire Light Railway, who both claimed that their rights were not protected, citing the lack of provision for running powers for the Shropshire Railways over part of the Tanat Valley line agreed in 1916 and insufficient provision for their traffic requirements. The Cambrian replied that as the Llanyblodwel branch and Nantmawr extension were worked and maintained by the Cambrian and the Shropshire Railways was in the hands of a receiver and owned no rolling stock, there was nothing in the Order that affected it and its position after the amalgamation would be unchanged. Regarding the Shropshire & Montgomeryshire, there was nothing in the Order that affected it and its position, too, would be unchanged.

Without the need for a public inquiry, the Cambrian Railways (Tanat Valley Light Railway Transfer) Order was made on 12 March 1921. As well as power for the transfer of the Tanat Valley to the Cambrian, it authorised the latter to work the line as a part of its existing system, requiring it to provide a service that met the needs of the district it served, and provided for the exchange of shares and the issue of stock to the Treasury. The Tanat Valley company was to be wound up as if it had been registered under the terms of the Companies (Consolidation) Act, 1908, and receiver James Fraser was appointed liquidator.

Notwithstanding the rebuttals to the Shropshire and Shropshire & Montgomeryshire objections, article 18 was provided for their protection, giving it running powers over part of Railway No 3 to enable it to reach the junction between Railways Nos 3 and 2 (Lord Bradford's curve) and exercise its existing powers over the Tanat Valley.

So, that was the end of the Tanat Valley Light Railway's existence as a (nominally) independent entity. It took a few months to wrap things up and the property transfer

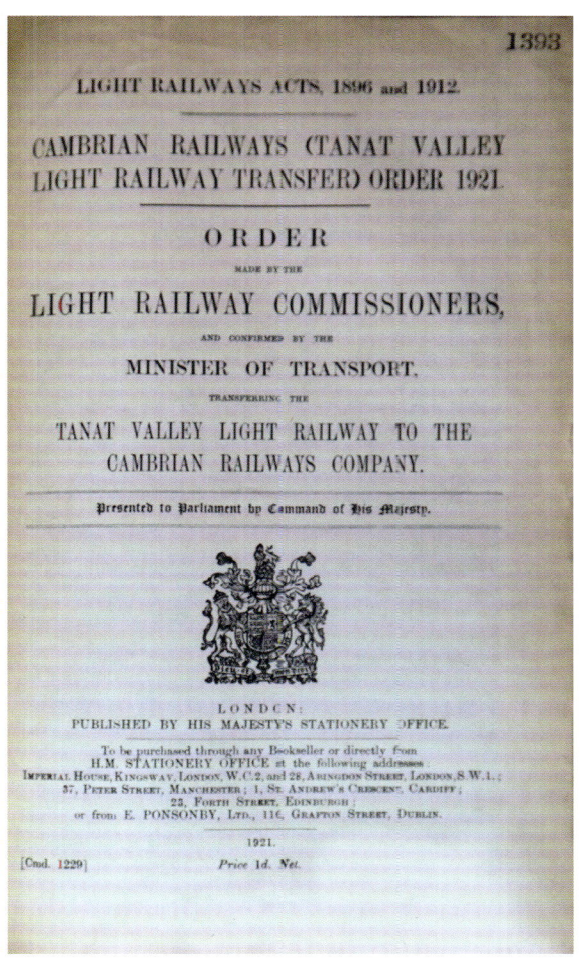

The Cambrian Railways (Tanat Valley Light Railway Transfer) Order, 1921.

was not validated by having a copy of the Order stamped by the Inland Revenue until October.

In the meantime, on 6 April William Kenrick Minshall (1871-1944), the Cambrian solicitor, reported that he was taking steps to release the Tanat Valley deposit and to carry out the winding up; a court order releasing it, £1,822 8s 5d in Consols and £7 19s 5d cash, to James Fraser for the benefit of the Cambrian was made by 1 December. In view of its own changing situation, the Cambrian had the Consols transferred to the GWR.

By 26 July the Cambrian had received certificates for £7,131 Tanat Valley shares. Naturally, there were problems. In one case, the executor of Robert Jones of Llangynog had found a banker's receipt for the third call for the deceased's £20 holding and asked for it to be accepted as evidence of title. The share register showed that all the calls had been paid on the due date, but did not indicate if a certificate had been issued. In another, the executrix of Robert Jones (1844–1909), also of Llangynog, who owned a £1 share, could not find the probate certificate, and wanted to use his will to prove her entitlement.

The directors authorised the first but had not responded to the other before their railway was taken over by the GWR. It was rather academic in any case, as when the GWR took over, the Inland stock was exchanged for deferred consolidated stock at the rate of 2.86%. If that was not bad enough, it would not pay dividends until 1929.

Alongside the negotiations over the Tanat Valley transfer, on 31 December 1918 the Cambrian and Liverpool Corporation had made an agreement whereby their 1900 agreement was terminated when the transfer Order was made and replaced by a new one. As well as covering the Corporation's traffic requirements, it called for the installation of additional facilities at Penybontfawr to accommodate timber being felled on the Corporation's Vyrnwy land. They included a roadway suitable for steam tractors hauling timber, a raised platform adapted for side and end loading alongside the existing siding and provision for a travelling crane. This work was done at the Cambrian's expense and on 13 June 1921 Williamson, the manager, notified the directors that it would cost £400, charged to capital. The cost had been £300 when McDonald had priced the works in 1918, twice what it would have been before the war.

Tanat Valley secretary John Williams maintained the same obstructionist stance towards the Cambrian during the transfer as he had done during the legal cases nearly twenty years before. Asked for the conveyances, he said that he would not part with them until he had been paid for his work for the light railway company. However, second thoughts prevailed, and he sent them on 13 September.

Reporting this to the directors a month later, Williamson reminded them that in 1919 they had approved a £50 payment to Williams for his services to the Tanat Valley and that he had been told this. On 25 October 1921 Williams submitted a claim for four years' salary to 30 September 1907 plus expenses to 1920 totalling £513 6s 10d, saying that he was also entitled to be paid a salary from 1907 until 1921. He settled for £250, unaware that Williamson had been authorised to go up to £300. When he asked the Cambrian chairman to sign the cheque, Williamson wrote, 'We had a good deal of trouble with Mr Williams and it was rather a trying business as his wife is dying at the present time, and whatever his faults may have been, he is in a pitiable condition at present and very hard up I think.' His wife, Mary Jane, died before the end of the year, aged 73, and was buried in Oswestry's public cemetery. Williams died in 1927, aged 77, apparently intestate.

Liquidator James Fraser had also not been paid. Discussing the matter with Williamson in January 1922, he suggested that 250 guineas would be a reasonable amount to cover his services; Williamson authorised the payment on 16 January. The liquidation was completed on 6 July.

Earlier, in 1920, in preparation for what became the railway grouping, the Ministry of Transport had established the Light Railways (Investigation) Committee, with a view of deciding whether they should be included in the proposed grouping or not. The Cambrian submitted the returns for the light railways under its control on 10 March 1921. In it, details of loadings give a snapshot of traffic before and after the war (Appendix 22). Two engines were steamed daily; other types were used on occasion. Mixed trains ran with two carriages, four wagons and a brake van. The regular locomotives could take ten four-wheeled carriages or fifteen loaded goods wagons. Carriage lighting was by oil or oil gas and footwarmers provided heating in winter. Personnel attached to the branch were four four-man gangs of platelayers, two drivers, two firemen, two cleaners, one guard, two porter guards, one signalman, three porter signalmen, two porters, and five stationmasters. One driver and one fireman worked on the line part time. The mileage figures show a significant decline (Appendix 23).

The Cambrian, and the Tanat Valley Light Railway, were absorbed into the GWR on 25 March 1922, several months before the main railway grouping. The Cambrian records do not say why the company amalgamated early but the implication is that it was about to run out of money.

Life for the Tanat Valley under the GWR was much the same as it had been since 1904, although the advance of motor buses and lorries and of private motoring had its inevitable effect on traffic. The GWR responded by running its own bus service to Oswestry, picking up passengers at Llanrhaeadr village centre, Hirnant and Llansilin, as well as along the valley. Probably because of the commitment made by the Tanat Valley company regarding the number of trains to be run, the GWR did not terminate the passenger service in 1931, as it did on other similar lines, including the nearby Welshpool & Llanfair Light Railway. The total of 67,762 tickets issued in 1913 fell to 35,153 in 1923 and to 11,670 by 1938.

The GWR waited three years before closing the former Potteries Railway line between Wern and Blodwel junctions in 1925, routing the Nantmawr traffic via Porthywaen and a reversal at Blodwel Junction.

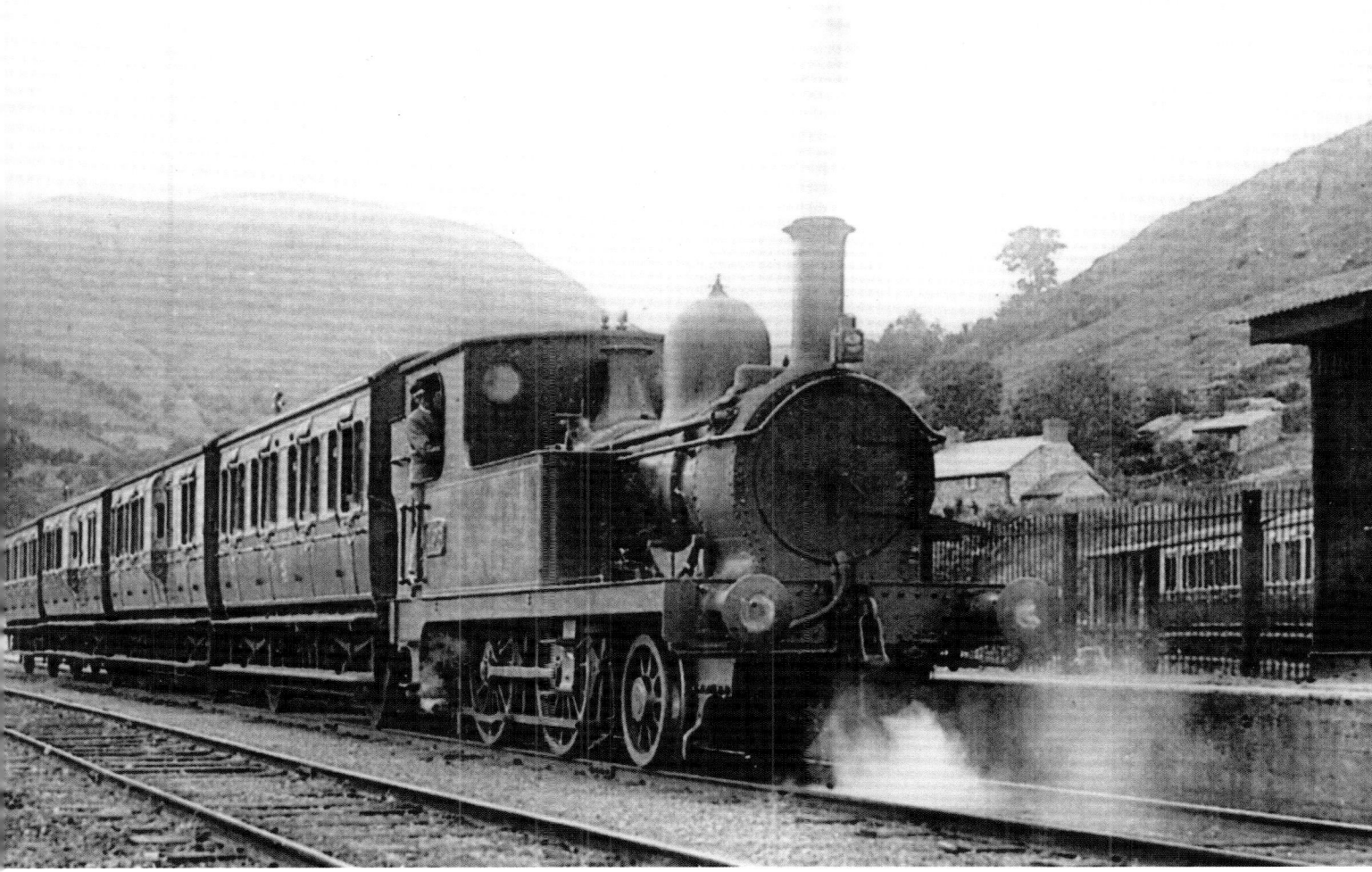

One of the Cambrian 'Seaham'-class locomotives as rebuilt by the GWR with a train at Llangynog. There are at least two other carriages in the yard, September 1929.

No 1197 in the GWR list was originally No 59 *Seaham* in the Cambrian list.

GWR No 2516 at Nantmawr, reached via Llynclys and Porthywaen, around 1950. (G. F. Bannister)

Under GWR auspices the Cambrian's 'Seaham'-class locomotives were soon rebuilt with new boilers and later had larger bunkers fitted. While one was transferred to Devon in 1927 and withdrawn in 1929, the others lasted until withdrawal by British Railways in 1948. The Lambourne Valley locomotives were also reboilered; two were sold into industry in 1930 and 1932 and the last remained in use until 1946.

Small tank engines, 2-4-0 and 0-6-0 types absorbed from other railways, were allocated to Oswestry after 1923, some being used on the light railway until they were sold or worn out. From the 1940s GWR 0-4-2Ts were used on the passenger trains. Photographs show that six-coupled tender engines reached Llangynog on occasion, which might have happened during the Cambrian era, too.

From 1926, the running lines were renewed with bull head rail, while sidings were renewed with similar second-hand rail, although the engine shed siding retained its original rail until it was lifted in the 1950s. The line was re-ballasted in 1946. There had been a brief revival in pipe traffic when Liverpool Corporation had renewed the Vyrnwy pipeline during the 1920s.

Newspapers reported five accidents during the inter-war years. Another derailment occurred near Llangedwyn on 22 May 1924, when the loco and two carriages left the rails. The attractions of the Powys eisteddfod meant that there

Ex-Liskeard & Looe Railway 2-4-0T *Lady Margaret* being prepared to leave Penybontfawr with a goods train in the 1920s.

CHANGES OF OWNERSHIP, AND CLOSURE • 101

A vintage scene at Llangynog in the 1930s. No 898 was Cambrian No 14 *Broneirion*, built by Sharp, Stewart in 1878. It had been rebuilt by the GWR but the round-top firebox and the tender betray its age, complemented by the four-wheeled carriages.

The location of this photograph is unknown, but it shows a temporary narrow-gauge railway laid to facilitate the movement of Liverpool Corporation's pipes. The locomotive's identity is also unknown. (United Utilities)

Liverpool Corporation installed a third pipeline to its Vyrnwy reservoir in the late 1920s, seen here near Penybontfawr, with no obvious effort made to protect the train from the works or vice versa. (United Utilities)

were few passengers on the train and apart from three women suffering from shock no one was injured (*Birmingham Daily Gazette*, 24 May). The location must have been close to that of the 1916 derailment. For the entire train to leave the rails maybe indicates that McDonald's renewals programme had not been completed.

In August 1925 14-year-old Fanny Edwards was staying with her aunt at Gartheyr Farm, Llangedwyn. Taking cows to a field on the far side of the railway, she was run down by a train and died of her injuries in hospital. Her death certificate records the date of death as 20 August, but as the *Liverpool Echo* the day before had said she had died 'this morning' then the certificate is wrong; the accident probably happened on 18 August. At the inquest the coroner regretted that no attempt had been made to apply a tourniquet as it would probably have saved her life (*Birmingham Daily Gazette*, 21 August). The cause of death was recorded as 'accidentally killed on the Great Western Railway at Llangedwyn'. She was buried in St Cedwyn's churchyard there on 22 August, her grave being unmarked. In an unusual move, in the margin of the burial register the vicar noted the cause of death.

A collision between Oswestry Rural District Council's Foden steam wagon and an engine running tender first at the Porthywaen level crossing on 18 March 1926 led to an appearance at Shropshire Assizes for the GWR on 4 July 1927, the wagon having been damaged beyond repair. The Foden driver, who was familiar with the crossing and knew to look out for trains, said that he had not seen or heard this one until it was upon him as he crossed. Trapped in the wreckage, he was taken to hospital with a leg injury. His fireman was thrown off but unhurt. The newspaper report does not say why the council thought the GWR was negligent, although as written it sounds as though the loco driver had not sounded his whistle. Awarding £450 damages, the jury said that it did not consider the arrangement at the crossing to be satisfactory (*Birmingham Daily Gazette*, 5 July 1927). It had been in use for twenty-two years without any reported problems.

The crossing at Pedairffordd, which crossed the road in the middle of a 90-degree bend, was the location of two accidents with different outcomes and one person involved in both. The first was on 13 July 1929, when Annie Ida Jones (1888–1945), of nearby Brynaber Hall, was driving home from Llanrhaeadr with her two children and collided with a train from Llangynog. She received head and leg injuries, her son a broken thigh and her daughter had cuts on her face. A motorist happening upon the scene drove to Llanrhaeadr to fetch Dr Micah and mother and son were removed to the Shropshire Orthopaedic Hospital at Oswestry (*Birmingham Gazette*, 15 July 1929).

In a tragic coincidence, the doctor, David John Micah, was killed instantly when his car collided with a train from Llangynog at the same crossing on 11 May 1935. He was 40 years old. At the inquest the assistant county surveyor gave evidence that the corner at the crossing was well signed but doubted that the loco crew or the motorist could have seen each other. The driver said that the train's speed had been reduced to 4 or 5mph and that he had sounded his whistle (*Gloucester Citizen*, 13 May / *Liverpool Echo*, 13 May / 20 May). Recording the location of death as Pedairffordd Halt, his death certificate recorded the cause as 'fracture of the skull, other injuries and shock accidentally sustained, the result of a collision with a railway train at Pedairffordd level crossing'.

Coincidentally, Micah was the son-in-law of John Kenrick Jones, his predecessor as Llanrhaeadr's doctor and one of the Tanat Valley company directors.

Apart from the restricted visibility, the problem with the crossing for road users was that they would have rarely seen trains using it.

Seen in 2023, the site of Pedairffordd level crossing, the location of two recorded collisions with trains. From Llangynog, the railway crossed the verge on the right before crossing the road. Not so long ago it was possible to see the former platform from the road.

With the advent of British Railways on nationalisation in 1948 it was not long before the viability of branch lines was subject to review. The Western Region's branch line committee reported in 1951, recommending that the Tanat Valley's passenger service be withdrawn. Road competition and increased use of private cars had seen tickets issued decline from 35,140 in 1923 to 5,944 in 1949. The report had been pre-empted, however, by the response to a coal shortage, which on 18 January had resulted in the withdrawal of the Tanat Valley passenger service.

Closure between Llanrhaeadr and Llangynog (exclusive) was in a list submitted by the Railway Executive to the British Transport Commission on 18 June 1951. It would save the gross replacement cost of a locomotive (£4,985) and a carriage (£2,495), the accrued renewals of buildings and platforms (£743) and signalling (£1,199) offset by the recovery value (£45) of displaced signalling.

In 1950 1,035 tons of freight had earned £1,046. The goods sheds at Penybontfawr and Llangynog were let to Imperial Chemical Industries, who had said that the tenancies would be surrendered on account of the additional cost of road transport from Llanrhaeadr if the train service ceased. Two coal merchants would be moved to Llanrhaeadr. 'Smalls' goods and parcels traffic was already delivered by road from Oswestry.

Successive Llanrheaedr doctors buried alongside each other in St Dogfan's churchyard, not only connected by profession but by marriage and by the railway. On the right is the grave of Dr D. Kenrick Jones, a director of the railway company, his estate being valued at £6,884 1s, £243,036 in 2022. He lies alongside his son-in-law, Dr D. J. Micah, who was killed in his car's collision with a train at Pedairffordd crossing in 1935. His estate was valued at £19,872 18s 5d, £1,116,337 in 2022. The broken column signifies a life cut short.

A busy scene at Llangynog on 5 July 1941. (R. E. Tustin)

Blodwel Junction looking east in March 1948. The Tanat Valley line runs in from the left; on the right the stub of the line to Llanymynech was used as a headshunt for the loop and for storing wagons.

CHANGES OF OWNERSHIP, AND CLOSURE • 107

A train of a single bogie carriage at Blodwel Junction in 1950, the presence of the heads of passengers and the guard at the windows suggesting that they know the photographer is present and might even be waiting for him to rejoin the train.

On 3 July, interest in the railway by local MPs and an expected objection by Liverpool Corporation led to one of the Commission's employees suggesting that as the case for closure was borderline it might be better to wait until permanent way renewals, estimated to cost £10,000, became necessary. An official at the Executive replied, on 3 October, that as renewals were not expected until 1955 and annual expenditure of £1,303 along with annual train working expenses of £800 would be incurred in the meantime, he thought that there was not much to be gained by deferring the closure. As there was some local opposition to the closure, however, the Area Transport Consultative Committee (later Transport Users' Consultative Committee) would be consulted. On 22 February 1952 the Committee signified that it had no objection to the closure proposal being

THE RAILWAY EXECUTIVE
(Western Region).

NOTICE.

TANAT VALLEY BRANCH

The Railway Executive hereby give notice that on and from the 1st July, 1952, the section of the Tanat Valley Branch between Llanrhaiadr Mochnant (exclusive) and Llangynog will be closed for all purposes.

The Zonal Collection and Delivery services based on Oswestry for conveyance of Goods "Smalls" and parcels will continue to be maintained.

Alternative facilities for dealing with full truck load traffic are available at Llanrhaiadr Mochnant station.

Information in respect of arrangements for dealing with traffic and any other matters arising out of the closing will be supplied on application to:—

MR. T. C. SELLARS,
District Traffic Superintendent,
OSWESTRY.
Telephone No. Oswestry 189.

K. W. C. GRAND,
Chief Regional Officer,
Paddington Station.
June, 1952.

Closure notice for the section beyond Llanrhaeadr, *Montgomery Times*, 28 June 1952.

implemented and the line was closed from 1 July 1952.

At first, the closed portion was used to stable over 1,300 crippled wagons while they awaited removal to Swindon works for repair. The delivery of 2,200 tons of pipes to Penybontfawr for Liverpool Corporation's fourth Vyrnwy pipeline from 2 November 1953 until the end of 1954 required 200 wagons to be relocated and was done without headquarters' approval. When it was no longer needed for wagons, the recovery of redundant assets for £12,981 was sanctioned on 22 July 1957.

In December 1953 Denbighshire Parish Councils' Association had complained to British Railways that the level crossing at Llanrhaeadr was not compliant with the 1898 Light Railway Order. An Association member thought that as the passenger service had ended and the trains not so regular, the crossing was more dangerous. Investigation, which included reference to the original deeds, revealed that the original gates had been replaced by cattle guards in 1936 and the crossing's non-compliance had been raised by the Minister of War Transport in 1942, drivers then being

One of the 1954 pipe trains nearly ready to leave Blodwel Junction for Llangedwyn. (John Milner)

CHANGES OF OWNERSHIP, AND CLOSURE • 109

Crossing the road at Porthywaen, this photograph is captioned to be the last train to Llangynog but as it is dated 1 July 1952, the day of the closure, it could be the first train to terminate at Llanrhaeadr. Either way, it is still an interesting and historic photograph.

Llangedwyn in 1954, with one of the Vyrnwy pipes on the left. (John Milner)

instructed to stop and confirm that the crossing was clear before proceeding. The Association was told that if it considered the safeguards inadequate it should complain to the Ministry of Transport.

Track lifting started on 25 January 1958, the contract let to Aldridge-based Pittrail Ltd, which used a second-hand Avonside four-wheeled diesel locomotive named *Attic* (2063/1932). With the track lifted, the land was sold piecemeal, several plots for around £20 an acre, but the 2 acres formerly occupied by Llangynog station fetched a remarkable £200 later in 1958.

The Stephenson Locomotive Society ran a farewell excursion to Llanrhaeadr on 20 September 1958, the first passengers on the line since and probably the only time that bogie carriages had run on the line. On 4 December 1960 flood damage to one of the piers to the river bridge west of Llangedwyn brought the goods service beyond Blodwel Junction to an end; the track was lifted in 1964–65.

Continuation of traffic from Nantmawr and Llanddu quarries was enabled by creating a headshunt just before the overbridge at Blodwel Junction. The simplified layout, while eliminating the use of a signalman, required the use of gravity to run the wagons past the locomotive, which was eliminated by the installation of a run-round loop in 1985. The Nantmawr traffic had ended in 1971 and that from Llanddu finished in 1989. The line was formally closed in 1992.

Activity at Blodwel Junction on 12 June 1957, the track flooded after heavy rain and with ballast wagons stabled in the loop and in the stub of the line to Llanymynech. For the extent on the flooding, see also the photograph on Page 144. (Hugh Davies)

Looking westwards at Blodwel Junction on 20 September 1958. (H. C. Casserley)

The end of the line as seen from the bridge at Blodwel Junction on 7 June 1969.

Shunting Whitehaven quarry at Porthywaen in 1954. (John Milner)

The Wirral Railway Circle ran a brake van tour to Nantmawr called 'The Welsh Dragon' on 24 May 1969. It apparently stopped for a photographic run past at Porthywaen and is seen here crossing the road. There are several enthusiasts in the bushes on the right. (V. J. Bradley)

CHANGES OF OWNERSHIP, AND CLOSURE • 113

The railtour train at Nantmawr. British Rail must have scoured the North-West to secure enough vehicles to make up the train. (V. J. Bradley)

A stone train at Llynclys in the 1970s. Depending on the exact date, it could be stone from either Nantmawr or Llanddu.

Abandoned track near Blodwel Junction in 2006. The branch to Llanddu quarry is on the right.

Porthywaen level crossing in 2023. The rails are still in the road, albeit covered in tarmac. The remains of the platform are on the left, Oswestry-bound, side of the road.

The stub of the Potteries Railway's Nantmawr Line and a tiny part of the Tanat Valley Light Railway was not dismantled and remained in the ownership of British Rail and its successors until 2004, when it was purchased by the Oswestry-based Cambrian Railways Society.

In 2005 it was taken over by the newly formed Tanat Valley Light Railway Company, a charity registered with the objective of preserving the railways and industrial heritage of the area, which is developing the former Nantmawr sidings site as a visitor centre.

The remains of the first bridge over the Tanat built by Strachan, between Blodwel Junction and Llanyblodwel, in 1902, seen 121 years later.

Deep in the Tanat valley, this 2023 view looking towards Llangynog between Pentrefelin and Pedairffordd shows the railway boundary running across the field towards a shallow cutting.

The Tanat Valley Light Railway was built too late to fulfil its potential, to improve the lives and livings of the Tanat valley's occupants. Any chance that it might have had of rewarding its investors, paying its debt interest and redeeming its debt was undermined by the First World War and the availability of motor lorries and buses. The Cambrian and Great Western railways kept it going, despite increasing losses, but under state ownership it did not last long enough to come to the attention of the infamous Dr Beeching. Rails that remain in situ between Llanyblodwel and Porthywaen might one day see trains running again but with some of the formation ploughed out and parts put to other uses, trains will not be heard running through the valley again.

APPENDICES

828 LIGHT RAILWAYS, 1896.

LIGHT RAILWAYS, 1896.

59 & 60 Vict. Cap. 48. An Act to facilitate the Construction of Light Railways in Great Britain. [14th August, 1896.]

Be it enacted by the Queen's most Excellent Majesty, by and with the advice and consent of the Lords Spiritual and Temporal, and Commons, in this present Parliament assembled, and by the authority of the same, as follows :—

Establishment of Light Railway Commission.

1.—(1.) For the purpose of facilitating the construction and working of light railways in Great Britain, there shall be established a commission, consisting of three commissioners, to be styled the Light Railway Commissioners, and to be appointed by the President of the Board of Trade.

(2.) It shall be the duty of the Light Railway Commissioners to carry this Act into effect, and to offer, so far as they are able, every facility for considering and maturing proposals to construct light railways.

(3.) If a vacancy occurs in the office of any of the Light Railway Commissioners by reason of death, resignation, incapacity, or otherwise, the President of the Board of Trade may appoint some other person to fill the vacancy, and so from time to time as occasion may require.

(4.) There shall be paid to one of the Commissioners such salary, not exceeding one thousand pounds a year, as the Treasury may direct.

(5.) The Board of Trade may, with the consent of the Treasury as to number and remuneration, appoint and employ such number of officers and persons as they think necessary for the purpose of the execution of the duties of the Light Railway Commissioners under this Act, and may remove any officer or person so appointed or employed.

(6.) The said salary and remuneration, and all expenses of the Light Railway Commissioners incurred with the sanction of the Treasury in the execution of this Act shall, except so far as provision is made for their payment by or under this Act, be paid out of moneys provided by Parliament.

59 & 60 Vict. ch. 48. i.

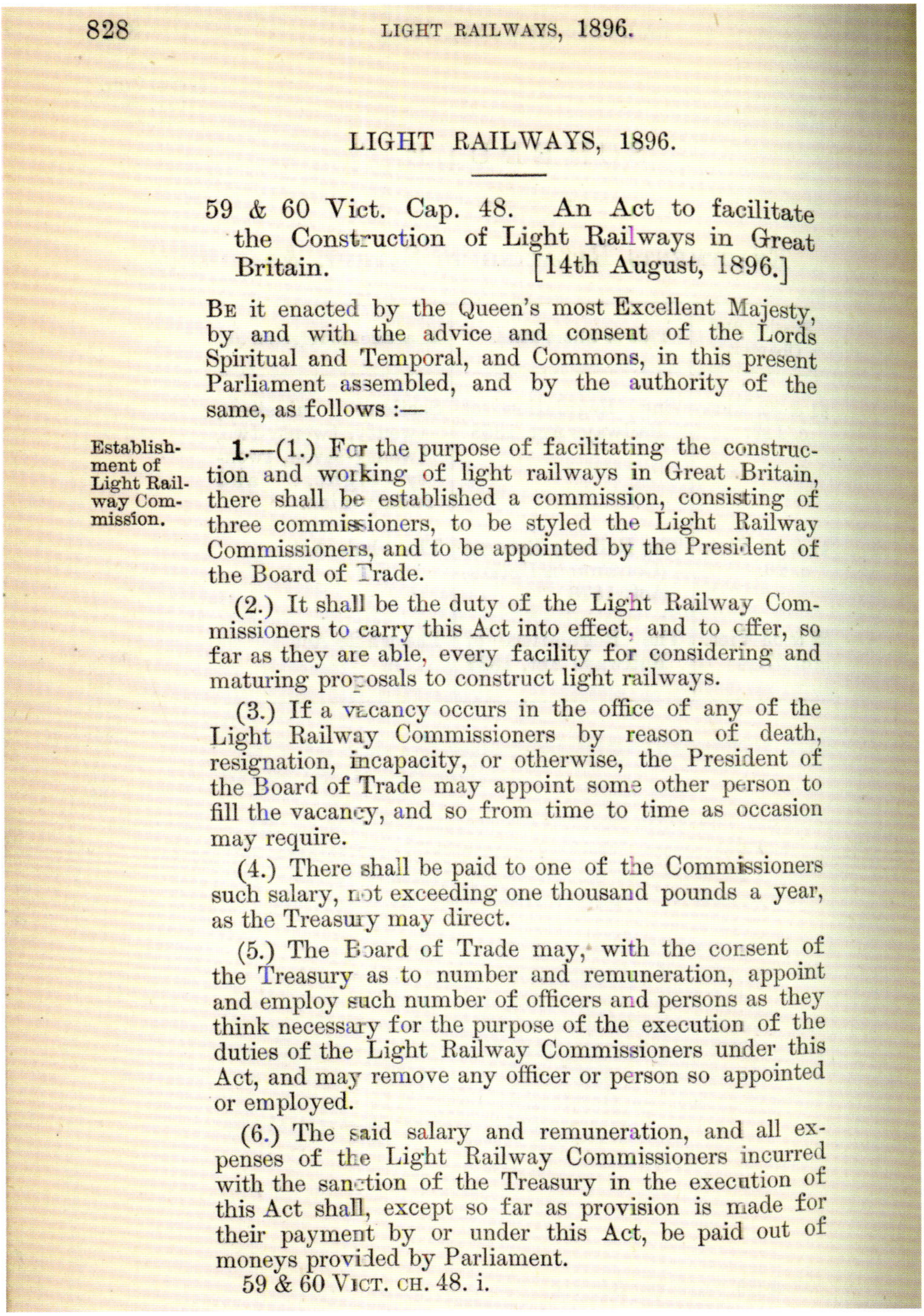

The first page of the 1896 Light Railways Act, the Act that enabled the construction of a railway to Llangynog after so many failed attempts.

APPENDIX 1
TANAT VALLEY PROPOSALS

Date	Promoters	Route	Comments
1860/1	West Midland, Shrewsbury & Coast of Wales Railway	Ford-Knockin, Porthywaen, Llanfyllin, Llanrhaeadr, Llangynog, Bala-Porthmadog	Failed standing orders
1862	Oswestry & Newtown Railway	Llanfyllin-Llangynog	No powers sought
1862/3	West Shropshire Mineral Railway	Llanymynech-Llanyblodwel-Llangynog	Failed standing orders
1863/4	West Shropshire Mineral Railway	Llanymynech-Llanyblodwel-Llangynog	West Shropshire Mineral Railway (New Lines) Act, 1864
1869/70	Not known	Oswestry-Llansilin-Llangynog	Narrow gauge, Bill deposited, landowners objected, Bill withdrawn
1872	Cambrian Railways' directors and officers	Llanfyllin-Llangynog	Narrow gauge, Llanfyllin & Llangynog Railway Act, 1873; Llanfyllin & Llangynog Railway (Abandonment) Act, 1876; lack of funds
1872	Oswestry residents	Oswestry-Llansilin-Llangynog	Bill withdrawn
1878	W. H. Spaull	Oswestry-Llansilin-Llangynog	Narrow gauge, scheme abandoned
1881	Liverpool Corporation	Llanyblodwel-Penybontfawr	Roadside tramway in connection with Vyrnwy reservoir construction
1881/2	Potteries, Shrewsbury & North Wales Railway	Porthywaen-Llangynog	Oswestry and Llangynog Railway Act, 1882; Oswestry and Llangynog Railway (Extension of Time) Act, 1886; Oswestry and Llangynog Railway (Abandonment) Act, 1889
1890		Oswestry-Llangynog	Initiated by Owen Roberts, Llangynog, and Oswestry residents; committee appointed but no action taken
1890	Shropshire Railways	Llanyblodwel-Llangynog	Failure to fund deposit resulted in Bill's withdrawal
1897	Llanfyllin & Llangynog Light Railway	Llanfyllin-Llangynog	Declined by Board of Trade
1897	Tanat Valley Light Railway	Llynclys-Llangynog	Tanat Valley Light Railway Order, 1899

APPENDIX 2

LLANFYLLIN & LLANGYNOG LIGHT RAILWAY – ESTIMATE OF EXPENSES 1897

Length of line 10m 3f 5ch Gauge 2 feet 6 inches Construction of line	Cu yd	Price/yd	£ s d	£ s d
Earthworks				
Cuttings – rock	7,660	3s	1,149 0 0	
Cuttings – soft soil	47,510	1s 4d	3,167 7 0	
Roads	170	2s 6d	21 5 0	
Total				4,337 12 0
Embankments, including roads – 49,820 cu yd				
Accommodation works				100 0 0
Viaducts over Rivers Cain, Hirnant and Tanat				1,100 0 0
Culverts and drains				818 0 0
Metalling of roads and level crossings				568 6 0
Permanent way, including fencing: cost per mile: 10 miles 3 furlongs 5 chains @ £950				9,915 0 0
Permanent way for sidings and cost of junctions				1,361 0 0
Stations, buildings, fittings and telephone				1,860 0 0
				20,059 18 0
Contingencies 10%				2,005 0 0
Land and buildings – 47 acres 2 roods 35 perches				2,685 0 0
Total				£24,749 18 0

(Signed) *Calthrop & Ward*, Engineers

APPENDIX 3

TANAT VALLEY LIGHT RAILWAY – ESTIMATE 1897

Length of line Construction of line	Cu yd	Price/yd	£ s d	14m 7f 0ch £ s d
Earthworks				
Cuttings – rock	28,326	1s 6d	2,124 9 0	
Cuttings – soft soil	126,058	1s	6,302 18 0	
Roads	390	1s	19 10 0	
Total			**8,446 17 0**	**8,446 17 0**
Embankments, including roads – 134,430 cu yd				
Bridges, public roads – none				
Accommodation bridges and works				1,697 0 0
Viaducts				1,850 0 0
Culverts and drains				816 0 0
Metalling of roads and level crossings				386 5 0
Gatekeepers' houses at level crossings, including gates and signals				1,240 0 0
Permanent way, including fencing: cost per mile: 14m 7fg @ £1,404 0 0				20,872 0 0
Permanent way for sidings and cost of junctions				2,498 15 9
Stations				1,249 0 0
Contingencies				3,324 3 0
Land and buildings – 71a 1r 34p				3,573 2 10
Total				**£45,953 13 7**

(Signed) *George Owen*

APPENDIX 4

TANAT VALLEY LIGHT RAILWAY – LOCAL AUTHORITY ADVANCES

Local Authority	1900	Interest	1901	Interest	Total
Denbighshire County Council	£3,000 loan	3%	£1,500 loan	3⅝%	£4,500
Montgomeryshire County Council	£2,500 loan	3%	£1,250 loan	3¾%	£3,750
Shropshire County Council	£2,000 loan	3½%	£1,000 loan	3½%	£3,000
Liverpool Corporation	£2,000 shares		£3,000 loan	3½%	£5,000
Oswestry Rural District Council	£2,000 loan, £1,000 shares		£1,000 loan, £1,000 shares	3¾%	£5,000
Llanfyllin Rural District Council	£3,000 loan	3%	£1,500 loan	3¾%	£4,500
Llansilin Rural District Council	£3,000 loan	3%	£3,000		£6,000
Total	£18,500		£13,250		£31,750

APPENDIX 5

TANAT VALLEY LIGHT RAILWAY – OTHER WORKS 1900

Permanent way material	£15,000
Alteration to Porthywaen branch	£2,000
Alteration to Nantmawr branch	£1,000
Signalling	£2,100
Electric telegraph and block working	£730
Station buildings	£450
Water supply and engine shed at Llangynog	£250
	£21,530

The 3rd Earl of Bradford was insistant that there should be a direct service between the light railway and Llanymynech, to the extent that the curve required attracted his name. He was interred in a vault alongside the mausoleum that he had had erected in the cemetery close to his family home at Weston Hall, Weston under Lizzard, Shropshire.

Appendix 6

Tanat Valley Light Railway – Estimate of Expenses 1901

In Parliament.
Session 1901.

TANAT VALLEY LIGHT RAILWAY.

ESTIMATE OF EXPENSE.

	Miles. f. chs. lks.			Single Line.
Length of Line	15 – 8 –			

EARTHWORKS:	Cubic yds.	Price per yd. s. d.	£ s. d.	£ s. d.
Cuttings— Rock	5,000	4 6	1,125 0 0	
Soft Soil	122,000	1 5	8,641 13 4	
Roads	3,000	1 9	262 10 0	
Side Cuttings	6,000	1 5	425 0 0	
Sundries	…	…	170 16 8	
TOTAL	136,000		10,625 0 0	10,625 0 0

Embankments, including Roads	136,000 cubic yards	…
Bridges—Public Roads, (none) Number.		…
Accommodation Bridges and Works		9,000 0 0
Viaducts, Bridges, and River Walls		6,107 16 8
Tunnel, yards, at £ per yard (none)		…
Culverts and Drains		1,495 0 0
Metallings of Roads and Level Crossings		2,504 0 0
Gatekeepers' Houses at Level Crossings		…
Permanent Way, including Fencing:		

MILES. F. CHS. LKS.	COST PER MILE. £ s. d.	
15 – 8 – at	1,916 11 4	28,939 13 10½
Permanent Way for Sidings, and Cost of Junctions		9,043 5 7½
Stations		2,515 3 10
	£	70,230 0 0
Contingencies		5,000 0 0
	£	75,230 0 0
Land and Buildings	A. R. P. 76 1 14	6,500 0 0
TOTAL	£	81,730 0 0

A. J. COLLIN, *Engineer.*

APPENDIX 7

TANAT VALLEY LIGHT RAILWAY – NECESSARY EXPENDITURE 1900

Lowest tender	£48,700
Other works	£21,530
Land	£6,500
Preliminary expenses, say	£2,000
Engineer's expenses	£3,000
	£81,730

The 4th Earl of Bradford continued with his predecessor's efforts to secure a direct service to Llanymynech for several years. With other members of his immediate family he was buried in the cemetery at Weston under Lizzard, close to the family mausoleum.

APPENDIX 8

TANAT VALLEY LIGHT RAILWAY – TENDERS 1901

Contractor	Location	Contract No 1 £ s d	Contract No 2 £ s d	Total £ s d
John Elwell	Birmingham	3,246 1 6		
Holme & King	Liverpool	3,932 10 4	37,115 14 3	40,980 4 7
E. C. & J. Keay Ltd	Birmingham	5,736 16 0		
S. E. Lucas	East Leake, Loughborough	4,102 4 9	33,361	37,463 4 9
F. Morton & Company	London	5,093 0 6		
Naylor Brothers	Huddersfield	5,496 0 0	42,462 11 6	48,958 11 6 ~
H. M. Nowell	Leeds	3,788 15 0	39,518 7 10	43,307 2 10
J. D. Nowell & Sons	Westminster	3,890 15 0	38,017 19 4	43,908 14 4
E. W. Palmer	London	4,425 10 7		
Pethick Brothers	Plymouth	6,166 0 0	37,973 0 0	44,139 0 0
D. Rowell & Company	London	5,850 18 5		
Rowland Brothers	Fenny Stratford	4,571 11 3		
J. B. Squire & Company	Westminster	4,700 0 0	39,650 0 0	44,350 0 0 #
J. Strachan	Cardiff	4,517 0 0	35,726 17 8	40,243 17 8 #
J. H. Tozer & Son	London	3,697 4 1		
P. Smith	Manchester			58,692 0 0 #
Braithwaite & Co	London			40,100 0 0

~ Would only accept both contracts; would not provide bond
# Would only accept both contacts

APPENDIX 9

TANAT VALLEY LIGHT RAILWAY – JOHN STRACHAN'S TENDER

Contract No 1, Fencing and gates	£4,517
Contract No 2, Earthworks	£11,181
Bridges and river walls	£6,125
Culverts and drains	£1,540
Permanent way	£13,892
Cattle pits	£804
Cattle creeps	£967
Metalling	£509
Stations	£708
	£40,243

Porthywaen platform looking towards the level crossing and Llangynog.

APPENDIX 10

TANAT VALLEY LIGHT RAILWAY – COST OF WORK DONE TO 20 NOVEMBER 1902

Estimate of Expense

Earthworks	Cu yd	Price/yd	£ s d	£ s d
Cuttings – rock	3,880	4 6	873 0 0	
Cuttings – soft soil	74,700	1 6	5,602 10 0	
Roads	503	1 9	44 0 3	
Benching	222	4	3 14 0	
Side cutting	9,980	1 6	748 10 0	
Total	89,285		7,271 14 3	7,271 14 3
Accommodation bridges and works				2,672 17 4
Viaducts				1,960 19 9
Culverts and drains				553 5 0
Metalling of roads and level crossings				81 12 0
Gatekeepers' houses at level crossings, including gates and signals				12,128 8 9
Permanent way, including fencing				10,317 18 1
				34,986 15 2
Engineering Commission				1,500 0 0
Contingencies 10%				
				£36,486 17 2

(Signed) A. J. Collin, Engineer

APPENDIX 11

TANAT VALLEY LIGHT RAILWAY – DETAILS RE ENGINEER'S COMMISSION

	£ s d	£ s d
Amount of Contract No 1		5,777 7 3
Amount of Contract No 2	43,059 6 1	
Daywork for extras	1,966 18 5	45,026 4 6
Cambrian Railways Company – materials	49 17 8	
Cambrian Railways Company – carriage	462 16 8	512 14 3
Guest, Keen & Company – rails		8,357 1 4
George Bowes – testing materials		3 15 6
Isca Foundry Company – points and crossings		372 19 6
Tyer & Company – signalling		2,480 11 3
J. B. Saunders & Company – telegraphs		1,700 10 7
J. Strachan – station buildings		800 0 0
W. H. Thomas – engine shed, &c		730 17 2
J. Minshall & Company – troughs		3 15 0
Clay & Davies – iron gates		11 19 9
Pooley & Son – weighing machines		240 0 0
		67,165 6 8
Cost of altering the Nantmawr and Porthywaen branches of the Cambrian Railways to make them fit for passenger traffic		2,993 10 10
		70,158 16 6
Engineer's fee		
5½% commission on £70,158 17s 6d		3,858 15 9
Less amount received on account		2,150 1 0
		1,708 15 9
For extra work		60 0 0
		£1,768 15 9

14 September 1904

APPENDIX 12

TANAT VALLEY LIGHT RAILWAY – JOHN STRACHAN'S LOCOMOTIVES USED ON CONTRACT

	Wheel arrangement	Maker	Works number/date of manufacture	Date arrived	Date left
J. Strachan No 3	0-4-0ST	Hunslet	365/1885	20 August 1901	31 July 1903
J. Strachan No 5	0-6-0ST	Manning, Wardle	373/1871	19 February 1902	16 October 1903
J. Strachan No 6	0-6-0ST	Manning, Wardle	1605/1903	17 August 1903	9 January 1904
J. Strachan No 7	0-6-0ST	Manning, Wardle	1576/1903	23 January 1903	7 December 1903

Locomotive data courtesy of the Industrial Railway Society. Dates of arrival/departure from 27 May 1905. Report compiled by Herbert Jones, locomotive superintendent, Cambrian Railways.

APPENDIX 13

TANAT VALLEY LIGHT RAILWAY – BALANCE SHEET, 15 JUNE 1903

To Share Capital:		By payments on account of preliminary expenses, law costs, etc per solicitors and general charges	£5,310 8s 8d
Received on account of calls	£13,323 10s 0d	Engineer, payments on account	£1,950
Amount received in respect of loans on mortgage less instalments of principal sums repaid	£24,475 8s 2d	Deposit with Board of Trade under provisional order	£1,500 0s 0d
Subscriptions to preliminary expenses	£173 19s 0d	Interest on loans	£432 11s 5d
The Treasury – moiety of free grant and subvention	£14,000 0s 0d	Cambrian Company rent due to 3 December for use of Shropshire Railways	£625
Lloyds Bank Ltd – amount of debit of account	£8,274 12s 10d	Purchase money for land taken, surveyor's fees, &c.	£7,020 11s 9d
		Tenants' compensation	£89 0s 0d
		Construction of railway, contractor on account	£32,810 0s 7d
		Rails, switches, fishplates, spikes, &c.	£10,514 17s 7d
	£60,252 10s 0d		**£60,252 10s 0d**

APPENDIX 14

TANAT VALLEY LIGHT RAILWAY – APPROXIMATE STATEMENT OF LIABILITIES, DECEMBER 1903

	£ s d
Cambrian Railways Company	10,447 8 2
Cambrian Railways Company (Moiety of retention money, not yet due)	2,480 0 0
Cambrian Railways Company (Amount due to contractor on final certificate)	(?)
Engineer's charges	(?)
Lloyds Bank (Amount overspent on capital account)	2,528 10 8
J. B. Saunders & Company	1,754 5 0
Tyer & Company Ltd	2,480 11 3
Isca Foundry Company	119 10 0
Pooley & Son Ltd	240 0 0
J. Minshall & Company	5 9 0
C. Drew & Company	14 8 6
Woodall & Company	17 4 10
Baker, Lees & Company	15 11 2
Clay & Davies	11 19 9
W. H. Thomas	730 17 2
Sundry creditors	109 4 3
	20,954 19 9

APPENDIX 15

TANAT VALLEY LIGHT RAILWAY – STATEMENT OF COSTS, JANUARY 1904

	£ s d	£ s d
Fencing and gates	6,424 13 7	
Earthworks	17,118 9 9	
Bridges, river walls, &c.	9,990 8 3	
Culverts and drains	1,750 0 2	
Permanent way	13,946 19 3	
Cattle pits	804 5 0	
Cattle creeps	1,200 0 0	
Metalling	897 19 8	
Stations	921 14 0	£53,054
Permanent way, rails, signalling, &c.		£18,530
Sundries		£606
		£72,191
Land conveyancing, &c.		£10,106
Engineer	4,000	
Bank charges	960	
Sundries	993	
		£5,953
Preliminary expenses		2,137
Shropshire Railways rent, interest on loans		1,856
		£92,243

APPENDIX 16

TANAT VALLEY LIGHT RAILWAY – LAND PURCHASE COSTS

	£ s d
Land	7,315 4 9
Conveyancing	804 6 2
Valuers' fees	559 7 8
Vendors' solicitors' costs	1,164 19 6
Stamp duty	52 15 6
Tenants' compensation	209 0 0
	£10,105 13 7

APPENDIX 17

TANAT VALLEY LIGHT RAILWAY – ESTIMATED AND ACTUAL COSTS

	Estimate	Actual	Difference
	£ s d	£ s d	£ s d
Fencing and gates	4,517 0 0	6,424 13 7	1,907 13 7
Earthworks	11,180 16 8	17,118 9 9	5,937 13 1
Bridges, river walls, &c.	6,124 5 10	9,990 8 3	3,866 2 5
Culverts and drains	1,540 5 0	1,750 0 2	209 15 2
Permanent way	13,892 3 4	13,946 19 3	54 15 11
Cattle pits	804 5 0	804 5 0	
Cattle creeps	967 8 6	1,200 0 0	232 11 6
Metallings	509 3 4	897 19 8	388 16 4
Stations	707 18 0	921 14 0	213 16 0
	£40,243 5 8	**£53,054 9 8**	**£12,811 4 0**

APPENDIX 18

TANAT VALLEY LIGHT RAILWAY – LIST OF BUILDINGS REQUIRED

(John Strachan's tender, 25 August 1903)

Station	Buildings	£ s d
Porthywaen	Waiting room (£15 0s 0d), small urinal (£5 0s 0d)	20 0 0
Old Llanyblodwel	Waiting room and booking office (£110 0s 0d), earth closet, urinal and lamp room combined (£8 10s 0d)	118 10 0
New Llanyblodwel	Waiting shed 10 x 6ft (£15 0s 0d), small urinal (£5 0s 0d)	20 0 0
Penybont (Llansilin Road)	Waiting shed and office (£20 0s 0d), new goods shed (£103 0s 0d), earth closet (£15 0s 0d)	138 0 0
Pentrefelin	Waiting shed 10 x 6ft, small urinal	20 0 0
Llangedwyn	Waiting room/booking office (£110 0s 0d), urinal and lamp room (£8 10s 0d), waiting shed 10 x 6ft (£15 0s 0d)	133 10 0
Llanrhaeadr	Waiting room and booking office (£110 0s 0d), urinal and lamp room (£8 10s 0d), waiting shed 10 x 6ft (£15 0s 0d), goods shed (£103 0s 0d)	236 10 0
Pedairffordd	Waiting shed (£15 0s 0d), small urinal (£5 0s 0d)	20 0 0
Penybontfawr	Waiting shed and office (£20 0s 0d), urinal and earth closet (£15 0s 0d), goods shed (£103 0s 0d)	138 0 0
Llangynog	Waiting room and booking office (£110 0s 0d), urinal and lamp room (£8 10s 0d), goods shed (£103 0s 0d)	221 10 0
		1,066 0 0
	Less 10%	106 0 0
	Total	£960 0 0

APPENDIX 19
TANAT VALLEY LIGHT RAILWAY – GROSS TRAFFIC RECEIPTS TO 30 JANUARY 1904

		£ s d
Passengers	5,414	134 13 1
Parcels	16 Cwt	6 11 4
Goods	1,676 tons	211 6 4
Minerals	1,272 tons	81 4 1
Livestock	11 wagons	4 7 3
		£438 2 3

Llanrhaeadr, looking over the level crossing towards Llangynog. The home signal, on the left, has been replaced, whereas the starter retains its original timber post.

APPENDIX 20

TANAT VALLEY LIGHT RAILWAY – GROSS TRAFFIC RECEIPTS FROM 6 JANUARY 1904 TO 30 JUNE 1907

Half-year ending	Passenger £ s d	Parcels £ s d	Goods £ s d	Minerals £ s d	Livestock £ s d	Total £ s d
June 1904	1,061 13 4	74 7 2	1,516 1 4	356 4 0	37 5 11	3,045 11 9
December 1904	1,326 10 3½	112 3 9	1,256 2 6½	451 2 10	66 17 6	3,212 16 11
June 1905	1,013 17 0	87 10 10	406 13 11	367 17 0	61 2 9	1,937 1 6
December 1905	1,197 16 5	122 11 4	411 8 8	506 2 5	107 12 10	2,345 11 8
June 1906	923 3 6	104 19 5	355 15 3	433 17 11	54 13 10	1,872 10 2
December 1906	1,151 13 0	137 0 0	405 3 0	441 15 11	109 1 5	2,244 13 5
June 1907 *	843 16 5	109 13 4	351 0 2	451 19 1	63 8 8	1,819 17 11
						£16,478 3 4

* Estimated traffic for the month of June

APPENDIX 21

TANAT VALLEY LIGHT RAILWAY – GROSS RECEIPTS AND WORKING EXPENSES 1905–1919

	1905 £	1906 £	1907 £	1908 £	1909 £	1910 £	1911 £	1912 £	1913 £	1914 £	1915 £
Running expenses											
Wages	454	417	432	404	369	389	393	378	379	402	409
Coal	467	523	509	616	511	367	323	358	461	532	345
Water, gas, stores	58	86	56	26	55	48	41	50	43	49	42
Repair and renewals											
Wages	71	91	64	108	44	86	37	76	70	28	63
Materials	179	230	126	38	43	68	65	34	23	11	7
Carriage & wagon repairs											
Carriages – wages	50	45	81	59	43	53	46	43	47	51	56
– materials	28	19	26	33	39	32	33	31	24	28	32
Wagons – wages	44	48	45	44	28	39	36	36	40	41	45
– materials	44	62	42	38	33	36	49	51	47	46	52
War bonus											12
Engineer's department											
Wages	1,192	846	1,057	940	813	710	770	794	745	743	1,117
Materials	43	76	135	32	182	138	185	207	236	174	193
Engine hire – ballasting						11	15				
Miscellaneous									17	12	21
War bonus											107
Traffic department											
Wages	914	864	840	833	750	670	621	695	696	700	688
Materials	69	70	74	93	60	55	43	42	64	72	86
War bonus											94

	1905 £	1906 £	1907 £	1908 £	1909 £	1910 £	1911 £	1912 £	1913 £	1914 £	1915 £
Sundries	37	35	36	43	48	48	47	53	54	55	61
National Insurance								16	21	22	21
Maintenance of telegraphs	115	115	115	115	113	114	115	115	115	115	115
Total expenditure	3,765	3,527	3,608	3,417	3,129	2,864	2,819	2,979	3,092	3,081	3,768
Gross receipts	4,294	4,133	4,058	4,239	3,922	4,412	4,146	4,061	3,933	4,285	3,973
Net revenue	529	608	450	822	793	1,548	1,327	1,082	891	1,204	205
Proportion of gross receipts paid to owning company	1,718	1,653	1,623	1,696	1,569	1,765	1,659	1,624	1,593	1,714	1,389
Loss to Cambrian Company	1,189	1,047	1,173	874	776	217	332	542	702	510	1,384

	1915 £	1916 £	1917 £	1918 £	1919 £
Running expenses					
Wages	409	396	393	360	426
Coal	345	608	683	555	737
Water, gas, stores	42	72	86	72	113
Repair and renewals					
Wages	63	37	109	56	97
Materials	7	14	79	17	76
Carriage & wagon repairs					
Carriages – wages	56	39	56	59	86
– materials	32	36	33	42	29
Wagons – wages	45	52	49	46	72
– materials	52	48	65	74	42
War bonus	12	125	184	354	545
Engineer's department					
Wages	1,117	781	752	865	952
Materials	193	297	267	286	750
Engine hire – ballasting					72
Miscellaneous	21	13	12	12	44
War bonus	107	230	518	949	1,348
Traffic department					
Wages	688	695	730	949	899
Materials	86	73	67	75	113
War bonus	94	196	440	760	1,066

	1915 £	1916 £	1917 £	1918 £	1919 £
Sundries	61	61	64	74	94
National Insurance	21	21	22	22	22
Maintenance of telegraphs	115	115	115	115	225
Total expenditure	3,768	3,929	4,724	5,480	7,828
Gross receipts	3,973	3,974	3,975	3,971	3,970
Net revenue	05	45	(749)	(1,509)	(3,858)
Proportion of gross receipts paid to owning company	1,389	1,590	1,590	1,588	1,588
Loss to Cambrian Company	1,384	1,545	2,339	3,097	3,446

The floods at Blodwel Junction on 12 August 1957. The road bridge remains in situ but there is now no sign of the station. (N. C. Simmons)

APPENDIX 22

TANAT VALLEY LIGHT RAILWAY – TIMETABLES 1913 AND 1920

Summer 1913 Service

Tanat Valley Light Railway and Nantmawr Branch

WEEK DAYS.

Miles from Oswestry	DOWN.		3 Goods	5 Mixed ¶	7 Goods	9 Mixed	11 Mixed Weds. excepted	13 Mixed Weds. only.	15 Mixed Thurs only to Sep. 4.	17 Pass.	19 Mixed Weds. & Sats. excepted	21 Mixed Weds. & Sats. only.	23 Mixed 1st Wed. in each m'nth
M. C.			a m	a m	a.m.	a m	a m	p.m.	p.m.	p m	p.m.	p.m.	p m
..	*b*Oswestry	dep.	7 20	8 30	8 45	..	11 50	1 25	1 50	..	4 15	5 35	7 45
3 48	*c*Llynclys Junction	,,	S	8 38	S	..	11 58	1 33	..	..	4 23	5 43	7 53
4 52	*c*Porthywaen	,,	..	8 42	..	..	12 3	1 38	..	..	4 28	5 48	7 58
6 8	*c*Blodwell Junction	arr.	..	8 47	9 20	..	12 8	1 43	..	..	4 33	5 53	8 3
M. C.													
..	*c*Llanymynech	dep.	8 15	..	R	11 25	..	..	2 11	2 25	..	..	Will also run on August 2nd
0 71	*c*Nantmawr Junc.	,,	..	..	..	..	..	..	..	..	..	..	
1 77	Rhydmeredydd Sid.	,,	..	..	..	..	..	..	..	..	..	..	
2 46	*c*Blodwell Junction	arr.	8 25	..	..	11 35	..	..	2 21	2 35	..	..	
	,,	dep.	8 30	..	..	..	..	..	..	..	..	..	
2 72	Llanddu	,,	S	..	..	..	..	..	..	..	..	..	
3 77	Nantmawr	arr.	8 50	..	..	..	..	..	..	..	..	..	
..	*c*Blodwell Junction	dep.	..	8 48	9 35	..	12 9	1 44	2×24	..	4 34	5 54	8 4
6 62	Llanyblodwell	,,	..	8 53	S	..	12 14	1 49	2 29	..	4 39	5 59	8 9
7 77	Glanyrafon	,,	..	*	*	..	*	*	*	..	*	*	*
9 17	Llansilin Road	,,	..	9 3	S	..	12 24	2 0	2 39	..	4 49	6 9	8 22
10 68	*c*Llangedwyn	arr.	..	..	10×10	..	..	2 ×5	..	..	..	..	..
	,,	dep.	..	9 9	10 30	..	12 30	2 7	2 45	..	4 55	6 15	8 28
12 59	Pentrefelin	,,	..	9 16	..	..	12 37	2 14	2 52	..	5 2	6 22	8 35
14 9	Llanrhaiadr Mochnant	,,	..	9 22	S	..	12 43	2 21	2 58	..	5 10	6 30	8 42
15 18	Pedair Ffordd	,,	..	9 27	..	..	12 48	2 26	3 3	..	5 15	6 35	8 47
16 75	Penybont Fawr	,,	..	9 35	S	..	12 56	2 34	3 11	..	5 23	6 43	8 55
19 39	*c*Llangynog	arr.	..	9 43	12 0	..	1 5	2 45	3 20	..	5 35	6 55	9 5

Miles from Llangynog	UP.		2 Mixed Weds. only.	4 Goods	6	8 Mixed	10 Goods	12 Mixed	14 Goods Tues. & Weds ex'cep R ¶	16 Goods Weds. only.	18 Mixed Weds. & Sats except	20 Mixed Wed. and Sats. only.	22 Mixed Thurs only to Sep. 4
M. C.			a m	a m		a m	noon	p.m.	p.m.	p.m.	p m	p.m.	p.m.
..	*c*Llangynog	dep.	6 40	..	..	9 55	..	1 35	2 0	3 20	5 50	7 5	7 15
2 44	Penybont Fawr	,,	6 48	..	..	10 3	..	1 43	S	..	5 58	7 13	7 23
4 21	Pedair Ffordd	,,	6 55	..	..	10 10	..	1 50	..	..	6 5	7 20	7 30
5 30	*c*Llanrhaiadr Mochnant	,,	a 7 0 d 7 5	..	..	10 15	..	1 55	S	S	6 10	7 25	7 35
6 60	Pentrefelin	,,	7 10	..	..	10 20	..	2 0	..	..	6 15	7 30	7 40
8 51	*c*Llangedwyn	,,	a 7 15 d 7 20	..	..	10×25	..	2 ×5	S	S	6×20	7 35	7 45
10 22	Llansilin Road	,,	7 30	..	..	10 32	..	2 12	S	S	6 27	7 42	7 52
11 42	Glanyrafon	,,	*	..	..	*	..	*	*	*	*	*	*
12 57	Llanyblodwell	,,	7 37	..	..	10 39	..	2 19	S	S	6 34	7 49	7 59
13 31	*c*Blodwell Junction	arr.	7 41	..	..	10 43	..	2×23	3 20	4×30	6 38	7 53	8 3
M. C.													
..	Nantmawr	dep.	..	10 20	..	..	..	..	..	..	..	..	..
1 5	Llanddu	,,	..	S	..	..	..	..	..	..	..	..	..
1 31	*c*Blodwell Junction	arr.	..	10 35	..	..	..	..	..	..	..	..	..
	,,	dep.	..	..	..	10 45	12 0	2 40	..	..	..	..	..
2 0	Rhydmeredydd Sid.	,,	..	..	..	..	S	..	..	..	..	..	..
3 6	*c*Nantmawr Junc.	,,	..	..	..	..	..	..	..	..	..	..	..
3 77	*c*Llanymynech	arr.	..	..	..	10 55	12 15	2 50	..	..	..	..	..
..	*c*Blodwell Junction	dep.	7 45	..	..	10 44	..	2 25	3 30	4 40	6 40	7 54	8 4
14 67	*c*Porthywaen	arr.	7 50	..	..	10 49	..	2 30	..	..	6 45	7 59	8 9
	,,	dep.	7 55	..	..	10 51	..	2 31	..	..	6 46	8 0	8 11
15 70	*c*Llynclys Junction	arr.	..	..	..	..	..	..	3 40	4 50	..	..	..
	b	dep.	8 0	..	..	10 56	..	2 36	4 45	5 30	6 51	8 5	8 16
19 39	*b*Oswestry	arr.	8 10	..	..	11 5	..	2 45	5 0	5 45	7 0	8 15	8 25

† Passengers from Llangynog, Blodwell Junction and intermediate stations for Llanymynech and stations beyond travel via Oswestry.

¶ Nos. 7 and 14 will not run on Thursdays when Nos. 15 and 22 run. On the first Thursday in each month No. 14 Goods will leave Llangynog at 10·30 a.m., arriving Oswestry by 1·15 p.m. in time to work No. 15.

No. 15 will run via Llanymynech.

Winter 1913 Service

TANAT VALLEY LIGHT RAILWAY AND NANTMAWR BRANCH.

WEEK DAYS.

Miles from Oswestry	DOWN.	1 Goods	3 Mixed	5	7 Goods R ¶	9 Mixed	11 Mixed Weds. excepted.	13 Pass	15 Mixed Wed. only.	17 Mixed Weds. and Sats. excepted.	19 Mixed Weds. and Sats. only.	21 Mixed 1st Wed. in each M'nth
M. C.			am	am	am	am	am	pm	pm	pm	pm	pm
...	bOswestry ......dep	...	7 20	8 30	8 45	...	11 50	...	1 25	4 15	5 35	7 45
3 48	bcLlynclys Junction ......,,		S	8 38	S		11 58		1 33	4 23	5 43	7 53
4 52	cPorthywaen ......,,		...	8 42	...		12 3		1 38	4 28	5 48	7 58
6 8	cBlodwel Junction ......arr		...	8 47	9 20		12 7		1 43	4 33	5 52	8 3
M. C.												
...	cLlanymynech ......dep	...	8 15	...	R	11 25	...	2 25	...	...	...	...
0 71	cNantmawr Jct. ,,		...		...	...		...				
1 77	Rhydmeredydd Sid. ,,		...		...	...		...				
2 46	cBlodwel Junction .. arr		8 25			11 35		2 35				
	,, ...dep		8 30									
2 72	Llanddu ,,		S									
3 77	Nantmawr ......arr		8 50									
...	cBlodwel Junction ......dep	...	...	8 48	9 35	...	12 8	...	1 44	4 34	5 53	8 4
6 62	Llanyblodwel ......,,			8 53	S		12 13		1 49	4 39	5 57	8 9
7 77	Glanyrafon ......,,			*			*		*	*	*	*
9 17	Llansilin Road......,,			9 3	S		12 23		1 59	4 49	6 7	8 22
10 68	cLlangedwyn......arr				10X10				2X4			
,,	......dep			9 9	10 30		12 29		2 7	4 55	6 13	8 28
12 59	Pentrefelin ......,,			9 16	...		12 36		2 14	5 2	6 20	8 35
14 9	cLlanrhaiadr Mochnant ... ,,			9 22	S		12 42		2 20	5 10	6 25	8 42
15 18	Pedair Ffordd ......,,			9 27	...		12 47		2 25	5 15	6 30	8 47
16 75	Penybont Fawr ......,,			9 35	S		12 54		2 32	5 22	6 38	8 55
19 39	cLlangynog ......arr			9 43	12 0		1 2		2 40	5 30	6 45	9 5

Miles from Llangynog	UP.	2 † Mixed Weds only	4 Goods	6	8 Mixed	10 Goods	12	14 Mixed	16 Goods except Tues. and Weds. R ¶	18 Goods. only.	20 † Mixed Weds & Sats excepted	22 Mixed Weds and Sats. only.
M. C.		am	am		am	noon		pm	pm	pm	pm	pm
...	cLlangynog ......dep	6 40	...		9 55	...	...	1 35	2 0	3 20	5 50	7 0
2 44	Penybont Fawr ......,,	6 48	...		10 3	...		1 43	S	S	5 58	7 8
4 21	Pedair Ffordd ......,,	6 55	...		10 10	...		1 50	...	...	6 5	7 15
5 30	cLlanrhaiadr Mochnant ,,	a 7 0 d 7 5	...		10 15	...		1 55	S	...	6 10	7 20
6 60	Pentrefelin ......,,	7 10	...		10 20	...		2 0	...	S	6 15	7 25
8 51	cLlangedwyn ......,,	a 7 15 d 7 20	...		10X25	...		2X 5	S	...	6 20	7 30
10 22	Llansilin Road......,,	7 30	...		10 32	...		2 12	S	S	6 27	7 37
11 42	Glanyrafon ......,,	*	...		...	...		*	S	S	*	*
12 57	Llanyblodwel ......,,	7 37	...		10 39	...		2 19	S	S	6 34	7 44
13 31	cBlodwel Junction ......arr	7 41	...		10 43	...		2 23	3 20	4 30	...	...
M. C.												
...	Nantmawr......dep	...	10 20		...	...		...	R			
1 5	cLlanddu ,,	...	S		...	...		...	...			
1 31	Blodwel Junction... arr	...	10 35		...	...		...	A			
,,	......dep				10T45	12 0		2T40				
2 0	cRhydmeredydd Sid. ,,	...	...		...	S		...				
3 6	Nantmawr Jct. ,,	...	...		...	...		...				
3 77	cLlanymynech ......arr	...	...		10 55	12 15		2 50				
...	cBlodwel Junction ......dep	7 45	...		10 44	...		2 25	3 30	4 40	6 38	7 48
14 67	cPorthywaen ......arr	7T50	...		10T49	...		2T30	...	...	6T43	7T52
,,	......dep	7 55	...		10 51	...		2 31	...	...	6 45	7 53
15 70	bLlynclys Junction ......arr								3 35	4 50		
,,	......dep	8 0	...		10 56	...		2 36	4 35	5§0	6 50	7 58
19 39	bOswestry ......arr	8 10	...		11 5	...		2 45	4 50	5§10	7 0	8 8

† Passengers from Llangynog, Blodwel Junction and intermediate stations for Llanymynech and stations beyond travel via Oswestry.

A Advertised to public to leave at 2·25 p.m.; Blodwel Junction to advise Llanymynech if any passengers.

¶ On the First Thursday in each month No. 7 Goods will not run, and No. 16 Goods will leave Llangynog at 1·0 p.m.   § Light engine.

Summer Service 1920

27

TANAT VALLEY AND NANTMAWR BRANCHES.

WEEK DAYS.

Miles from Oswestry	DOWN	1 Goods	3 Pwaen Goods	5 Mixed	7 Goods ¶	9 Goods Weds. only.	11 Mixed Weds. and Sats. excepted	13 Mixed Wed. and Sats. only.	15 Mixed Weds. and Sats. excepted	17 Light Engne Tues. only.	19 Mixed Weds. and Sats. only.	21 Mixed 1st Wed. in each M'nth
M. C.		a m	a.m.	a m	a m	a m	a m	p m	p m	p m	p m	p m
...	bOswestry ....dep	6 30	7 0	8 0	8 50	9 45	11 35	2 15	4 20	...	5 0	8 0
3 48	bcLlynclys Junction ...... ,,	S	7 10	S X 8	S	9 58	11 43	2 23	4 28	4X35	5 X 8	S 8
4 52	cPorthywaen .... ,,	...		8 12	...	...	11 48	2 28	4 33	...	5 13	8 13
6 8	cBlodwell Junction ...... arr	...	...	8X16	S	10X15	11 52	2 32	4 38	...	5 18	8 18

M. C.												
...	cLlanymynech ......dep	7 10										
0 71a	Llanfyllin Brch. J. ,,	7 15				Wednesdays excepted.						Will also run on July 31st.
1 77	RhydmeredyddSid. ,,											
2 46a	Blodwell Junction . arr	7 30										
,,	dep	7 45										
2 72	Llanddu ,,	S										
3 77	Nantmawr ...... arr	8 15										

...	cBlodwell Junction ......dep	...	...	8 17	...	10 30	11 53	2 33	4 39	...	5 19	8 19
6 62	Llanyblodwell ,,	...	...	8 20	S	...	11 58	2 38	4 44	...	5 24	8 24
7 77	Glanyrafon ,,	...	..	*	...	...	*	*	*	*	*	*
9 17	Llansilin Road ,,	...	...	8 30	S	...	12 8	2 48	4 54	...	5 34	8 35
10 68	cLlangedwyn.. arr	...	...	...	10 0	...	12 13	2 53	...	...	...	...
,,	dep	...	...	8 35	10X15	S	12 16	2 55	5 0	...	5 41	8 42
1 59	Pentrefelin ,,	...	...	8 41	...	...	12 22	3 2	5 7	...	5 49	8 50
14 9	cLlanrhaiadr Mochnant ,,	...	...	8 47	S	...	12 29 / 12 30	3 8	5 13	...	5 X 55	8 56
5 18	Pedair Ffordd ,,	...	...	8 52	...	...	12 35	3 13	5 18	...	6 5	9 1
16 75	Penybont Fawr ,,	...	...	9 0	S	S	12 43	3 21	5 26	...	6 13	9 9
19 39	cLlangynog ...... arr	...	...	9 10	11 30	12 0	12 53	3 31	5 36	5X50	6 23	9 19

Miles from Llangynog	UP.	2 Mixed Weds only	4 Goods	6 Mixed	8 Mixed Weds. and Sats. only.	10 Mixed Weds. and Sats. excepted	12 Goods Weds. and Sats. excptd ¶	14	16 Goods. Weds. and Sats. only.	18 Mixed Weds. & Sats. excepted	20 Mixed Weds. and Sats. only.	
M. C.		a.m.	a m	a m	p.m.	p.m.	p m		p m	p m	p m	
...	cLlangynog ....dep	7 5	...	9 35	12 50	2 10	2 35		5 0	5X50	6 45	...
2 44	Penybont Fawr ...... ,,	7 13	...	9 43	12 58	2 18	S		S	5 58	6 53	...
4 21	Pedair Ffordd ,,	7 15 / 7 23	...	9 50	1 5	2 25	...		...	6 5	7 0	...
5 30	cLlanrhaiadr Mochnant ,,	a 7 28 / d 7 33	...	9 55	1 10	2 30 / 2 35	...		SX	6 10	7 5	...
6 60	Pentrefelin ,,	7 38	...	10 0	1 15	2 40	...		...	6 15	7 10	...
8 51	cLlangedwyn ,,	a 7 43 / d 7 48	...	10X 5	1 20	2 45	S		S	6 20	7 15	...
10 22	Llansilin Road ,,	a 7 55 / d 8 0	...	10 12	1 27	2 55	S		S	6 27	7 22	...
11 42	Glanyrafon ,,	*	..	*	*	*	...		...	*	*	...
12 57	Llanyblodwel ,,	8 8	...	10 19	1 34	3 2	S		S	6 34	7 29	...
13 31	cBlodwel Junction ...... arr	8X13	...	...	1X38	3 6	3 40		6X35	..	7 33	...

M. C.												
...	Nantmawr ...... dep	...	10 0	...	...	...	...		...	...	...	...
1 5	Llanddu ,,	...	S	...	...	...	...		...	...	...	...
1 31a	Blodwell Junction arr	...	10 50	...	...	...	...		...	...	...	...
,,	dep	...	11 5	...	...	...	...		...	...	...	...
2 0	RhydmeredyddSid. ,,	...	..	...	...	...	...		...	...	...	...
3 6c	Llanfyllin Brch. J. ,,	...	11 15	...	...	...	...		...	...	...	...
3 77c	Llanymynech ...... arr	...	11 25	...	...	...	...		...	...	...	...

...	cBlodwell Junction ......dep	8 16	...	10 24	1 41	3 7	3 50		6 45	6 38	7 34	...
14 67	cPorthywaen ... arr	8T20	...	10T28	1T46	3T12	...		...	6T43	7T39	...
,,	.........dep	8 25	...	10 30	1 50	3 15	...		...	6 45	7 40	...
15 70	cLlynclys Junction ...... arr	...	...	10 35	1 55	3 20	4 15		6 55	6 50	7 45	...
	...... dep	8 30	...	10 40	2 0	3 25	4 35		7 15	6 55	7 50	...
19 39	bOswestry ...... arr	8 40	...	10 45	2 5	3 30	4 50		7 30	7 0	7 55	...

¶ No. 7 Goods will not run on the days following those on which No. 19 runs, and No. 12 Goods will leave Llangynog at 12 0 noon on those dates.

Winter Service 1919-20   27

TANAT VALLEY AND NANTMAWR BRANCHES.
WEEK DAYS.

Miles from Oswestry	DOWN	1 Goods	3 Pwaen Goods	5 Mixed	7 Goods ¶	9 Mixed Wed. and Sats. only.	11	13 Mixed Weds. and Sats. excepted	15 Light Engne Tues. only.	17 Mixed Weds. and Sats. only.	19 Mixed 1st Wed. in each M'nth
M. C.		a m	a.m.	a m	a m	p m		p m	p m	p m	p m
...	bOswestry ....dep	6 15	7 0	8 0	9 0	2 15	...	4 20	...	5 0	8 0
3 48	bcLlynclys Junction ...... ,,	S	7 10	8 8	S	2 23	...	4 28	4X30	5 X	8 8
4 52	cPorthywaen .... ,,	...	...	8 12	...	2 28	...	4 33	...	5 13	8 13
6 8	cBlodwell Junction ... arr	...	...	8X16	S	2 32	...	4 38	...	5 18	8 18
M. C.											
...	cLlanymynech ......dep	7 0	...	...	...	...	...	...	...	...	Will also run on Dec. 24, April 3, and May 22.
0 71a	Llanfyllin Brch. J. ,,	7 5	...	...	...	...	...	...	...	...	
1 77	RhydmeredyddSid ,,	...	...	...	...	...	...	...	...	...	
2 46a	Blodwell Junction . arr	7 20	...	...	...	...	...	...	...	...	
	,, ...dep	7 40	...	...	...	...	...	...	...	...	
2 72	Llanddu .... ,,	S	...	...	...	...	...	...	...	...	
3 77	Nantmawr .... arr	8 5	...	...	...	...	...	...	...	...	
...	cBlodwell Junction ...dep	...	...	8 17	...	2 33	...	4 39	...	5 19	8 19
6 62	Llanyblodwell .... ,,	...	...	8 20	S	2 38	...	4 44	...	5 24	8 24
7 77	Glanyrafon .... ,,	...	...	*	...	*	...	*	...	*	*
9 17	Llansilin Road .... ,,	...	...	8 30	S	2 48	...	4 54	...	5 31	8 35
10 68	cLlangedwyn .... arr	...	...	...	10 0	2 53	...	...	...	...	...
	,, dep	...	...	8 35	10X15	2 55	...	5 0	...	5 41	8 42
12 59	Pentrefelin .... ,,	...	...	8 41	...	3 2	...	5 7	...	5 49	8 50
14 9	cLlanrhaiadr Mochnant ... ,,	...	...	8 47	S	3 8	...	5 13	...	5 X 55 6 X c	8 56
15 18	Pedair Ffordd .... ,,	...	...	8 52	...	3 13	...	5 18	...	6 5	9 1
16 75	Penybont Fawr .... ,,	...	...	9 0	S	3 22	...	5 26	...	6 14	9 8
19 39	cLlangynog .... arr	...	...	9 10	11 30	3 32	...	5 35	5X50	6 25	9 17

Miles from Llangynog	UP.	2 Mixed Weds only	4 Goods	6 Mixed	8	10 Mixed Weds. and Sats. only.	12 Goods Weds. and Sats. exceptd ¶	14	16 Goods. Weds. and Sats. only.	18 Mixed Weds. & Sats. excepted	20 Mixed Weds. and Sats. only.
M. C.		a.m.	a m	a m		p.m.	p m		p m	p m	p m
...	cLlangynog ....dep	7 5	...	9 35	...	12 50	2 0	...	5 0	5X50	6 45
2 44	Penybont Fawr .... ,,	7 13	...	9 43	...	12 58	S	...	S	5 58	6 53
4 21	Pedair Ffordd .... ,,	7 15	...	9 50	...	1 5	...	...	...	6 5	7 0
5 30	cLlanrhaiadr Mochnant ... ,,	a 7 23 d 7 28	...	9 55	...	1 10	S	...	SX	6 10	7 5
6 60	Pentrefelin .... ,,	7 33 7 38	...	10 0	...	1 15	...	...	...	6 15	7 10
8 51	cLlangedwyn .... ,,	a 7 43 d 7 48	...	10X 5	...	1 20	S	...	S	6 20	7 15
10 22	Llansilin Road .... ,,	7 55	...	10 12	...	1 27	S	...	S	6 27	7 22
11 42	Glanyrafon .... ,,	d 8 0 *	...	*	...	*	...	...	...	*	*
12 57	Llanyblodwel .... ,,	8 8	...	10 19	...	1 34	S	...	S	6 34	7 29
13 31	cBlodwel Junction ... arr	8X13	...	...	...	1X38	3 20	...	6X35	..	7 33
M. C.											
...	Nantmawr ....dep	...	9 45	...	...	...	...	...	...	...	...
1 5	Llanddu .... ,,	...	S	...	...	...	...	...	...	...	...
1 31a	Blodwell Junction arr	...	10 35	...	...	...	...	...	...	...	...
	,, dep	...	11 0	...	...	...	...	...	...	...	...
2 0	RhydmeredyddSid ,,	...	...	...	...	...	...	...	...	...	...
3 6c	Llanfyllin Brch. J. ,,	...	11 15	...	...	...	...	...	...	...	...
3 77c	Llanymynech ...... arr	...	11 20	...	...	...	...	...	...	...	...
...	cBlodwell Junction ......dep	8 16	...	10 24	...	1 41	3 30	...	6 45	6 38	7 34
14 67	cPorthywaen .... arr	8T20	...	10T28	...	1T46	...	...	...	6T43	7T39
	,, ... dep	8 25	...	10 30	...	1 50	...	...	...	6 45	7 40
15 70	cLlynclys Junction ...... arr	...	...	...	...	...	3 35	...	6 55	...	...
	b ,, dep	8 30	...	10 35	...	1 55	4 35	...	7 10	6 50	7 45
19 39	bOswestry .... arr	8 40	..	10 45	...	2 5	4 50	...	7 25	7 0	7 55

¶ No. 7 Goods will not run on the days following those on which No. 19 runs, and No. 12 Goods will leave Llangynog at 12 0 noon on those dates.

APPENDIX 23
TANAT VALLEY LIGHT RAILWAY – RETURN TO LIGHT RAILWAY (INVESTIGATION) COMMITTEE, LOADINGS

	1913, 14 & 16	1919
	Tons	Tons
Grain	1,491	914
Timber	734	981
	107	**338**
Manures (Patent)	82	194
Cake	72	81
Coal	4,424	4,625
Bricks	260	405
Lime	603	174
Slates	108	93
Roadstone	10,558	22,313
Goods	512	2,261
Minerals	14,155	596
Livestock	596 wagons	335 wagons
Passengers	52,951	54,620

Appendix 24
Tanat Valley Light Railway – Return to Light Railway (Investigation) Committee – Mileages

	1913	1919
Coaching	27,514	18,500
Freight	27,514	18,500
Shunting	2,000	1,000
Total	**57,028**	**38,000**

BIBLIOGRAPHY

Baughan, Peter; *A Regional History of the Railways of Great Britain Vol 11 North and Mid Wales*; David & Charles, 1980, 2nd Edition 1991

Bridges, Alan J. (Editor); *Industrial Locomotives of Cheshire, Shropshire & Herefordshire*; Industrial Railway Society, 1977

Johnson, Peter; *An Illustrated History of the Shropshire & Montgomeryshire Light Railway*; Oxford Publishing Company, 2008

Johnson, Peter; *The Shropshire & Montgomeryshire Light Railway*; Pen & Sword Transport, 2024

Johnson, Peter; *The Welshpool & Llanfair Light Railway – the story of a Welsh rural byway*; Pen & Sword Transport, 2020

Lake Vyrnwy and the Vyrnwy water supply of Liverpool Corporation; *The Engineer*, 15 July 1892

Lloyd, Mike; *The Tanat Valley Light Railway*; Wild Swan Publications, 1990

Mitchell, Vic & Smith, Keith; *Branch Line to Shrewsbury – The Shropshire & Montgomeryshire*; Middleton Press, 1991

Perkins, T. R. & Fox Davies, F. E.; 'The Tanat Valley Light Railway'; *The Railway Magazine*, May 1904

Wren, Wilfrid J.; *The Tanat Valley – Its railways and industrial archaeology*; David & Charles, 1968

Wren, Wilfrid J.; *The Tanat Valley Light Railway*; Oakwood Press, 1979

Prometheus was one of three Sharp, Stewart 0-4-0STs supplied to the Oswestry & Newtown Railway in 1863 and retained by the Cambrian for use on the Porthywaen and Nantmawr branches. Two were withdrawn in 1905 and *Prometheus* followed in 1907 so all three were likely to have run to Nantmawr via Porthywaen instead of Llanymynech.

The Stephenson Locomotive Society's special train to Llanrhaeadr on 20 September 1958 carried the last passengers to travel on the Tanat Valley Light Railway. It is also the only occasion known that bogie carriages were used. (Chris Gammell)

The abandoned trackbed looking towards Llangynog from Llanrhraeadr on 20 September 1958. The tour participants in the foreground are waiting for the locomotive to detach from the train, to run round for the return journey. (Chris Gammell)

INDEX

Accidents, 71/2, 91, 94, 101, 104
   Construction, 57
Accounts, 55, 76, 88, 90, 94
Acts of Parliament
   Companies (Consolidation), 1908, 97
   Light Railways, 1896, 12, 28-30, 51, 86, 117
   Light Railways (Ireland), 1889, 28
   Llanfyllin & Llangynog, 1873, 19/20, 43, 118
   Llanfyllin & Llangynog (Abandonment), 1878, 24, 118
   Locomotives on Highways, 1896, 29
   Oswestry & Llangynog, 1882, 18/9, 22/3, 118
   Oswestry & Llangynog, 1886, 24, 118
   Oswestry & Llangynog (Abandonment), 1889, 24, 118
   Railway Construction Facilities, 1864, 28
   Regulation of Railways, 1868, 28
   West Shropshire Mineral (New Lines), 1864, 14, 118
Afon Iwrch, 60, 87
Afon Tanat, 10, 53, 54, 55, 56, 57, 60, 87, 111, 116
Afon Vyrnwy, 10
Arbitration, 48, 52, 55, 75, 79, 80, 81
Area Transport Consultative Committee, 108
Armstrong, W. Y., 79

Baldwin, S., MP, 96
Bell, H., 36
Berwyn mountains, 10, 12
Bickerton, W. H., 25, 38, 67
Bickerton, W. H. (Jnr), 67
Bills (deposited in Parliament),
   Llanfyllin & Llangynog Railway, 21
   Oswestry & Llangynog Railway, 16, 21-23
   Shropshire Railways, 14, 1626
   West Shropshire Mineral Railway, 118
   West Midland, Shrewsbury & Coast of Wales Railway, 12/3, 14
Blodwel Junction, 58, 81, 111, 115
Blodwel loop, 34, 57, 65, 70, 81, 82
Board of Agriculture, 30, 74
Board of Trade, 21, 28, 29, 30, 37, 38, 39, 40, 41, 48, 51, 56, 62, 64, 70, 74, 86, 90, 94, 96,
   Inspections, 56/7, 64, 80
   President, 29, 86
Book of reference, 36
Bradford, Earl of
   3rd Earl, 37, 38
   4th Earl, 49, 51, 57, 68, 81, 82, 88, 98
Bradford Estate, 10, 34
   Mausoleum, 122, 124
Bridges, 38, 51, 53-8, 60, 65, 87, 111, 116
   Pipeline, 46, 48, 58, 74
   Underbridge, 65
British Railways, 7, 101, 105, 109, 114
British Transport Commission, 105, 108

Calthrop, E. R., 32, 36, 37, 119
Cambrian Railways, 18, 22, 29, 32-4, 38, 41, 43-5, 47-51, 53-66, 68, 69, 70, 71, 72-81, 83, 85, 86, 88, 90-9, 101, 116, 118
   Agreements, 45, 47, 83
   Capital, 38, 98
   Debentures, 70, 83
   General manager, 24, 32, 34, 38, 51, 66, 68, 90, 98
   Solicitor, 23, 32, 44, 76, 79, 81, 88, 95, 97
   Transfer Order, 97, 98
Cambrian Railways Society, 115
Closure, 108, 109, 110, 111
Conacher, J., 24
Construction, 43-67
   Contract, 44, 50, 64, 80
   Contractor, 43, 44, 46, 47, 48, 49/50, 58, 63, 125
   Flooding, 57, 79
   Inspections, 55, 57, 58, 61, 64, 80
   Pipe traffic, 58, 62/3
   Sunday working, 58/9
Court of Appeal, 21, 85
Creditors, 79, 85, 88, 90, 91

Debentures, 50, 70, 77, 78, 85, 86, 88
Debt, 72, 73, 75, 77, 79, 83, 85, 86, 90, 91, 95, 116
Demolition, 111
Denbighshire County Council, 121
Denbighshire Parish Councils' Association, 109
Denniss, C. S., 32, 34, 35, 38, 39, 51, 57, 58, 59, 60, 62, 63, 64, 68, 69, 70, 72, 73, 74, 75, 76, 77, 78, 81, 83, 85, 86, 88, 90
Directors, 39, 43, 43-51, 55-65, 67, 72, 74-8, 81, 83, 85, 86, 88, 95, 96, 98
Drew, J., 39, 40, 131
Druitt, Colonel E., 57, 64, 65, 66, 70, 80
Dugdale, J. M., 37

Engineer,
   Collin, A. J., 38, 43, 46-49, 51-4, 56-60, 62, 64, 65, 73-6, 78/9, 83, 85
   McDonald, G. C., 74, 79, 91, 92, 98, 104
   Owen, G., 18, 21, 30, 32, 43, 46, 56
Eshelby, H. D., 78, 79
Estimates, 46, 48

First sod ceremony, 45, 46, 66
First World War, 91, 95, 116
Flood relief channels, 57, 79
France, R. S., 13, 14, 25, 38, 67

George, D. Lloyd, 86
Gough, W. H., 53, 58, 64, 69
Great Western Railway, 50, 79, 84, 97-102, 104
Green-Price, Sir R., 26
Grouping, 96, 98, 99

Hamer, J. L. P., 62
High Court, 47, 76, 79, 94, 97

Holme & King, 50, 60, 62, 63, 67, 78, 125
Holme, A. H., 60, 63
Holme, C. J. W., 67
Hughes, J. M., 52, 53
Hughes, R. E., 44, 95

Investing authorities, 49, 53, 72, 75, 76, 78, 81, 83, 85, 88, 90
Isca Foundry & Engineering Company, 75, 76, 90, 128, 131

Joint Committee, 76, 78, 83, 96
Jones, C. R., 32
Jones, Dr J. K., 39, 95, 104, 106
Jones, J. Parry, 32, 45, 49, 50, 51, 56, 60, 62, 64, 67, 68

Lead mine, 6, 10, 11, 18
Level crossings, 27, 40, 41, 91, 92, 101, 104, 105, 106, 109, 110, 111, 113, 115, 140
Light Railway Commissioners, 29, 30, 34, 36, 37, 38, 51, 53, 74, 77, 85
Light Railway Orders, 28-42, 48, 49, 50, 51, 83, 96/7, 109, 118
    Applications, 33, 34, 39, 48, 49, 78, 96/7
    Inquiry, 34-37
Light railways investigation committee, 98, 145/6
Liquidator, 97, 98
Liverpool Corporation, 24, 37, 47, 57, 60, 63, 70, 71, 74, 78, 83, 85, 88, 96, 98, 101, 103, 108, 109, 121
    Pipeline, 25, 38, 40, 46, 48, 57, 58, 60, 62-3, 64, 67, 77, 78, 80, 86, 101, 102, 103, 109, 110
Llanddu, 111, 114, 115
Llanfyllin, 10, 13, 17/8, 30, 31, 33, 35, 37, 38, 55, 88
    Branch, 24, 78
    Intermediate School, 35, 37
    Highway Board, 24
    Market, 10
    Rural District Council, 32, 34, 44, 45, 74, 83
    Town Council, 32, 38, 44, 49
Llanfyllin & Llangynog Light Railway, 35, 36, 118
Llanfyllin & Llangynog Railway, 19/20, 21, 118, 119

Llangedwyn, 10, 16, 21, 40, 51, 62, 67, 71, 76, 104, 110, 111
    Hall, 52
Llangynog, 6-7, 10-27, 29, 30, 32, 34, 37, 54, 57, 60, 62, 66, 88, 94, 107, 118
    Granite Company, 92/3
    Methodist Chapel, 11, 56
    Mineral extension, 92/3, 94
    Parish Council, 32
    Proposed tunnel, 12
    Railway, 25
    St Melangell, 11, 12
Llanrhaeadr ym Mochnant, 10, 13, 14, 15, 16, 22, 30, 71, 79, 81, 88, 99, 118
    Level crossing, 109
    Parish Council, 37
    Waterfall, 11, 12
Llansilin, 16, 18, 21, 30, 31, 33, 99, 118
    Rural District Council, 45, 49, 74, 83, 121
Llanyblodwel, 13, 24, 33, 34, 40, 41, 46-9, 51, 53/4, 57, 59, 61, 62
    St Michael, 11, 62
    Branch, 34, 47, 48, 59, 97
Llanymynech, 13, 21, 34, 37-9, 49, 50, 51, 57, 62, 65, 68/9, 81, 107, 111, 118, 122, 124
    Plascerrig brickworks, 81
Llanymynech Parish Council, 33
Lloyds Bank, 51, 74, 85, 90, 130, 131
    Overdraft, 51, 72, 74, 85, 90
Llynclys, 37, 41, 49, 51, 57, 58, 69, 83, 91, 100, 114, 118
Loans, 28, 29, 30, 32, 34, 41, 44, 45, 49, 50/1, 75, 78, 79, 81, 83, 85, 86, 90/1, 95, 96, 121, 130, 132
Local authority advances, 30, 32, 34, 37, 41, 44, 49, 75, 85, 121
Local Government Board, 21
Locomotive superintendent, 55, 59, 62, 64, 70, 129
Locomotives, 42, 59, 70, 71, 78, 98, 99, 101
    Contractor's locomotives, 55, 60, 129
London Gazette, 77, 97
'Lord Bradford's Loop,' 82, 88, 97
Lucas, S. E., 50, 125

Micah, Dr D. J., 104, 106
Mickleburgh, C., 21
Ministry of Transport, 96, 98, 111

Minshall, A. C., 45, 85
Minshall, T. E., 16
Minshall, W. K., 97
Montgomeryshire County Council, 32, 83, 88, 121
Motor bus competition, 99, 116

Nantmawr, 10, 14, 16, 38, 100, 111, 113, 114, 147
    Branch, 14, 16, 21, 33, 34, 39, 48, 76, 99, 115, 128
    Junction, 65, 69
    Quarry, 100, 111, 114
    Tramway, 33, 39, 48

Oswestry, 17, 18, 25, 26, 37, 38, 39, 70
    Highway Board, 21, 24
    Market, 10, 32, 58, 68
    Public cemetery, 40, 43, 67, 71, 95, 98
    Rural District Council, 33, 104, 121
    Town Council, 30, 34, 49, 56
Oswestry & Llangynog Railway, 16, 18, 19, 21, 22/3, 24, 43
Oswestry & Newtown Railway, 13, 14, 16, 66, 118, 147

Parry, J., 38
Payne, A. E., 50, 51
Penybontfawr, 10, 24, 30, 40, 55, 63, 72, 103
Permanent Way, 33, 41, 48, 53, 54, 56, 57, 64, 81, 91, 92, 108, 111, 115, 119, 120, 126, 127, 132, 134
Pethick Bros., 50, 125
Pierce, E. W., 85, 86, 88, 90, 96
Piercy, B., 16, 21
Plans, 13, 20, 21, 43, 73, 75, 76
Plascerrig brickworks siding, 81
Pooley & Son, 90, 128, 131
Population, 10, 28
Porthywaen, 11, 12, 14, 21-23, 33/4, 39, 45/6, 49, 65, 83, 113, 116, 118
    Branch, 39, 53, 60, 65, 76, 83, 91, 99, 100, 122, 128, 147
    Level crossing, 91, 104, 110, 113, 115, 126
    Lime Company, 41, 42,
Potteries, Shrewsbury & North Wales Railway, 13, 14, 21, 22, 25, 26, 38, 61, 67, 99, 115, 118
Powis, Countess of, 45, 66

Powis, Earl of
    4th Earl, 39, 45, 46, 47, 51, 52, 53, 56
    Estate, 10, 32, 34
Pughe, W. A., 44, 45, 49

Quarries
    Llanddu, 111, 114, 115
    Llangynog, 88
    Llwm Bar, 77
    Nantmawr, 111, 114
    Rhiwarth, 10, 25, 39, 56, 77
Quarrying, 12

Railtour, 111, 113, 114
Railway Executive, 105, 108
Receiver, 74, 76, 77, 85, 91, 93, 95, 97, 98
Resident Engineer, 16, 52, 54, 57, 74
Roberts, O., 25, 39, 43, 56, 118
Robinson, N., 51, 52, 59
Rolling stock, 30, 59, 64, 92, 97
Royal Commission on
    Agriculture, 28/9

Saunders, J. B. & Company, 62, 72-6, 83, 1128, 131
Savin, T., 18, 21
Secretary, 43, 47, 54, 57, 74, 83, 85, 90, 96, 98
Seal, 43
Shrewsbury, 18, 32, 39
    Town Council, 34
Shropshire & Montgomeryshire
    Light Railway, 97
Shrewsbury & Welshpool Railway, 12
Shropshire County Council, 49, 50, 121
Shropshire Railways, 24, 25, 26, 33, 34, 39, 46-8, 50/1, 57, 62, 65, 66, 90, 97, 118, 130, 132
Shropshire Union Canal, 21
Signalling, 33, 41, 46, 47, 50, 60, 62, 65, 81, 84, 91, 99, 105, 111, 120, 122, 127, 128, 132
    Electric train staff, 70
Spaull, W. H., 21, 22, 32, 67, 118
Speed, 28, 41
Stations, 37, 62, 64, 66, 73, 78, 96, 119, 120, 126, 132, 134
    Blodwel Junction, 58, 61, 62, 69, 81, 99, 108, 108, 109, 111, 112, 115, 140

Llangedwyn, 40, 55, 64, 76, 109, 110, 135
Llangynog, 40, 62, 68, 69, 70, 71, 77, 78, 81, 92/3, 99, 101, 102, 105, 107, 111, 122
Llanrhaeadr, 40, 55, 62, 64, 69, 70, 71, 76, 79, 105, 109, 111, 135, 140
Llansilin Road, 27, 62, 69, 75, 135
Llanyblodwel, 40, 62, 69
Nantmawr Junction, 65, 69
Pedairffordd, 37, 62, 69, 104, 105, 106, 116, 135
Pentrefelin, 37, 57, 62, 69, 77, 135
Penybont Mill, 40
Penybontfawr, 40, 69, 70, 80, 88, 98, 105, 109, 135
Porthywaen, 62, 69, 84, 126, 135
Stephenson Locomotive Society, 111, 148
Strachan, G. L., 52, 78, 81
Strachan, J., 46, 48, 50-66, 72-4, 76, 78, 79, 80, 81, 116
    Locomotives, 55, 61, 129
    Tenders, 48, 50, 125, 126, 128, 135
    Tickets, 58/9
    Train service, 54, 58
Stationmasters, 69, 99

Tanat Valley, 10-12, 13
Tanat Valley Light Railway, 28
    passim
    Borrowing, 38, 45, 48, 53, 88, 90
    Capital, 34, 41, 45, 48, 49, 56, 77, 78
    Debt, 72, 73, 75, 77, 79, 83, 86, 90, 91, 95, 116
    Opening, 66-8
    Operating, 68, 70, 75, 78, 91, 136
    Costs, 142-3
    Purchase by Cambrian Railways, 81, 83, 95, 96-9
    Revenue, 74, 85, 88, 141, 143, 144
    Shareholders' meetings, 21, 44, 45, 48, 51, 52, 55, 60, 76, 78, 79, 88, 96
    Shares, 29, 37, 41, 49, 50, 55, 56, 88, 96, 97, 121
Through carriages, 57, 68, 69
Timetable, 68, 141-4

Tenders, 46, 48, 49, 50, 60, 62, 72, 78, 124, 125, 126, 135
Thomas, W. H., 39, 45, 72, 95, 128, 131
Track lifting, 111,
Traffic, 86, 98, 99
    Goods, 77, 86
    Livestock, 86
    Mineral, 88, 91, 92/3, 99, 111
    Parcels, 105
    Pipes, 58, 60, 62, 63, 77, 80, 86, 101, 110
    Passenger, 86
Transport, Ministry of, 96, 98, 111
Transport Users Consultative
    Committee, 108
Treasury, 28-30, 36, 56
    Grants, 37, 38, 44, 45, 49, 72, 74, 75, 81, 90, 130
    Loans, 78, 81, 83, 85/6, 91, 96, 97
Triffit, F. L., 52, 54, 57, 74
Tyer & Company, 60, 75, 76, 83, 86, 128, 131

Vyrnwy reservoir, 24, 25, 38, 103
    Pipeline, 38, 40, 57, 60, 63, 67, 101, 103, 109

Weighbridges, 62, 72, 78, 79, 90
West Midland Railway, 13, 14, 118
West Midland, Shrewsbury & Coast
    of Wales Railway, 14, 118
West Shropshire Mineral Railway, 13, 14, 16, 118
Western Region, 105
Whalley, G. H., 18
Whitehaven quarry, 42, 53, 84, 113
Williams, C. E., 39, 43, 45, 60, 66, 72, 77, 78, 79, 83, 95
Williams, J., 43, 47, 54, 57, 74, 83, 85, 91, 96, 98
Williams Wynn, Dowager Lady, 45, 46, 47, 66, 67
Williams Wynn, Sir Watkin 10, 52
    6th Baronet, 16, 21
    7th Baronet, 47, 52
Williamson, S., 90, 91, 94, 95, 98
Wirral Railway Circle, 113

One day in the later 1950s members of a Festiniog Railway Society (London Area Group) working party returning from a weekend's work on the railway stopped to view the abandoned Llangynog station. Despite having been out of use for several years the site does not look to be too neglected. (Norman Gurley)